137, 8,
D

Monograph 64

THE AMERICAN ETHNOLOGICAL SOCIETY

Robert F. Spencer, Editor

*

MOUNTAIN OF THE CONDOR

Metaphor and Ritual in an Andean Ayllu

JOSEPH W. BASTIEN

WEST PUBLISHING CO.

St. Paul   New York   Los Angeles   San Francisco

Library of Congress Cataloging in Publication Data

Bastien, Joseph William, 1935-
  Mountain of the condor.

    (Monograph - The American Ethnological Society ; 64)
    Bibliography: p.
    Includes index.
        1.   Callahuaya Indians—Religion and mythology.
2.   Callahuaya Indians—Medicine.   3.   Indians of
South America—Bolivia—Religion and mythology.
4.   Indians of South America—Bolivia—Medicine.
5.   Ayllus.   I.   Title.   II.   Series: American
Ethnological Society. Monographs ; 64.
F3320.2C3B37   299'.7   78-17223
ISBN 0-8299-0175-2

To Judith A. Bastien, who traveled
to the mountain with me.

*

Pariya Qaqa (Igneous Rock), main divinity of the ayllu,
was born in the form of five eggs, five hawks, and five humans
on *Kuntur Qutu* (Mountain of the Condor).

Huarochiri ms. 3169, Chapter V

*

Contents

*

Illustrations

†

Acknowledgments

I thank Leighton Hazlehurst who taught me anthropology and assisted most in this study.

I am indebted to Professors James Boon, David Davidson, Charles Hudson, David Maybury-Lewis, Luis Millones, Dianne Peters, Miles Richardson, Lester Robbins, William C. Sturtevant, Victor Turner, and Frank W. Young who critically evaluated the manuscript for subsequent revisions. Hank Cabaniss drew the maps and illustrations. Secretaries at the Universities of Texas in Arlington and in Odessa typed the manuscript. Latin American Studies at Cornell financed my research. I completed this book at Tulane University where the National Endowment for the Humanities provided me with a grant during 1976 and 1977. Professors Don Robertson and Arden King greatly assisted me at this time.

Andeanists beyond repute, John V. Murra taught me Andean ethnohistory, Jorge Urioste taught me the symbolism of the Huarochiri oral tradition, and Richard Schaedel helped me clarify important concepts.

Most of all, I thank the Qollahuayas, especially Marcelino, Carmen, Damaso, Elsa, and Sarito, who taught me the expanse of their knowledge and the limits of my own. They shared with me, as I try to do with the reader, their religion, which doesn't emphasize ideas and dogmas, but rather considers the earth and nature for its understanding of life, and which is still richly embellished in mythology, mystery, and ritual.

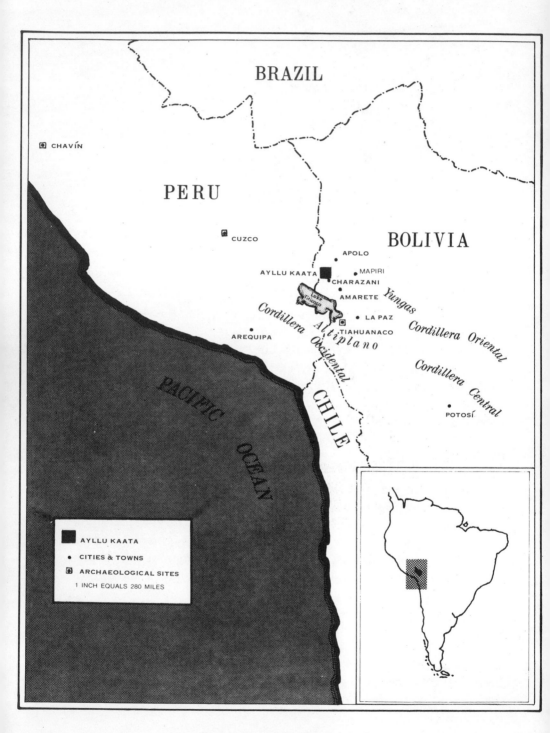

General Map of the Central Andes

Preface

My love for Aymaras began in 1963. I had worked as a missionary priest among the Bolivian Indians and, for six years, had directed a leadership school in a tiny Indian village on the Altiplano. I taught Indian leaders how to start credit cooperatives and raise chickens which, I thought, would benefit their communities. Dressing in a poncho and sandals, I spoke with them in Aymara and Quechua. Many people at that time saw these Indians as backward or as obstacles to progress, and I wanted to incorporate them into the mainstream of Bolivian life.

Most of the projects I undertook, such as providing potable water, electricity, and consumer cooperatives, were not accepted by the Indian communities. My evangelistic activity was even less effective. The Catholic religion was as foreign to them as I was; the Indians put up with it because they had to.

By the end of the sixties, I realized that my endeavors had failed because I was oblivious to an ancient Andean religion, rich in symbolism and ritual. Deeper symbolic patterns governed the lives of these Indians who preferred to worship land instead of spirits. It appeared to me that anthropologists had been successful in interpreting these patterns, so I decided to become an anthropologist to better understand the Aymaras. I resigned from the priesthood in 1969 and began studies in anthropology at Cornell University.

Most ethnographic studies of the Aymaras have depicted them as a negative and violent tribe. "The Aymara's nature is suspicious," wrote Paredes (1936:137), "and profoundly pessimistic; he doubts all and in everything supposes evil to be more possible than good. It seems that the eyes of the Indian have no sight save to perceive the dark side of things." Tschopik (1951:173) called this "the most extended and penetrating estimation of Aymara personality," and he added that Aymaras were anxious, hostile, irresponsible, submissive, disorderly, and mean. La Barre (1948:39, 51) said they were treacherous, violent, turbulent, pugnacious, emotionally unstable, and bad humored. More recent scholars, Carter (1968:258) and Bolton (1972), confirmed these negative traits and added their own—all equally bleak![1]

But few, if any, of these ethnographers spoke the Aymara language, and many of them used mestizo informants, who were racially prejudiced against the Indians. Once the prototype of the Aymaras as "the tough culture" had been established by earlier anthropologists, their students accepted this assumption without substantive verification by either psychological testing or cross-cultural comparisons. By contrast, my experiences with the Aymaras revealed a friendly, sensitive, and intelligent personality.

After I completed graduate course work in anthropology at Cornell, my wife Judy and I journeyed to Bolivia in January, 1972. Beginning a year of fieldwork for a doctoral dissertation, we wanted to understand Aymaras far more deeply than previous scholars who had negatively and superficially stereotyped them. In contrast, we endeavored to understand Aymara behavior and personality in terms of deep symbolic patterns, and to do this, we became engaged with Andeans in their way of life.

Carmen and Marcelino Yanahuaya invited Judy and me to live with them in Kaata, a community of 205 families in midwestern Bolivia. We did so from January until December of 1972. The Yanahuayas belong to Qollahuaya Andeans, an important group of the Aymara nation. Although the Qollahuaya Indians cure with herbs and divine with coca throughout the central Andes, Marcelino and Carmen are neither curers nor diviners, but rather elders and leaders of Kaata.

Carmen and Marcelino became elders after Marcelino had led the community for twelve years, serving as secretary, sheriff, treasurer, and mayor. Carmen, moreover, had helped Marcelino sponsor four major fiestas for each of which they had fed the community for five days, costing them almost a year's supply of food. After this, the elders of Kaata called Carmen and Marcelino *"pasado runakuna,"* which literally translated means "completed adults" or "elders." Presently, Carmen and Marcelino, with about twenty elders, not only make community decisions, such as when and where to plant, but they also guard and teach Qollahuaya traditions. For this reason, we chose to live with the Yanahuayas.

The Yanahuayas, suspicious at first, after awhile grew to love Judy and me. We lived in a small hut alongside their courtyard and shared meals with them. Our participation in Andean activities was very important to the Yanahuayas; Carmen taught Judy weaving, and Marcelino taught me farming. I learned how to plow with oxen, and Judy wove a Qollahuaya belt with a design finer than Sophia, Carmen's ten-year-old daughter, could weave. Carmen was proud of Judy because she had mastered the technique and design of Qollahuaya weaving.

Weaving is an important tradition to Andeans. Cloth is used not only for warmth and dress but also to signify wealth. When a Kaatan girl marries, for example, she presents a dowry of woven cloth to her husband. In raising daughters, consequently, mothers carefully teach them how to weave. Carmen, an excellent weaver, had both failed and succeeded in teaching five daughters to weave.

Not all the daughters have followed the teachings of their parents. Rejecting Qollahuaya traditions, Carmen's third oldest daughter Gloria did not learn how to weave and, when she became an adult, moved to La Paz where she now lives and wears store-bought dresses. Although Carmen daily placed coca leaves inside Gloria's Qollahuaya hat beseeching the mountain to bring Gloria back to Kaata, she seldom spoke about her. But the other daughters stayed in the community and continued the traditions. Carmen delighted in Celia, her second oldest daughter. Remaining on the mountain, Celia married Martin Mejia and lived with him in the lower hamlet of Kaata.

Carmen sang with joy when Celia gave birth to Margarita on April 10, 1972. The next day, Carmen and Marcelino asked us to be godparents for Margarita's baptism, an initiation ritual of birth, and for first haircutting, an initiation ritual from crawling to walking. We accepted. Carmen gave Judy a Qollahuaya headband to wear, and Marcelino gave me a red poncho. And, of even greater significance, Carmen called Judy "daughter," and Marcelino called me "son."

After Judy and I became involved in the Yanahuaya way of life, we began to realize the importance of the mountain metaphor to Andeans. I had first studied about the mountain metaphor at Cornell. Jorge Urioste, my professor of Quechua, had translated the Huarochiri legends, preconquest oral traditions of the central Andes which described the mountain as a human body. The mountain had a head on the summit, a chest and shoulders on the central slopes, and, where two rivers diverge from below the central slopes, a crotch and legs. This human mountain, according to Huarochiri legends, lived with divinities dwelling in its earth shrines. The mountain, moreover, was a metaphor of Andean social organization before the conquest of Peru in 1530 and gave the Andeans a cultural understanding of their lineage and marriage principles. Most Andean research has emphasized how much Andeans had changed since the conquest, which initiated four hundred years of acculturation. From Spanish colonial institutions to modern republican innovations, Andeans had been influenced by foreigners. Consequently, when we arrived in Kaata we thought that the mountain metaphor was archaic and obsolete, but Marcelino showed us that it remained the metaphor of social organization in the Qollahuaya region.

We were approaching the end of our third month in Kaata when Marcelino Yanahuaya first spoke to us of the mountain. He led us to the edge of a terraced field, a balcony overlooking a vertical world. To the north, Aqhamani mountain towered over us, and a tumbling white stream ran through a valley below us. The wind rustling the trees temporarily suspended the stillness. We looked across the valley, and then at Marcelino. A tall Indian, Marcelino was dressed in a red poncho woven from alpaca threads and brilliantly layered with designs of animals and people. The poncho sloped down the length of his arms almost to his hands and covered coarsely woven black pants, worn over another white pair. His rough, sandaled feet stood firmly on the ledge as he raised his hands with coca to Aqhamani.

"Aqhamani, Lord of the Harvest, grant us food as we give you coca," Marcelino prayed. His wide face was faintly marked from smallpox and slightly wrinkled from age, wind, and sun. He smelled of smoke and earth.

Marcelino helped us offer coca to Aqhamani, slowly speaking the Quechua prayer so that we could follow. He was as patient with us as he was gentle with the plants and children around him. A careful observer, Marcelino loved to reflect on nature and society, always examining, questioning, and verifying the nuances of the weather, land, and community. He could collect countless herbs for curing, plant many varieties of potatoes, and list the genealogies of all the families living in his hamlet.

"The mountain is like us, and we're like it," Marcelino explained. "The mountain has a head where alpaca hair and bunchgrass grow. The highland herders of Apacheta offer llama fetuses into the lakes, which are its eyes, and into a cave, which is its mouth, to feed the head. There you can see Tit Hill on the trunk of the body." He pointed to a large knoll high on the central slopes surrounding Kaata. "Kaata is the heart and guts, where potatoes and oca grow beneath the earth. The great ritualists live there. They offer blood and fat to this body. If we don't feed the mountain, it won't feed us. Corn grows on the lower slopes of Niñokorin, the legs of Mount Kaata." In other words, Kaatans understand Apacheta, Kaata, and Niñokorin, the high, central, and low communities, according to the head, trunk, and legs of a human body. It was then that we realized the continuing importance of the mountain metaphor to Kaatans, and to other Andeans as well.

The mountain is the unifying and holistic metaphor for Kaatans. Judy and I participated as members of the Yanahuaya family in twelve rituals which dealt with sickness, death, lineage, and land. In some way, every ritual centered around the mountain metaphor. Sickness, for example, was cured by symbolically putting the body of the mountain together. Marriage rituals gathered together people and produce from three levels of the mountain to symbolize that marriage unites the people of the mountain. Furthermore, statistical patterns from 24 marriages in the eighteenth century as well as 205 in the twentieth century verified that the people of Mount Kaata evenly exchanged spouses in marriage between low, middle, and high communities on the mountain. Metaphorically, then, social principles corresponded to a mountain understood as a human body with three parts—head, trunk, and legs. Agricultural rituals symbolically awoke and fed the mountain so that the mountain was kind to Kaatans and gave them food and life.

Rituals, moreover, reminded Kaatans of the integrity of their mountain, especially when the parts of Mount Kaata did not correspond to the human metaphor. The governor of Charazani usurped the lower lands of Mount Kaata in 1592. He turned this land into a hacienda, and forced the Indians to work as serfs. As a record of their battle to regain this land, Kaatan Indians hold in Kaata legal documents dating from 1592 until 1799, which are validated replicas of originals now in Seville. The Indians, testifying in these documents, argued that the land on the lower part of Mount Kaata belongs to the middle and high communities because it is part of the mountain's body. Not only by this argument, however, but also by legal strategy did Kaatans convince the Crown to restore the lower part of the mountain in 1799. For two hundred years, Kaatans have been reminded of the wholeness of their mountain by metaphors and rituals which lend cultural solidarity to distant and divided communities.

RELEVANCE THROUGHOUT THE ANDES

The symbolism of Mount Kaata and its rituals provide deep insight into Andean society, and so perhaps Mount Kaata can be called a "keystone of Andean culture." The mountain metaphor is not only important to Kaatans but to other Andeans as well. The people of Kaata divine throughout the central Andes, and because the symbolism of their rituals centers on the mountain metaphor, Andeans are united by a shared cultural understanding of the mountain.

The replication of the mountain metaphor across the Andean chain provides insight into the cultures of all Andeans; it lets the Andeans understand themselves and lets us understand them. This shared understanding of the mountain comprises a cultural unity for divided Andeans. The mountain metaphor unites divisions of people, language, and land.

The Andeans are the largest group of Indians still existent in the New World of which the Qollahuayas are a part. Qollahuayas' mountainous land is similar to other Andean areas where twenty-eight million Indians and mestizos live (Bennett 1946:6). Roughly one-fourth of this total population are Indians living and speaking as they did before the Spanish Conquest. These seven million Indians are spread across the mountains of Columbia, Ecuador, Peru, Bolivia, Argentina, and Chile where they constitute the major race. Their large and growing population, coupled with cultural conservatism, has presented a considerable problem of assimilation for the governments of these republics for many years. The governments' political and economic manipulation of the Indians' land without regard for their metaphorical understanding of it has posed an even greater problem for Andeans.

In addition to demographic density and diversity is the linguistic and historical complexity of the Andes: 5,500,000 Andean Indians speak Quechua; 600,000 Aymara; 300,000 Araucanian; and 100,000 speak any of fifteen other languages.[2] Qollahuayas, and other Andeans as well, are able to converse with each other because they are biaudial and monolingual. Qollahuayas can understand Quechua and Aymara, but speak only one language. This solves the problem of two languages being spoken in adjacent territories.

Aymara and Quechua emphasize guttural sounds. They employ six different phonemes for K, each distinguishing a meaning. Whereas English expresses concepts with word phrases, these languages add suffixes to word stems; *warmi,* for example, is the root word for "woman" and with five suffixes, the following word, *warminakara-quiniwachejjaya,* means "Also for the women in the future"! Aymara and Quechua are similar but distinct languages, related remotely in the past. They probably descended from Hokan-Siouan, a linguistic phylum originating thousands of years ago in North America (Mason 1963:197).

The Aymara and Quechua languages spread through the Andes along with the conquests of the Aymara and Inca kingdoms. Aymara is generally termed the "older" language: it had wider extent in pre-Inca days, but yielded ground to Quechua after the Inca conquest. The Aymara nations arose after the decline of Tiahuanaco, a Florescent era from 200 to 600 A.D. which spread throughout the central Andes from 800 to 1100 A.D. (Mason 1975:16). Tiahuanaco was a religious center with intricately carved rock shrines on the Altiplano (Bennett 1946:130; Posnansky 1945). The Aymara nation was a loose federation of diverse ethnic groups throughout the central Andes (Tschopik 1946:503) of which the Qollahuayas were a part. At this time, Qollahuayas spoke Aymara and Pukina. Pukina became extinct in the seventeenth century, but its vestiges continue in the secret language of the Qollahuaya curers (Stark 1972).

Nevertheless, in spite of ethnic and linguistic diversity, central Andeans shared prominent shrines and participated in similar rituals during the periods of Tiahuanaco and the Aymara nation. Archaeological evidence (see Wassén 1972) indicates Qollahuayas were curing at the end of the Florescent era of Tiahuanaco, and, in addition, contemporaneous Kaatan rituals indicate symbolism from the periods of Tiahuanaco and Aymara. Throughout these early periods, then, Qollahuayas performed rituals to the mountain and provided a common metaphor for ethnic diversity.

During the time of the Inca, the mountain metaphor symbolically unified not only ethnic diversity but also feuding groups. The Aymara tribes feuded with each other, and by 1430, civil war had divided the Colla tribe from the Lupaca. When Viracocha, the Inca emperor, began pushing south from Cuzco, he absorbed the Aymara tribes of Canchi and Cana and formed an alliance with the powerful Lupaca. Emperor Pachacuti (1438-71) broke the alliance, defeated the Lupaca, and extended Quechua reign into the Altiplano (see Rowe 1946).

The Aymara tribes became still more divided by the Inca conquest. In addition to the civil feuding among the Aymara-speaking tribes, Aymaras resisted Inca conquest. And the Incas used this divisiveness as a political tool in controlling these resistant and heterogenous tribes. The Inca rulers divided each tribe and sent its members to colonize other areas. Territories, where once there had been homogenous communities, now had settlers from other parts of the Andes. The emperors also sent Incas to colonize and control the newly formed groups in each territory. By 1530, the Incas ruled the Andes from Colombia to Chile by garrisons and colonists.

Colonization meant people were scattered all over. The Incas sent Aymaras to other parts of the Andes, to northern Chile to mine salt and to the jungle to grow orchids, which flowers decorated Inca homes. Qollahuayas traveled to Cuzco where they performed ritual functions such as carrying the chair of the Inca emperor, a descendant of God. Members of the Inca class moved to a mountain near Kaata, which they named ayllu Inca. The Incas thought colonization would not only divide the feuding Aymaras but also split the potentially dangerous ethnic groups. The Incas, however, still had to tie the empire together so they built roads and supplied them with runners (*chasquis*), capable of crossing the empire in days.

Although each ethnic group was spread out, two factors, verticality and the ayllu, unified them. Verticality is an underlying principle of Andean social, political, and economic organization (Murra 1972:429-468) and means the strategy of one group's controlling as many distinct niches as possible. In the Andes, altitude is the great ecological variable, and so is an extremely important factor for control. Andean civilizations arose through successful efforts to control as many vegetational zones as possible so as to furnish these civilizations with a variety of produce. The mechanisms of vertical control include colonization, seasonal migration, resource exchange, and kinship relations. The Inca empire, for example, controlled the ethnic and ecological diversity of the Andes by colonized "islands" far away from Cuzco (Murra 1972:465). The "islands" of Incas vertically controlled many distinct ecological niches and distant ethnic groups in order to supply their empire with produce and resources from the lowlands to the highlands.

But verticality, which interprets Andean unification by economic and political control of distant and diverse vegetational zones, is not a complete explanation. Although verticality explains how the Inca empire was able to subjugate many ethnic groups, it narrowly considers political control and resource extraction as the dynamic principle unifying Andean communities. Verticality does not consider basic symbolic patterns. Still more basic to verticality is the ayllu, which in its variant forms has survived the economic and political changes of the Incas, Spaniards, Republicans, and Reformists. The metaphorical nature of the ayllu has made it difficult for scholars to define it. They have described the Incan ayllus in different and incomplete terms as communal land (Cobo 1892:248), a lineage-based community (Cunow 1891), and a clan (Bandelier 1910:255). In other words, each of these several interpreters considers only one side of the ayllu's solidarity-corporate land or lineage. Were these scholars to have looked at the whole picture, that is, the mountain metaphor, they would have represented more aspects of Andean culture.

More recent community studies suggest that ayllu solidarity is a combination of kinship and territorial ties, as well as symbolism (Albo 1972; Duviols 1974; Tschopik 1951; and Urioste 1975). These studies, however, do not explain how the ayllu is a corporate whole, which includes social principles, verticality, and metaphor. As a new approach to the Andean ayllu, then, this book interrelates the metaphorical understanding of the mountain not only to social principles but also to territorial ties. When Kaatans speak of Mount Kaata, they refer to three communities, Apacheta, Kaata, and Niñokorin, corresponding to the high, central, and low lands. But when Kaatans say that Mount Kaata is ayllu Kaata, they add a metaphorical dimension to territorial unification. They understand the mountain as a human body. Such an understanding lends solidarity to the group of three communities. Furthermore, the body has three parts, and each part is a community. Ayllu means that like a family the mountain has one ancestor, *huh yayayuh*. In Kaatan language, Niñokorin means lower child, and Apacheta, ancestor or leader, *apu*. The low people are the descending generation, which is open and spreading horizontally, whereas the upper are the closed generation coming to an apex. In other words, Kaatans conceive of genealogy as we do—as a pyramid spreading from one ancestor at the apex.

The mountain is a metaphor for Kaatans' descent groups, *jatun ayllu*, which means erect penis, like the mountain where the founders of the ancestral line are buried. The men then hold permanent claim to land, always remaining on the level of their dead ancestors. Their wives belong to the *masi ayllu*, level ayllu. Marriage looks to the mountain for its social structure in that people on one level must select a spouse from one of the other two gradient levels, that is, a person from the central lands must marry someone from a lower or higher level. In marriage, women cross the levels of the mountain according to virilocal settlement patterns, thus bringing a solidarity to the mountain by linking levels.

However, membership in an ayllu is not always limited to social principles. Ayllu also refers to people who live in the same territory (*llahta*) and who feed the earth shrines of that territory. Peruvian migrants, for example, moved to Kaata around 1920 and became members of that level's descent groups by feeding the ancestors of the native Kaatans. Similarly, Incan colonists became members of the territorial ayllu by living there and ritually feeding the same earth shrines. Peruvians and, many years earlier, the Incas also maintained solidarity with their ethnic groups by descent, marriage, and exchange ties, forming additional ayllus. By living on the mountain and ritually feeding its shrines, people became a part of the mountain ayllu, no matter where they came from.

Ritual is essential to the ayllu. Ritual maintains integration among society, earth, and religion; it is a process that enables these peoples to express, through symbols, their *oneness* with the mountain. They feed it and eat it. They become the mountain and the mountain becomes them. Wearing symbols of the mountain, they dress like the mountain that gives them their clothes—and the designs for the clothes. Their oneness with the mountain is their integrity.

Finally, the mountain metaphor provides imagery for our own society. North American Indians understand land differently than we do, and we must interpret their struggle for it as a religious endeavor. Most of the land taken from the Indian will never be returned, but what we have possessed, we have also destroyed. Pollution and the energy crisis, for example, indicate an environment hostile to its holders. Andeans, in contrast, are in harmony with their land, and this oneness creates a human mountain.

NOTES

1. Other ethnographers who have negatively characterized the Aymara are: Forbes 1870:198; Bandelier 1910:19, 35, 70; Romero 1928:173-174; and Squier 1877:304.

2. The following is the location of minor Andean languages: Atacama in northern Chile, Catacao (extinct) in northern Peru, Chibchan (stock of languages extending into Central America) in Colombia and Ecuador, Chimu (extinct) in northern Peru, Choco in northern Colombia, Diaguit (Quechua-nized) in western Argentina, Huarpe (extinct) in southern Argentina, Huma-huaca (extinct) in northern Chile, Jirajara in Venezuela, Lule (Quechuanized) in Argentina Chaco, Pukina (extinct) on the eastern coast of Lake Titicaca, Sechura (extinct) in northern Peru, Timote (extinct) in Venezuela, Uru-Chipaya (Aymaraized) around Lakes Poopo and Titicaca, and Yurimanqui (extinct) in northern Colombia (Bennett 1946:6; Loukotka 1968; Mason 1963; Voegelin 1965).

The Community of Kaata

1

Introduction to an Ayllu

In midwestern Bolivia, northeast of Lake Titicaca, stands Kaata, a sacred mountain. On its central slopes, in a community also called Kaata, live forty-six men and sixty-one women diviners. Kaatan diviners have been ritual experts in the Andes for more than a thousand years; they performed brain surgery as early as 700 A.D. (Rydén 1957; Wassén 1972) and carried the Inca emperor's chair in the fifteenth century (Guaman Poma, ed. 1936:331). Kaatan diviners are Qollahuaya Indians,[1] which is a special cultural subgroup of the Aymara nation (Tschopik 1946:569).[2] Kaata is renowned throughout the central Andes as a community of diviners. Seeking these soothsayers, Andeans travel across the mountains to Kaata where famous diviners read their fortune.

Mount Kaata is centrally located in the Bolivian province of Bautista Saavedra which borders on the provinces of Muñecas to the south, Larecaja to the southwest, Caupolican to the north, and Peru to the west. Throughout Bautista Saavedra, communities of Qollahuaya Indians live on the mountains of the Carabaya range. Approximately fifteen thousand Qollahuayas live in this province, a mountainous area about the size of Delaware.

Americans and Europeans rarely ventured into the remote

1

Qollahuaya region before 1948 when a dirt road was completed from La Paz to Charazani, the capital of Bautista Saavedra. Two hundred miles long, the road crosses a high plateau, the Altiplano (12,500 feet), and a mountain range, the Cordillera Oriental (around 18,000 feet); consequently, the trip takes anywhere from twenty hours during the dry season to several days during the rainy season when the roads become muddy and impassable. Even today, few non-Andeans risk their lives on the dangerous journey from La Paz to Charazani. Because of Bautista Saavedra's inaccessibility to non-Andeans, Kaatan diviners still practice Andean rituals, which, in more accessible areas of the Andes, have been suppressed by missionaries. For this reason, an early ethnographer to South America, Bandelier (1910:103), described the Qollahuayas as the "Wizards of the Andes." He thought that an analysis of their rituals would provide the key to understanding Andean religion.

Following Bandelier's suggestion, my wife Judy and I traveled to Mount Kaata to do dissertation research on the interrelationship of Andean religion and social organization. Kaatan rituals, I thought, would be the most authentic and characteristic expression of the Andean symbolic system. Unfortunately, it was at the height of the rainy season, January 20, 1972, when Judy and I traveled from La Paz to Charazani. We boarded a six-ton truck, called *Yawar Mallku* (Blood of the Condor) at one-thirty Wednesday morning. We climbed into the back of Yawar Mallku which was already loaded with sacks of sugar, coca and rice, tins of alcohol and lard, bundles of clothes and food, and thirty-five Indians perched on top. The Indians had arrived hours earlier to reserve a place on the truck. Andeans, nevertheless, share their shelter with strangers at night, and this rainy night was no exception. An Indian family awoke, crouched together to give us room, and then wrapped their blankets around us.

Blood of the Condor traveled through the dark streets of La Paz. Circling around the cone-like basin in which La Paz sits, we climbed to the rim of the Altiplano. This basin probably once held a lake, whose shores reached the Altiplano and whose depths descended to Calaqota. The lake washed away, and today Calaqota, at 11,000 feet, is the greenest and wealthiest settlement of La Paz. El Alto, the highest (13,300 feet) and fastest growing settlement with 100,000 people, overlooks the rim of La Paz from the Altiplano. With a population of a half-million people, La Paz is the largest city in Bolivia and resembles the whole of Bolivia in that the surface area of both places extends up and down. But, in contrast, Bolivia extends over a much wider altitude than La Paz: the regions of Bolivia ascend from sea level to 22,000 feet. Ecological zones change with altitude, and consequently, Bolivia has many levels of land on which a variety of resources are found. Lowland peoples, for example, lumber mahogany and rubber in tropical areas of the Beni and Pando Departments, northeastern Bolivia. Ranchers graze cattle and farmers cultivate sugarcane on the prairies surrounding Santa Cruz in central Bolivia. Coca, fruit, and vegetables abound on the lower eastern slopes of the Andes, a rainfall forest area from 3,000 to 6,000 feet. Corn, wheat, barley, oca, and potatoes grow on both sides of the Andes at elevations from 6,000 to 14,000 feet. And beyond 14,000 feet, alpacas, llamas, and sheep graze up to the mountains' snow line at 18,000 feet. Each level exploits its resources, and, as a result, Bolivians enjoy many products from the different regions.

La Paz, however, is not characteristic of Bolivia in regard to settlement patterns. The majority of Bolivians live in scattered small settlements, isolated from one another and from the outside world by physical barriers and linguistic differences. According to the census of 1967, Bolivia has a population of 4,561,400 people, who inhabit an area of 424,162 square miles, approximately the area of Oklahoma, New Mexico, and Texas. Of all the countries in South America, Bolivia has the smallest proportion of agricultural land to total area (0.3 percent), because of mountains, deserts, and jungles. Many Bolivians live on the high Altiplano (12,500 feet) of Lake Titicaca and in the valleys of the Cordillera Oriental. Escarpments, windswept plateaus, and towering ranges of mountains separate these settlements from each other. These clusters are further divided by languages of Aymara, Quechua, and Uru-Chipaya, as well as the European language of Spanish. Consequently, Bolivia is a divided republic.

Trucks transport resources from one region of Bolivia to another and thereby tie the diversified regions together. Transportation by truck, however, is quite different in Bolivia than in the United States. Bolivia, for example, has only three hundred miles of paved highway, which crosses lowlands from Cochabamba to Santa Cruz, and most Bolivian roads are wide paths cut into the sides of mountains, such as the road Yawar Mallku traveled to Charazani.

By late Wednesday afternoon, Blood of the Condor had crossed the Altiplano, passed through Escoma, and was climbing the pass of Italaque, 17,000 feet high, through the Carabaya mountains. Zigzagging back and forth up the switchback road, Yawar Mallku tilted from its load and a broken spring. Embankments which were washed out in several places precariously held our truck as it crossed precipices thousands of feet high.

Melted snow made the road muddy and Yawar Mallku slid sideways with the rear right wheel spinning into the side of the mountain. The tracks became trenches and embedded the truck. Everyone shoveled and pushed the truck through the mud. We gasped for breath in the thin air and wiped our faces splattered with mud from the spinning wheels.

Finally, as the sun was sinking into the Western Sierras, Blood of the Condor ascended to Italaque pass. It is an ancient Andean custom for travelers to deposit coca quids and rocks on the earth shrine of the pass. This rite of passage symbolized the removal of tiredness and the restoration of strength. For this reason, earth shrines on passes are called *apachetas*, which is a substantive of the verb *apachiway*, meaning "remove this burden from me." In thanksgiving, then, to Blood of the Condor and in renewal from the mountain, we removed wads of coca from our mouths and threw them on the rock pile near the apacheta.

"Be gone pain, hunger, and tiredness," we prayed. "Mother Earth give us health, food, and strength."

Snowcrested mountains ascended before us in the north, and a beautiful valley descended below us in the east. The valley stretched on forever until it finally disappeared in the dark green hills and cumulus clouds of the Yungas.

We had arrived in the land of the Qollahuayas.

Descending from the pass at Italaque, Yawar Mallku traveled through the night to Charazani. The truck rolled and bounced on the rock-laden road switching from one side of the valley to the other. The stream became deeper and wider each time we crossed it, and near the bottom of the valley, the stream flooded the truck bed. But Blood of the Condor kept going through the stream and darkness. We could smell the earth and feel a warm moist breeze as the truck crossed the ridge above Charazani. The whine of the engine awoke the town to welcome us, and some kids jumped on the tailgate. The driver screamed at them to get off. We circled a soccer field, school, police station, and passed through a tollgate into the plaza of Charazani at 5:30, Thursday morning. We had traveled twenty-eight hours. Another traveler, Eulogio Oblitas, invited us to stay at his small hotel in Charazani. We gratefully accepted his invitation and were ushered to a second-story loft, where we slept on a straw mattress until the next day.

QOLLAHUAYA AYLLUS

During our stay in Charazani, Eulogio told us about the Qollahuayas and their ayllus. Eulogio, a curer and a merchant, had observed many things about the Qollahuaya region during his travels. Moreover, he had studied Andean religion with his uncle, Enrique Oblitas, who had written several books on Qollahuaya folklore (see Oblitas 1963, 1968, 1969).

Qollahuayas, and many other Andeans as well, distinguish their communities according to the mountain on which the community is located. They call these mountains *ayllus*, and each ayllu has communities on low, middle, and high levels of the mountain. Qollahuayas have nine ayllus, namely, Amarete, Chajaya, Chari, Chullina, Curva, Inca, Kaalaya, Kaata, and Upinhuaya. Without calculating vertical relief, these ayllus cover 975 square miles (2,525 square kilometers).

Although valleys and rivers separate the Carabaya mountains, resource exchange unifies the Qollahuaya ayllus. According to an ayllu division of labor, the communities on each mountain specialize in some profession. The ayllus exchange services and supply each other, as well as other parts of the central Andes, with necessary resources. Ayllus Amarete, Chajaya, and Upinhuaya, for example, provide the potters, jewelers, tool and hat makers for the province. The people of ayllu Amarete mold pottery and carve wooden tools, and ayllu Chajaya, famous for jewelers who once fashioned ornaments for ruling Incas, furnishes all Qollahuaya jewelry. According to a unique technique, Upinhuayas press sheep wool into dress hats. All Qollahuayas wear these white hats with wide brims and rounded crowns for fiestas. The craftsmen from these ayllus practice skills learned from their ancestors. Following a long tradition, these craftsmen developed a technology tested through time. As a consequence, the complexity of each craft encourages ayllu specialization, and this specialization, in turn, requires exchange between ayllus for complementary resources.

Qollahuayas not only trade crafts but they also balance their diet. Since vegetational zones change with altitude, the ayllus, situated at varying altitudes, grow and exchange a variety of foods. In the eastern and lower area of Bautista Saavedra, for example, ayllu Chullina borders the rainfall forest region of the Yungas. On the lower slopes (7,000-9,000 feet) of Chullina mountain, Indians cultivate apple and orange orchards. Near the center of the province, the people of ayllu Inca and Kaata cultivate wheat on lower slopes (10,500-11,500 feet) of their mountains and grow potatoes on the central slopes (11,500-14,000 feet). And on the highest mountains in the western part of Bautista Saavedra, herders from ayllu Chari graze alpacas, llamas, and sheep from 14,000 to 17,000 feet. In other words, the vegetational zones of the Carabaya mountains provide the ayllus with the necessary carbohydrates, cereals, minerals, and proteins for a balanced diet.

After the Indians harvest their crops, the people of the ayllus come together at fiestas, which are sponsored twice a year in each community. They bring their community's produce and trade it for other necessary goods. The herders from ayllu Chari, for example, swap dried meat (*charqui*) for bread, fruit, and potatoes from ayllus Inca, Chullina, and Kaata. Furthermore, the people of the ayllus gather at fiestas to share a meal. The people pool their food, and the Indians feast upon the products from the Qollahuaya mountains. As a balance of diet and as an exchange between ayllus, the banquet is also an important symbolic gesture for Andean rituals. While the variety of food and people at a banquet symbolizes area specialization, the common meal symbolizes area integration.

Ayllu specialization, moreover, is an efficient strategy for utilizing the resources of Bautista Saavedra. Farming and herding require great skill in the Andes where the soil is marginal and the climate is variable, and the people of each ayllu must study the climate, soil, and plants of the ayllu's levels. The elders of each community, for example, know agricultural methods which are successful on their land. They can read signs of nature to determine when to plant and harvest in places where frost sets two hundred days of the year. Breeding seeds to grow in barren and high places, they carefully select and cross-fertilize plants which can resist the frost and snow. Consequently, the people of each ayllu adapt to the vegetational zones of their mountain and specialize in farming or herding techniques peculiar to their levels. By specializing and trading, then, the Qollahuaya ayllus are able to skillfully utilize complex resources within Bautista Saavedra.

Qollahuayas also take advantage of resources found outside Bautista Saavedra. The people of ayllu Upinhuaya, for example, travel three days by foot to the Yungas where they harvest incense. Upinhuayans slash trees for resin which is dried and crushed into incense. Loading the incense on their backs, Upinhuayans carry hundred-pound sacks up the tumultuous Ayllu River to the Qolla-huaya mountains. They market the incense in Bautista Saavedra and the southeastern Altiplano; Andeans burn large quantities of incense in their rituals. Upinhuayans reek with incense, and they are known throughout the Andes as the "Walking Incense Pots."

More than incense, however, Qollahuayas use coca not only for their rituals but also for survival in the Andes. Andeans divine from coca and serve it to the earth shrines during rituals. But magical qualities of the "divine leaf," as Andeans call coca, are interrelated to its physical properties; dried coca leaves contain the bitter alkaloid of cocaine, whose anaesthetic properties are also used by dentists to deaden dental nerves. As fortification against the higher altitudes, Andeans masticate coca for its narcotic effect; cocaine alleviates the pains of cold, hunger, and tiredness, as well as protects Andeans against hypoxia (altitude sickness). Not surprisingly, then, Andeans use coca as a symbol in all rituals. They say that *Pachamama* (Mother Earth) gives them power through coca and that coca is the "Divine Plant."

Coca, however, does not grow in the Qollahuaya region, but rather in the Yungas. The Yungas is the rainy and heavily forested slope of the Eastern Cordillera, where these mountains abruptly descend to the eastern plains. A line drawn north of due west from Santa Cruz to the edge of the Altiplano, passing north of Cochabamba, marks the southern end of the Yungas (James 1959:209). South of this line, a high-level surface (12,000-14,000 feet) stands, known as the Puna. Above this surface are high mountains and below it are valleys and basins. Most Bolivian Andeans occupy the northern basins of the Altiplano and the basins and valleys of the Eastern Cordillera along the line of transition between the very wet Yungas and the very dry Puna (James 1959:211).

Qollahuayas live between the Yungas and Puna, and ayllu Kaalaya has utilized this central location to harvest coca in the Yungas and to market it in the densely populated areas of the Puna. The trip, nevertheless, from Kaalaya to Apolo, coca center of the Yungas, takes seven days by mule. Kaalayans travel this journey three times a year to exchange coca for Qollahuaya products—hats, jewelry, pots, tools, charqui, potatoes, and salt. When they arrive in Apolo, Kaalayans trade with their relatives who have settled in the Yungas and grow coca in that area. The coca traders are linked to the coca producers by ayllu and kinship ties which guarantee exchange. The coca traders transport the coca to Bautista Saavedra where they barter it for items marketable in Apolo. The coca traders are important links between the Puna and Yungas zones because they provide the Yungas area with crafts and the Qollahuaya area with coca.

Like the coca traders, Qollahuaya medicine men link the Puna and the Yungas; they descend to the Yungas where they gather natural remedies, and then ascend to the Puna where they cure the sick. Qollahuaya curers live in ayllus Curva and Chari whose valleys descend to the Yungas and whose mountains ascend to the Puna. Skilled wildcrafters, these herbalists travel to the Yungas, gather animal products, herbs, and minerals, and dispense them throughout the central Andes. Qollahuaya curers can, for example, calm mental illness by guayasa (*Ilex guayasa*), set bones with plaster of Paris casts, and stretch muscles with frog skins. Their pharmacy includes more than one thousand remedies (Girault 1972), some of which are nature's equivalent of aspirin, penicillin, and quinine, and others which have yet to be discovered by Western medicine.

People unable to be cured by doctors have been healed by Qollahuaya herbalists. Domingo Flores, a famous herbalist, cured the daughter of Augusto Leguía, ex-President of Peru (Oblitas 1969:11-18). Although she was diagnosed incurable and dying by Lima's best doctors, Flores cured her within fifteen days. Leguía awarded Flores an honorary M.D. diploma, and the ex-President, moreover, publicly acclaimed the competence of Qollahuaya medical practices.

Medical doctors and missionaries, nevertheless, have tried to extirpate Qollahuaya pharmaceutical practices. Doctors and missionaries inculcate doubts into the Indians' thinking about the spiritual and material powers of the Qollahuayas. At the turn of this century, for example, curers stopped bloodletting and trepanning because of pressure from doctors, who said these practices were dangerous. At the present time, according to Andean informants, Methodist missionaries preach that Qollahuaya herbalists do the devil's work in the Garden of Eden. At the Methodist clinic in Ancoraimes doctors refuse to admit Andeans who have been cured with herbs. Because of this discrediting, Aymaras from Ancoraimes ridicule Qollahuayas and deride them as they travel by.

"Hey you dumb Indian with the medicine bag," they shout at Qollahuayas. "What tricks you got to cure me?"

These mysterious medicine men, rapidly passing from the scene, still remain the hope of all incurables and the healers of the Indian. Doctors and missionaries are scarce in the Andes, and traveling curers treat sick people in places where doctors refuse to live; they travel throughout five Andean nations and cure all classes of people. As hope for incurables throughout the world, Qollahuaya medicine men have remedies for diseases which Western medicine cannot cure. For this reason, Andeans call the land from which these herbalists come Qollahuaya or "Land of the Medicine."

"Qollahuaya" also means "Sacred Land" and refers to Mount Kaata, an ayllu of diviners. Anthropologists and historians have emphasized that Qollahuaya curers are famous throughout South America;[3] these scholars, however, have seldom mentioned Qollahuaya diviners and their religious influence upon the Andes. Nonetheless, Qollahuayas consider diviners to be different from and more important ritualists than medicine men. Qollahuayas distinguish the two specialists according to curers (*curanderos*) who cure with natural remedies and diviners (*yachaj*) who not only cure with supernatural remedies but also arrange tables to feed the earth. Qollahuayas don't mix the two professions; an herbalist, for example, never feeds the mountain blood and fat nor does a diviner cure with herbs. Although several herbalists perform earth feeding rituals outside Bautista Saavedra, Qollahuayas frown upon this practice and call them *farsantes* (quacks). Each profession requires such specialized expertise that rarely can anyone master both skills. It takes years of apprenticeship before an herbalist can know the interrelationship between the property of plants and the symptoms of sicknesses, or the ritualist can successfully divine from coca and the signs of nature when to plant and harvest. If crops fail in the Andes, Indians die of starvation; and divinatory skills, as curing, determine the fate of Andeans. Qollahuayas, consequently, have ayllus specialized in each profession so that Andeans have competent curers and diviners. Chari and Curva are ayllus of curers, and Kaata is an ayllu of diviners.

THE ONE WHO KNOWS

After Eulogio had told Judy and me about Kaata and its diviners, we decided that the best way to learn about Andean religion would be to live in Kaata. It is not wise for foreigners to be pushy in the Andes, so we waited until the appropriate time before we discussed the matter with Eulogio.

The right moment approached when Eulogio asked us to be godparents for his son, Federico, who was seven years old and unbaptized. After we had agreed to sponsor Federico, Eulogio accepted us into his family as ritual kin. He called us *"compadres"* or "coparents"; this meant that we shared, at least financially, in the upbringing of Federico. And reciprocally, Eulogio became indebted to us, as is the custom between Bolivian compadres.

Some time after Federico's baptism, I asked Eulogio to introduce Judy and me to a famous diviner in Kaata. Eulogio pondered the question before he replied; he knew that diviners practice in secret not only to guard their knowledge but also to escape suppression.

"Kaata has three *sumah yachajkuna* (great diviners). Sarito is the best," Eulogio said.

Eulogio believed in Sarito's divinatory powers and recounted numerous predictions Sarito had made and how they had come true.

"A colonel," Eulogio continued, "had dismissed his wife for

suspected infidelity. She called him a liar. To settle matters, they called Sarito to La Paz. Paid him 600 pesos ($50). The coca said the wife was faithful." Eulogio also explained that a prominent lawyer had traveled to Mount Kaata to have his son cured of epilepsy. Sarito fed the body of the mountain; and the boy never suffered another attack. "Sarito can cure madness," he added.

Sarito had studied to be a diviner under the tutorship of his classificatory father, Ambrosio Quispe, who had preceded him in divining throughout the Andes for more than fifty years.

"Sarito knows the names and is a good friend of the ancestors, shrines, and places of the mountain," Eulogio said, "and he knows how to prepare tables for them. Sarito performs rituals for my family."

Eulogio advised us to live with Marcelino Yanahuaya in Kaata; Marcelino was a close friend of Sarito, and if Marcelino trusted us, then he would take us to Sarito.

Shortly after, Eulogio introduced us to Marcelino, who had come to buy supplies in Charazani. Marcelino was dressed in leather sandals, black knee pants, a coarsely woven brown poncho, and a knit cap (*lluchu*). His deep dark eyes were quizzical as he shyly took my hand in his, moist with perspiration.

"Marcelino Yanahuaya, my godchild, has come from Kaata," Eulogio said. "My cofather, Sebastián, and comadre, Judith, have come from the United States."

We exchanged coca bags (*ch'uspas*), and talked in Quechua. Eulogio told Marcelino that we wanted to study Qollahuaya ritual, and after some time asked him if he would introduce us to Sarito. Marcelino pondered the question. Marcelino wondered whether Sarito and the people of Kaata would accept us; these Indians had suffered greatly from the deceits of the white usurpers. On the other hand, Marcelino trusted Eulogio who was a friend of Sarito.

"Tomorrow we will travel to Mount Kaata," Marcelino told us. Eulogio sprinkled us with confetti and flour which reminded us of Carnival, *"el tiempo del diablo."* We toasted each other with drinks and danced through the streets together.

The day after Carnival, Monday, February 14, 1972, we walked twelve miles to the community of Kaata. Marcelino and his horse, "Kisichu," carried foot lockers on their backs, while Judy and I carried pack sacks loaded with notecards and canned goods. We followed "Kisichu" ("Black Beetle") who, like a beetle, walked slowly but sure-footedly down a ridge below Charazani, across the Ayllu River and up an abrupt escarpment to Mojata Pass (14,500 feet). In four hours we had climbed three thousand feet up the southern slope of Mount Kaata. From there we could see the community of Niñokorin, which is situated on the lowest slopes of Mount Kaata (10,500-11,500 feet). The rest of the trip was easy as we walked down the gradually descending northern slope to the community of Kaata.

Kaata sets into the side of the mountain like steps on a circular staircase. Where the central slopes rise abruptly to the summit, a hill, separated from the slopes by two saddle-shaped dales, juts into the sky. Kaata consists of three hamlets settled geographically on high, middle, and low levels of land. The hamlets of Chaqahuaya (12,400 feet) and Qollahuaya (12,650 feet) rest within the low and middle dales, sloping up the hill which Kaatapata, the highest hamlet (12,800 feet) circles and crowns. Kaatapata looks down upon a deep valley with a white stream, appearing thread-thin in the distance, and upward to the imposing snowcrested mountain of Aqhamani (17,454 feet). Like Shangri-la nestled into the mountain, not only the natural beauty of valleys and mountains surround Kaata, but also the imaginary aspects of legend.

"In ancient times," Marcelino later explained to us, "a great flood destroyed the world because the people were wicked. Our ancestors feared another flood so they built a city on top of the hill and called it 'The Terrace-Roof' or Kaatapata."

Unfortunately, the people of Kaatapata were not spared from lightning. The archaeological ruins of Kaatapata indicated older and abandoned dwellings which were destroyed by fire. Lightning often strikes the top of the knoll, kills the Indians, and burns their straw-roofed huts to the ground. Only 36 families now live in Kaatapata; the others abandoned their homes out of fear and moved several hundred feet down the mountain to Chaqahuaya hamlet, where 139 families live.

Chaqahuaya population has also grown because of an influx of Peruvian immigrants in the 1920s. In an endeavor to be part of ayllu Kaata, they speak Quechua and are diviners. Moreover, they have modeled their hamlet according to the three levels of the mountain ayllu. Chaqahuaya hamlet, for example, has three levels of high, center, and low: it has a high settlement, Pachapata; a central,

Chaqapampa; and a low, Pachaqochu. Consequently, Chaqahuaya illustrates how Andeans have adapted the ayllu to social change.

As we approached his home, Marcelino led us up an inlaid rock path to the hamlet of Qollahuaya, where he and his wife, Carmen, lived with thirty other families. Along the path were gardens overflowing with vegetables and vibrant with flowers. Passing through a gate, we entered the patio of the Yanahuaya household, where they lived in small adobe houses (14 by 10 feet). Red, bell-shaped flowers protruded like trumpets from beneath the gables of the thatched roofs. The houses formed three sides of a courtyard, and a wall with a gate enclosed the patio which faced Aqhamani mountain to the north and Chaqamita Lake to the east. Kaatans believe that the sun is born each morning in Chaqamita Lake and that it is a well of fertility. With good reason, then, Chaqamita is the earth shrine for the mother of the house, Carmen Yanahuaya.

Carmen was weaving in the center of the courtyard. The loom was stretched between four poles in the earth, and Carmen sat on the cool clay floor. Slowly she wove designs of suns, butterflies, birds, animals, people, and the sacred mountain into cloth.

Carmen smiled when Marcelino introduced us, and the curvature of her wide mouth blended into her cheekbones and orbital ridges so that her large black eyes became brilliant and wistful while her nose became flat and friendly. She had a mole in the center of her forehead, another on the side of her nose, and a third within the crease of her chin. Her braided hair extended to her waist, and around the crown of her head, she wore a headband, whose designs of livestock, crops, and children symbolized fertility. Carmen and Marcelino's daughters were also working around the courtyard. Marcelino introduced us to four of his five daughters: Elsa (24), Celia (23), Gloria (20), Sophia (14), and Valentina (10). Alongside Carmen, Sophia and Valentina were learning how to weave, and in the corners of the patio, Celia and Elsa were sorting seeds. Gloria, however, was absent from Kaata; she had moved to La Paz where she worked as a maid.

Although Carmen greeted us with a smile, she was afraid that we might bring hail or a landslide to the mountain. On the trip there, Marcelino had told us that Carmen was suspicious of visitors and that she would be the one to decide whether or not we stayed in Kaata. He had explained that Carmen's suspicion of foreigners increased in 1967 when Bolivian and French filmmakers had stayed twenty days in Kaata. In their film *Yawar Mallku*, Marcelino played the lead role of a rebellious Indian, who was married to a beautiful Chilean actress. This angered Carmen who, because she had never seen a movie, could not distinguish between actual romance and role playing. In addition to Carmen's anger, Kaatan leaders blamed the filmmakers for involving the community in a political movie which advocated a socialist revolution to overthrow imperialistic institutions. After the movie had become a success, Bolivian officials blamed Kaatans for their part in the movie and said they were communists, even though these Indians knew nothing about communism or the political overtones of the movie. The Indians had been exploited by the filmmakers, just as the filmmakers argued that imperialists exploited Bolivians. The leaders of Kaata attributed their community's loss of reputation, as well as some crop failures, to the "bad luck" brought by the filmmakers. For this reason, then, when Carmen realized the intent of our visit, she walked away.

Following Carmen into the cooking house, Marcelino argued with her for several hours. Carmen finally agreed that we could stay with her family only if Sarito Quispe read the coca leaves and saw our visit as a good omen. The Yanahuayas had no doubt about Sarito's prophetic powers to predict the effects of our stay on the mountain. Several years before, Sarito had predicted the death of two Yanahuaya children.

"My only two sons, Sabino and Roberto, died," Marcelino said, weeping. "When they were sick, Sarito divined from coca.[4] The leaves revealed the time and place where they would die. I cursed him and said he was wrong. I doubted the leaves and took my sons to doctors in La Paz. I had to sell my cow to pay for their treatments, but they died as Sarito had prophesied."

Later that evening, Sarito came to the Yanahuaya house to divine the effects our research would have on their community.

"*Buenos dias, Machula Watayuh Purijchej,*" ("Ancestor, Lord of the Seasons, Guide") Marcelino greeted Sarito. Sarito was the only person on Mount Kaata given this title. As an "Ancestor," Sarito was anointed by the sacred dead who influenced the community and crops. The Indians planted and harvested whenever Sarito divined from reading the coca leaves. He was their Guide and Lord of the Seasons. Moreover, Sarito was the most powerful ritualist within a community renowned for its diviners; more than one hundred diviners had chosen Sarito to be their Lord. Carmen bowed before Sarito, kissed his feet and hands, and gave him coca.

As I looked into Sarito's eyes, I became afraid. I feared their power. These eyes would study coca leaves to determine whether Judy and I stay in the village or depart that night.

Sarito began reading the coca leaves before the sun set. He made the sign of the cross and then selected fourteen perfect leaves. Three brown leaves were called "bad luck" and three bright green ones "good luck." He earmarked the others with neat insect-like bites and called them Kaata community, Marcelino Yanahuaya, Carmen Yanahuaya, Joseph Bastien, Judy Bastien, Bastien's book, and the road. The reading would be to see which leaves paired with good luck and which with bad luck. If the leaves marked Bastien and the road came together, then we would depart from Kaata.

Sarito grasped the leaves with his right hand. He held them close to his heart and prayed to the earth shrines of the mountain.

"Cocamama,[5] advise us," he prayed.

He then tossed the leaves, skipping them across the table so they formed an arc of pairs.

"You'll travel safely to La Paz," Sarito said after reading the coca. When we heard this subtle expression of good-bye, we saddened.

Again the leaves were cast. Fortune leaves had fallen upon the community and our research.

"Sumah suerte!" ("Good luck!") Marcelino exclaimed.

Sarito read the leaves for the last time. "You've come to Mount Kaata. It's your shrine and it'll help you in your work. Your book is written. Don't worry and don't drink."

I chewed the coca leaves which had brought us luck. Carmen hugged me, happy that success had come. She asked me and my wife to stay with them for the year.

The leaders of Kaata still had to approve of our visit because we would eat their food, which is scarce in the high mountains. After Sarito informed the leaders, twelve secretaries, that the coca leaves associated us with good fortune for the community, the secretaries met with the people in the village and received their approval. Finally, they marched in procession to the hamlet of Qollahuaya and visited Judy and me. Carrying poles with rhea feathers in one hand

The One Who Knows

and ebony staffs in the other, the secretaries entered Marcelino's courtyard. Following the secretaries, six Indians piped away on bamboo flutes. The secretaries sat on the benches of the patio where we kissed their feet and hands, a reverence due Kaatan leaders. I poured each secretary several glasses of cane alcohol, a popular drink in the Andes, and filled their ch'uspas with coca. We drank alcohol and chewed coca for over an hour. After we were "high," they began to question me in Quechua, first asking my name.

"Sebastián," I replied, giving the name which other Andeans had called me because of my last name. Marcelino said that Sebastián resembled the name of Sabino, his dead son. A few secretaries speculated whether I could be Sabino returning to Carmen and Marcelino, so they inquired where we had come from and along which paths we had traveled to Kaata. They were curious to know the levels of land around Cornell University, and from which direction the roads entered the university. They discussed whether our earth shrines, *mallkus*, should be on Mount Kaata, the hill of Cornell, or the banks of Cayuga Lake.

Finally, they asked why we were there.

"You are the best diviners in the Andes," I said. "I want to write a book about your rituals so that your children and other people will always remember you." The secretaries were aware that many youths not only refused to become ritualists but also moved to La Paz where they abandoned Qollahuaya customs.

Genero Tipula, the secretary general or mayor of the community, listened understandingly. His eyes gleamed in his ruddy face as he made his final decision. We anxiously waited until he definitively said, *"Huh chacrata quysahku,"* or "We give you a field." We would have to farm potatoes, oca, and barley. This surprised us; we whispered to Marcelino that we had no time to farm, but Marcelino told us to accept the field, which we did. We celebrated long into the evening; everyone was happy that we had become members of Kaata.

As we later studied Kaata's incorporation rituals, we realized that we too were involved in a process of entering the community: we were incorporated, at least symbolically, into a family; we had names, Sebastián and Judith, which corresponded to people the secretaries knew; and we were given a plot of land to cultivate. However, the secretaries could not decide the location of our earth shrines, because, as Sarito said, "You have traveled far to Kaata; perhaps, then, Mount Kaata is calling you to return, like the condor, to one of its earth shrines."

NOTES

1. Qollahuaya has different spellings: Callawaya, Qollawaya, and Calla-huaya. Qollahuaya also means place of the *Qolla*, a term refering to the peoples of the highlands, as contrasted to the lowlanders, called *Cambas* by Andeans. Kaatans use a word sounding the same but with two different meanings in Quechua and Aymara. Both Aymara-speaking Apachetans and Quechua-speaking Kaatans understand *qolla* as both herbs and highland people, whereas *qolla* in Aymara is translated as herbs, and in Quechua is translated as highland people.

2. Studies concerning the Aymaras begin with Diez's *Visita* (1567), an ethnohistorical source concerning Chucuito Aymaras, and Murra's interpretation of Diez (1972). Much later Tschopik (1951) studied the rituals of this same group and Hickman (1963) did a follow-up study of Tschopik's data. Bandelier (1910) and La Barre (1948) completed ethnographic studies of the Bolivian Aymaras. Paredes (1936) and Costas (1961) collected and classified Bolivian folklore. Nordenskiöld (1953 trans.), Ponce (1957, 1969), and Posnansky (1945) pioneered in archaeological investigations of Aymara and Qollahuaya regions. Carter (1964), Buechler (1971), Heath (1969), and Leons (1967) have studied the sociological effects of the Bolivian Agrarian Reform upon the Aymaras. Bourricaud (1967) compared Indians with mestizos in Puno, Peru. Monast (1966) studied the religious universe of the Altiplano Aymaras, and Marzal (1971) wrote a sociological analysis of religious beliefs and practices of Andeans living around Urcos, Peru.

3. The following scholars have emphasized the impact of the traveling curers: Bandelier 1910:103-105; Girault 1969; Oblitas 1963, 1968, 1969; and Ponce 1969:150.

4. Coca (*Erythroxylum coca*) is an important Andean symbol. Andeans believe that coca has knowledge, and diviners share this knowledge. Its slightly narcotic effects alleviate bodies tired and cold from a harsh environment, and they chew it constantly.

Greetings and all activities are initiated with an exchange of coca, and contracts are sealed with it. Indians work for coca; its currency value is more stable than any Andean country's money.

5. Cocamama is Mother Coca, also referred to as Mother Earth. Early legends describe her, "Cocamama was first a beautiful woman whose body was evil so they killed her, dividing her in two. From these halves a tree was born, named Cocamama. Anyone eating these leaves, eats her. We carry her in a bag, which we cannot open until we have had intercourse with a woman in memory of her. This tree has many branches, so we call it coca." (Francisco de Toledo: 1882:197-98).

Qollahuaya Mountains

2

History of the Mountain

Qollahuaya ritualists, who antedate the Incas, gain their power from the ancestor graves (*chullpa machulas*) on Mount Kaata. Kaatans' ancestors, wrapped in weavings, were buried in these cists and the mummies were carried around the fields during land rituals. Missionaries later burned the mummies, but left the rock cubicles, which remained ritual sites and shrines to the Qollahuaya ancestors. Diviners sprinkle blood and fat inside these niches in the rocks where corpses once faced the top of the mountain. When archaeologist Stig Rydén (1957:7) uncovered the grave of an ancient medicine man near Niñokorin, he found a medicine man's outfit "with containers, spatulas, enema syringes, some extraordinary interesting snuff trays and a corresponding tube, bag-like pouches with leaves, *Ilex guayasa*, and, finally, an artificially deformed and trepanned cranium" (Wassén 1972:13). In eastern Ecuador, the Jibaros still force guayasa, a species of holly containing anesthetizing and stimulating chemicals, up the rectum with an enema syringe made from a pig's bladder and bamboo tube. The Qollahuayas did this a thousand years ago. By carbon 14 dating method, we know that the items discovered at Niñokorin were buried around 800 A.D.

Qollahuayas also operated on the brain. They drilled into the skull with a stone knife and removed part of the bone. The trepanned cranium had three holes, and a skilled anatomist described the trepanation as a "handsomely drilled crater-like opening" (Hjortsjö 1972:157). Surgical perforation and deformation of the skull were practiced by Qollahuayas from the Tiahuanaco horizon (Bennett 1946:36) to the early twentieth century (Bandelier 1904:441). This practice has recently disappeared, but modern curers still set bones and patch head wounds.

Medicine men were on Mount Kaata sometime after Chavín horizon (700 B.C.-150 A.D.) and throughout the Tiahuanaco (800-1100 A.D.) and Inca (1400-1532 A.D.) horizons. Chavín, Tiahuanaco, and Inca were three pan-Peruvian horizons, which were widespread styles adopted in separated areas of the Andes (see Bennett 1946; Mason 1975). Each style influenced the Qollahuayas. The massive shrines of Chavín, in the northern highlands of Peru, and Tiahuanaco, in the Bolivian Altiplano, point to the importance of religion during these epochs. Although symbols on weavings express varied beliefs, the ethnic groups probably united to build these temples. Both sites were located in an area where the resource base could not feed a permanent population while it constructed such edifices. For this reason, distant ethnic groups periodically visited these sites and contributed to their construction. Chavín's temple, for example, was a three storied platform, whose bottom floor covered the same area as a football field and whose top floor rose to a point of forty-five feet from the earth (Bennett 1946:82). Chavín de Huantar was probably a shrine to which pilgrimages were made from large surrounding areas. The religion of Chavín is centered around the treatment of the dead who were buried with mortuary offerings, jewelry, and pottery containing food and drink.

Tiahuanaco, the second pan-Peruvian horizon, spread from northern Chile to parts of Ecuador from a site by the same name, located thirty miles from Lake Titicaca on the Bolivian Altiplano. This site's pyramid has a 690 square foot base and rises 50 feet. Sporadic workmanship and the pyramid's monumental proportions suggest that this site was also a religious center. Indians came from all over the Andes to lay the stones and carve the surfaces of this earth shrine (Bennett 1946:118).

The Niñokorin tomb and other ancestor graves scattered on Mount Kaata are associated with the Chullpa period (900-1400

A.D.). Appearing throughout the central Andes, ancestor monuments were the distinguishing feature of this intermediate period between Tiahuanaco and Inca (Bennett 1946:505). Chullpa refers to the rock monument above the subterranean cist, which was round or square, about six feet high and four feet wide. Ancestors who were leaders or founders of the lineage were buried in chullpas with funeral pottery and personal belongings. Geometrical designs, vertical and horizontal bands with squares and parallelograms, decorated the pots (see Nordenskiöld 1953 and Ponce 1957:115). The cult of the dead was, and still is, an important part of Andean religion. Graveyards and chullpas remain earth shrines where Andeans reverence their dead ancestors. Kaatan diviners, moreover, still claim their power comes from these graves on Mount Kaata.

Following the Inca conquest of the Aymaras, the Qollahuayas became religious specialists for the Incas. The Inca emperor was believed to be a descendant of the sun, and it can be assumed that only the most sacred people of the Andes could carry him. A sixteenth century pictograph by Guaman Poma (ed. 1936:331) illustrates the Inca being carried by four men. "The Indians Qollahuaya carried the Inca" is the caption beneath this drawing. An early Quechua legend from Huarochiri says, "The ethnic group called Qollahuaya were chosen by the Inca to carry him around in his chair because they were strong. It is reported that these people would carry out in a few days a many days' journey" (*Huarochiri* ms. 3169:f. 91r). Their strength enabled them to rapidly transport herbs from the Qollahuaya region to sick Incas in Cuzco, a distance of several hundred miles.

The Qollahuayas also divined for the Inca ruling class. All activities of the Inca emperor, including warfare, depended on divination, "no move being made without favorable auguries" (Rowe 1946:281). During the war between Huascar and Atahuallpa, both sides consulted the oracle of Pachacamac and made sacrifices to gain its favor. Inca conquests were charged with the mission of converting other Indians to their beliefs; it was the Inca emperor's duty to spread the worship of *Wiraqocha*, the sky gods, and earth shrines throughout the Andean world (Polo 1940:132).

Wiraqocha (Sea of Fat) was the eternal creator of animals and humans and the divine prototype of the Inca emperor. His other titles named him the Ancient Foundation of the Earth (*Ilya Tiqsi*) and its Lord (*Pachaya Caciq*). The Incas depicted Wiraqocha as a gold man with one hand clenched and the other pointing as if in command. Qollahuayas continue to reverence Wiraqocha when they offer llama fat to the earth shrines and they associate fat with the energy of Wiraqocha, who is also Lord of the Earth. Symbolized by a golden disk with rays and a human face, the Sun, Wiraqocha's servant, ripened the crops for the Lord of the Earth. The Qollahuayas still consider the sun as an ancillary deity to the Lord of the Earth; they offer ritual items to the earth in collaboration with the power of the sun.

The Incas characterized Lightning Flash as a person attired in shining garments with a war club in one hand and a sling in the other. "The thunder was a crack of the sling, the lightning the flash of his garments as he turned, and the lightning bolt was his slingstone" (Rowe 1946:295). Lightning Flash (*Intuillapa*) was a mediating divinity between the sun and earth. The Qollahuayas still believe that lightning imparts divine powers to ritualists and earth shrines when it strikes them. The Moon (*Mama Qilla*) was the wife of the Sun and regulated the Inca festival calendar. Earth was especially important to the highland Indians who were concerned chiefly with agriculture, whereas Sea was the divinity of the fishermen of the coast (Rowe 1946:295). Earth shrines (*huacas*) were sacred places or objects of local importance to the people living near them. Cuzco, for example, had 350 earth shrines within a radius of twenty miles, and the city itself was considered a huaca (Rowe 1946:296). Before going to war, the Incas lessened the powers of enemy earth shrines by sacrificing wild birds on a fire of thornwood. The priests chanted, "May the earth shrines of our enemies lose their strength." They sacrificed a black llama and prayed, "as the heart of these animals faint, so may those of our adversaries" (see Rowe 1946:281).

Throughout the Spanish conquest, the Qollahuayas practiced many Andean religious beliefs and rituals which were characterized by earth shrines and divination. Kaatan diviners, for example, continued to sacrifice llamas at agricultural rites and to divine for Andeans. Kaatan religious practices, moreover, date further back than the Incas to the time of the ancestor mummies, a thousand years ago, and past that time to the earth shrines associated with Tiahuanaco and Chavín. Most research on pre-Columbian Andean religion has been done by studying archaeological data and early chronicles. Contemporaneous Kaatan rituals provide a fresh look into

Andean religion as a symbol system spanning the three horizons of Chavín, Tiahuanaco, and Inca. Although one can detect aspects of each horizon in Kaatan rituals, this is not a synchretized religion, which snatches bits from every horizon, but rather a symbolic system that is metaphorically linked to Mount Kaata. It is the mountain understood as a human body with three levels; this metaphor gives meaning to the earth shrines and rituals still celebrated at these sites.

CONQUISTADORES AND MOUNT KAATA

The first challenge to the ayllu's integrity was the Spanish colonialism. The Spaniards had conquered the central Andes by 1532, and by the turn of that century the governor of Charazani had usurped Niñokorin for his hacienda and the friars had gathered all the mountain's Indians into a catechetical mission. Kaatans resisted both encroachments; they proudly hold in Kaata 133 pages of documents which portray their struggle for survival. These manuscripts, signed by notaries of the Crown, express a two hundred year battle to restore Niñokorin to ayllu Kaata. They argued that Niñokorin belonged to Mount Kaata because it was a member of its body. The metaphor of the mountain as a body with three parts supported their resistance against the conquistadores.

The earliest papers, written sixty years after the conquest of Peru, ordered that the neighboring Indians of ayllu Chullina be a reduction and mission (*doctrina*) under the supervision of the Franciscans. Reduction implies the congregating of neophytes into a community (see Gibson 1966:82).

> The Captain Arias Pando Maldonado, by the King, our Lord, commands that the Indians of ayllu Chullina be a reduction and mission; do not disturb these Indians, neither destroy their gardens and thatched huts, nor steal their crops. Leave them alone. The priests of this parish (Charazani) will go to say Mass before planting and harvesting. A fine of 100 pesos and severe punishment will be meted to those who violate this order (1592:32).[1]

Ayllu Kaata was similarly a reduction and mission, as the manuscript later indicated (1611:22-24). Spaniards had always conceived of religious conversion in America as a broadly civilizing process, and they aimed at a full social and cultural reorientation of Qollahuaya life. The Franciscans imposed a discipline of Christian duties, with manual labor, partially common property, and strict daily schedules. The friars answered to the Crown, who according to the Royal Patronage, had absolute authority over the Church and its subjects in the New World.

Viceroys, the highest ranking representatives of the Spanish Crown in America, were responsible for Indian welfare in addition to civil and military order. The Qollahuaya area belonged to the Viceroyalty of Peru from 1535 until 1776, when it became a part of the Viceroyalty of La Plata. As early as 1611, however, the Qollahuayas were under the Royal Audience of La Plata, which was a subdivision of the viceroyalty, as well as an appellate court for political abuses of the viceroyalty and its provinces over which governors ruled. The Qollahuaya area belonged to the province of Larecaja (Ponce 1957:71) with the governor living in Charazani. Charazani was a characteristic Spanish American town with a central plaza surrounded by municipal offices, the residence of the governor, the church, and a few shops, all dominated by the white aristocracy. The governor received an average salary of three to five hundred pesos per year, in contrast to sixty thousand pesos that was the viceroy's salary (Gibson 1966:171). Yet, Spaniards often purchased these offices, because as the local leaders, they could confiscate Indian land.

Kaatan Indians, hospitable at first to the governor of Charazani, soon discovered his interest in their land. Cajra Ycho, an ayllu leader, complained to the Royal Judge:

> My father, as a friend, allowed Tome Coaxete, Governor of Charazani, to grow a little corn, so he could eat corn on the cob. Now he has taken all my land, which I inherited from my ancestors since the time of the Incas, and I have no land to plant (1604:12).

The judge said that the governor could keep only the small parcel given to him by Ycho's father, but from this foothold the governor later invaded Niñokorin, the left leg of Mount Kaata. He enslaved the Indians as serfs (*yanaconas*) for his hacienda (1609:12) and usurped the land of seventy Indians who paid tribute of seventy pesos a year to the Crown, and the land of old men, women, and children. The Indians retaliated by attacking his hacienda and recaptured their land. They cut down his fruit trees and burned his barn (1609:9).

Seeking legal sanction for Indian possession of land, the Protector of the Indians informed the Crown that these Indians could not pay tribute if they were serfs without land. He testified in 1609 before the Royal Audience:

> I say to the Royal Crown that these Indians lived from time immemorial and from the time of the Inca on these lands. These same Indians and their ancestors have lived, in ownership and possession . . . they have sown crops, paying their quotas and living peacefully on this land. Three years ago the governor and *cacique* of Charazani forcefully and violently usurped this land (1609:9).

The Royal Audience later decreed that Niñokorin, Quiabaya, and Kalla Kalla belonged to the Indians of ayllu Kaata and that whoever usurped their land would be given 200 lashes and four years in the galleys (1611:22-24). The governor temporarily retreated from Mount Kaata, smug in his knowledge that the galleys were a long way from the mountain and that his power granted him immunity from the whip.

Powerful Indian leaders also wanted a part of the mountain as their private property. Cajra Ycho, who twenty years earlier had fought the governor, claimed in 1633 that Quiabaya (the right leg of Mount Kaata) belonged to him and not to the ayllu. "I have cultivated this land," Cajra petitioned the judge, "as my own from 1611 until 1633. I am sending my titles asking you to separate Quiabaya from the commune of ayllu Kaata" (1633:29).

The Royal Decree of 1633 defined all ayllu land as communal:

> It is declared that these lands belong to ayllu Kaata without Cajra Ycho nor any other Indian in particular maintaining ownership or possession, but rather as if these lands were in the name of all the community of the ayllu. (1633:28).

Despite the decree, the left leg was not returned to the mountain's body until the end of the colonization. Niñokorin hacienda remained the property of the governors, passing from the Coaxetes to Martín Sirena in the late 1600s, who bequeathed it to his son Juan. The governors were sometimes supported by the friars, who were supposed to protect the Indians. In one instance, Friar Pedro Durán ordered the Indians to build a fence around Niñokorin, warning them to keep outside it. "The guardian Friar deceived us," they testified to the Crown, "saying it was easy to cheat the King out of Indians' land" (1797:111).

During his long term as governor in the eighteenth century, Juan Sirena had accumulated four haciendas. His will bequeathed large haciendas in Azangaro, ayllu Amarete, ayllu Chullina, and ayllu Kaata to his wife, Micaela, and year-old son (1760:52). The Niñokorin hacienda in 1760 included all of the lower fields, where Indians planted corn and wheat, and most of the acreage of the rotative fields, where they grew potatoes and oca. On these lands the governor grazed 1,500 sheep, 100 cows, 60 horses, 5 yoke of oxen, and 100 llamas (1757:50; 1760:52).

After Sirena died (circa 1760), the governorship moved to Sorata, Bolivia, which was more accessible to the rising administrative centers of La Paz and Sucre. Sirena's young son did not inherit this position, but he and his mother remained on the Niñokorin hacienda. The power of governorship no longer guaranteed their dubious title to this land, nor could the Indians be suppressed; they forcibly occupied Niñokorin in 1790. Micaela, realizing the weakness of her position, made an impassioned appeal, indicative of how the mestizos and administrative class of the eighteenth and nineteenth centuries viewed the Qollahuayas:

> The Indians of the Kaata community are despots. They entered my hacienda to cultivate the best lands. They act with crazy and sensual consciences, totally devoid of reason and justice. They have land in abundance, more than enough to cultivate without disturbing my land. Acting with insatiable greed, they have entered my property, treating me with vengeance and hatred. Their deeds are unchristian and they follow the ways of nature, thinking like trees.
> See and recognize the nature of these Indians, who have no

foundation to their intrusions and who hide the truth, being totally stupid natives (*originarios*), ignoring the light of day (1796:64).

The Royal Judge ordered the Indians to stop rebelling and molesting Micaela, and said that if they had any documents in their favor they should present them (1797:66). The commissioner delivered this decree to ayllu Kaata. The men were purposely absent, leaving their women to speak. The women shouted nasty insults at the commissioner, denying his authority as a representative of the Crown. "We will never obey the hacienda owner," they asserted, "nor will we perform services for her" (1796:66). A solidarity movement of angry Indians demanded freedom and the return of their mountain.

Returning for the final match, the Qollahuayas, who had become astute legal fighters, presented copies of every document concerning the mountain since the time of the conquest. The Kaatan manuscript also included sworn statements by aged Indians, who attested to the solidarity of Niñokorin with communities Kaata and Apacheta. Near the end of the eighteenth century, Pocomallcu, eighty years old, testified before a representative of the Crown.

"Niñokorin belongs to Kaata," he swore, "because it is the leg of its body" (1797:109).

Witnesses from other ayllus said that the Indians of ayllu Kaata were authorized to cultivate all of the body, which they had cultivated from time immemorial (1796:66). Since the mountain constituted one geographical and anatomical unit, its land and communities belonged together. The geographical and anatomical body, more than a metaphor of comparison, was the grounding and vitalizing of ayllu Kaata. Their argument was that the three communities and their land belonged together on Mount Kaata. The budding Republicans, interested in gaining support against the Crown, returned Niñokorin to ayllu Kaata at the dawn of the Republic.[2]

The Republicans threatened the ayllu's integrity by continuing to transform ayllus into cantons, as the colonialists did. The Qollahuaya ayllus, grounded in their mountains, with communities tied together by symbols and exchange, became cantons, communities united by external economic and political networks. The sixteenth and seventeenth century Qollahuaya ayllus were Kaata, Chari,

Chajaya, Inca, Amarete, Upinhuaya, Chullina, and Kamata (*Matrimonial Libro* No. 1, 1783-1786). Their centers were Curva and Charazani, two cities (*pueblos*) built by the Spaniards for religious and political administration of the region. Charazani, no longer a provincial capital in the nineteenth century, became a canton and assimilated ayllus Chari and Kaata.

A parochial mayor and corregidor governed the Charazani canton, and they demanded work and respect from their satellite communities. Kaatans supplied laborers for Charazani officials, similar to the *pongo* tribute on the hacienda, or rotative peonage, supplying free work for their estates. Sarito Quispe explained what he had to do for the corregidor: "I gave him a sheep and a sack of potatoes each year. In addition, I worked thirty days a year and performed rituals for their feasts. They still did not pay me for this." This tribute and deference was abolished by the Agrarian Reform Laws,[3] and Kaata became a canton with its own corregidor; however, Charazani does not recognize Kaata as a canton.

The Indians still mistrust most of the mestizos of Charazani, but fraternize with them for economic, religious, and political mediation with the Bolivian Republic. In February, 1972, the Indians battled several mestizo families. The mestizos supported a subprefect who favored their interests more than those of the Indians. Troops were sent from La Paz, and another subprefect was appointed, but two Indian leaders were jailed.

Charazani is once again the provincial capital of the Qollahuaya region with a subprefect, chief of police, judge, notary, and, until recently, a priest.

The subprefect, the maximum political authority in the province, approves the nomination of political leaders for Kaata's communities and assures the proper fulfillment of these secretarial offices as outlined by the Agrarian Reform. The subprefect also oversees the maintenance of roads between the communities by requiring the Indians to repair them. The provincial chief of police and sheriff arrest criminals for acts of violence, murder, and serious theft. The provincial judge, who is subordinate to the Supreme Court in La Paz, holds court for these grievances and settles land disputes. When the priest arrives on monthly visits from Sorata, the Indians travel to Charazani for baptisms, weddings, and funeral masses.

Charazani, the commercial center of the Qollahuaya area, has a dozen small stores, which market such goods as alcohol, beer, coca, sugar, rice, noodles, sandals, sweaters, blankets, kerosene, lard, and candy, brought from La Paz, Peru, and the Yungas. About ten mestizo families manage these stores and operate the six-ton trucks which travel from La Paz to Charazani. The Indians travel in the rear of these trucks, transporting their produce to La Paz, a journey of anywhere from one to three days in duration, depending upon the condition of the roads. Ritual kinship serves to link these mestizos with Kaatan Indians. The ritual parents and the natural parents refer to each other as godfather and godmother. The mestizos receive ample produce and service from their ritual kin, and the Indians in turn receive the protection of a godfather and godmother.

The Indians' battle for their mountain continued into the twentieth century. Four centuries of litigation gave them a mastery over the legal-bureaucratic Spanish "sense of justice," whose intricacies many Spaniards and Republicans never understood. Charazani officials usually bypassed legal arguments and employed racial slurs against Kaatans by calling them "rebels, savages, barbarians, naturals, devoid of reason, and unenlightened." In 1919, Eduardo Pastén of Charazani, for example, forced two Indians to give him their house plots in payment for a loan. Kaatans reclaimed this land and sent their leader, Vicente Vega, to authorities in La Paz. Vega astutely argued that according to article three of the Law Fifth of October 1874, and article fifty of the Supreme Court of the Law First of December 1880, commoners held indivisibly and in common all lands corresponding to their communities. The sale of land to Pastén was, therefore, invalid, since no Kaatan commoner had total proprietorship over communal land. The La Paz prefect agreed with Vega's arguments, even though, in his conclusion, he referred to Kaatans as members of the disgraceful indigenous race. Pastén ignored the decree, threatened Vega's life, and had him arrested. Vega, however, sought asylum with Ulla Ulla's subprefect, and the argument was resolved in Kaata's favor. This Charazani mestizo used prejudice and violence against the Indians, and they resorted to justice and the law.

This century's concern has not been so much the removal of ayllu land as the division between its communities brought about by boundary disputes. Bolivian laws (1833, 1874, 1888) emphasized proprietorship and indivisibility for the community rather than the ayllu. Whereas during the Crown and early Republic, the Qollahuaya ayllus were united against the mestizos, presently they are internally divided by boundary disputes. Such disputes resulted in inter-ayllu wars, such as the following eyewitness account of Upinhuaya's invasion of Kaata.

> Six Kaatans were fixing their terraces, clearing brush and removing rocks. Forty Upinhuayans crossed the Kunochayuh River. They beat and stabbed the workers. The Upinhuayans claimed that land to be theirs (Kaatan ms. 1904: October 27).

Kaatans regained their land shortly afterward, but the crossing of the Kunochayuh is still remembered by Kaatans.

The Agrarian Reform tried to incorporate Qollahuaya communities into the social, political, and economic life of Bolivia. These reformers disregarded the more traditional cultural unit of ayllu Kaata. Apacheta, Kaata, and Niñokorin were legally incorporated into the statutes of the reform as independent, autonomous, and territorially defined communities. Each community now has its own leaders, who are linked to Charazani and La Paz instead of to its neighbors on the mountain. The Bolivian government, moreover, requires that each community build a school, where Indians should learn the "new" language, economics, politics, mathematics, civics, and Spanish and Bolivian history. New links have been formed between the communities by a common civic pride as well as by competition between them with soccer matches and tournaments which rank the winners and losers with trophies and awards.

The definition of boundaries has split the communities of ayllu Kaata not simply by stating that levels are distinct to the communities, but by making these differences explicit in relation to external sources of authority. Especially after the Bolivian laws of the 1880s the communities defined and redefined their boundaries. The Agrarian Reform further insisted on clearly defined community boundaries.[4] The resultant feuding has been a strong centrifugal force which separated the parts of the ayllu body from each other and made them dependent on the legal chicaneries of La Paz. The Indians complain that they have spent 6,000 pesos (a day's wage for 1200 laborers) in legal fees against Chari and Apacheta within the last twenty years. They explain it simply by recalling the day when the surveyor "photographed their mountain."

Laws of supply and demand determined by national and international markets create new relationships on Mount Kaata. Apachetans, for example, have linked themselves economically with the pastoral herders of Chari; they realize the advantages of consolidating pastoral lands and flocks, as well as utilizing Chari's truck to ship hides and wool to La Paz. Apacheta has sided with ayllu Chari in another land battle with Kaata. Niñokorin now ships more resources to La Paz than it exchanges with the central and highlands. The three levels of ayllu Kaata are exchanging fewer resources than before; they prefer to sell them in La Paz, where they can buy the traditional goods and the "new" world products such as clothes, sewing machines, radios, Japanese wool, and plastic pots. Competition between sellers and buyers slowly discourages the amiable ties of reciprocal exchange between levels, as these farmers compete with their neighbors in an economic world of supply and demand.

Airports and roads have created new economic relationships between sectors of Bolivia, which are different from traditonal exchange patterns within the Qollahuaya area. Before the advent of trucks, roads, and airplanes, the Qollahuaya area was an important central level between the highlands (Altiplano) of Bolivia and Peru, and the lowlands of the Yungas. Coca, incense, quinine, and fruit traveled up to the highlands in exchange for meat, salt, wheat, and pots, which were sent down to the Yungas. In contrast to the present time, fifty years ago Charazani was a village of muleteers exchanging Yungas produce (as well as gold and rubber) with the highlands of Bolivia, Peru, and Argentina. The traveling curers and ritualists followed this expanding exchange. The Chaco War of the 1930s cut off the supply of mules from Argentina by tightening national boundaries between Bolivia and Argentina. More direct routes to the Yungas were made from La Paz, bypassing the Qollahuaya region. The airplane has made direct contact with large urban centers and the productive Yungas areas easier. Now, as a result, intermediate marketing communities are on the decline.

Kaalaya and Cañisaya, neighboring communities of Kaata, illustrate these new economic relationships. These people travel to Apolo to exchange coca for the produce of the Qollahuaya ayllus. Ten years ago, they traveled three times a year to Apolo, a journey of seven days each way by mule. Kaalayans and Cañisayans distributed coca to the southeastern parts of the Altiplano in exchange for charqui, potatoes, pots, and salt. Today, half the Cañisaya coca traders now live in La Paz, and they fly to Apolo, often renting a DC-3 for 8,400 pesos ($700.00) a flight. They buy and sell the coca for cash and control a large part of the La Paz coca market.

For many Andean areas, colonialism, republicanism, and modernization have obliterated the ayllu's integrity. Many people consider ayllu Kaata to be an archaic and inoperant social organization with the Aymara pastoral people of Apacheta, who are politically and economically associated with Chari, and the lowland people of Niñokorin who are associated with Charazani. The people of Charazani consider ayllu Kaata to be nonexistent; they argue that the three communities are no longer linked to one another, but rather to Charazani. These observers and many anthropologists, as well, have identified Andean unification with political and economic associations, and, consequently, they have overlooked deeper symbolic ties. At different historical periods, Mount Kaata's land and people appeared to be divided, yet they were metaphorically united. This symbolic solidarity spurred them on to restore the mountain integrity. Their rituals, for example, continued to feed Mount Kaata as a whole body, even though its legs had been expropriated for several centuries.

NOTES

1. To facilitate the reading, the references will give the year of the document and the page of the manuscript.

2. *En Challapampa, Partido Larecaxa, 28 Febrero 1799.* Juan Bautista Rebollo, *Protector de los Naturales.*

3. The Agrarian Reform divided the haciendas, distributed the land to the peasants, and abolished the tribute system. By 1952, two-thirds of the land on the Altiplano was occupied by estates (Carter 1964:9). Managers ran these estates for owners, who lived in the city or abroad. The Indians worked as serfs on these haciendas for nothing; and when they were free, they tilled a plot alloted them by the manager. The Agrarian Reform began after the April, 1952 revolution. Peasants and miners defeated the military and land owners in the bloodiest combat since the Chaco War. The revolutionary leader, Victor Paz Estenssoro, and the *Movimiento Nacional Revolucionario* (MNR) established the Agrarian Reform Commission on January 20, 1953, and by the end of that year they had drafted laws with six fundamental objectives:

1. To allot cultivable land to the peasants. . . .
2. To restore to the indigenous communities the lands which were usurped from them and to cooperate in the modernization of their agriculture. . . .
3. To free rural laborers from their conditions as serfs. . . .
4. To stimulate commercialization of the agricultural industry. . . .
5. To conserve natural resources of the nation, adopting technical and scientific means. . . .
6. To promote migration of the rural population concentrated in the interAndean zone to the eastern tropical areas of Bolivia ("Preamble" to *Decreto Ley de La Reforma Agraria* as found in Carter 1964:10).

After the Agrarian Reform law was signed, ninety per cent of the landlords abandoned their estates, and the countryside belonged to the Indians. It was the end of feudalism in Bolivia.

4. Personal sources told me that President Victor Paz (1952-1956) initially opposed land definitions, which he saw as dividing the communities.

UQHAMAPAN

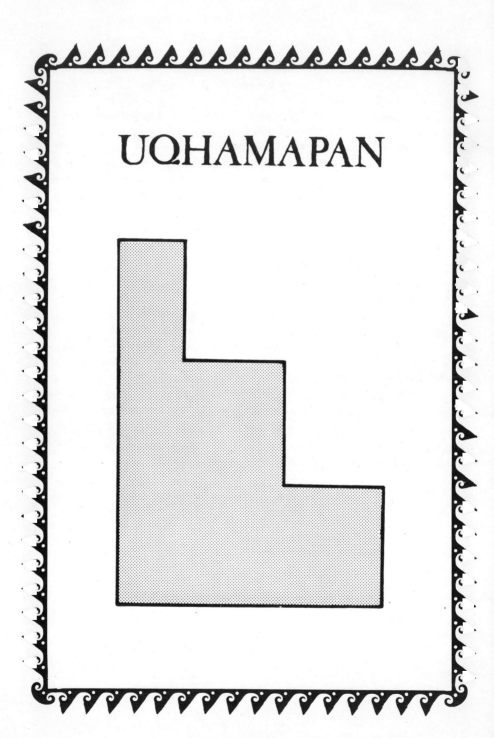

Symbol of the Mountain

3

The Mountain Metaphor

Legends and rituals symbolize Mount Kaata as a human mountain.
Kaatans name the places of the mountain according to the anatomy
of the human body. Apacheta, for example, is the head, Kaata is the
bowels and the heart, and Niñokorin is the legs of the body. Diviners
live in the community of Kaata where they can pump blood and fat,
principles of life and energy, to the rest of the mountain's metaphorical
body. These ritualists serve the earth shrines on Mount Kaata foods
from all three levels: chicha made from lowland corn, blood and fat
from Kaata, and llama fat and fetuses from Apacheta. When diviners
feed the mountain, in other words, they symbolically represent it as
a human body. This geographical body ritually eats produce from all
three communities and in return provides food for the people.
Mount Kaata is sacred because Andeans metaphorically refer to it as
having a human body. Andeans associate sacredness with wholeness,
similar to our traditional meaning of 'holy'. Ritualists provide the
symbols which create the geographic mountain into a human
mountain. More than rhetoric and imagery, the mountain metaphor
cements together the mosaic of ayllu Kaata, apparently falling apart
from economic and political forces of foreigners.

Ayllu Kaata has three major communities of Niñokorin, Kaata,

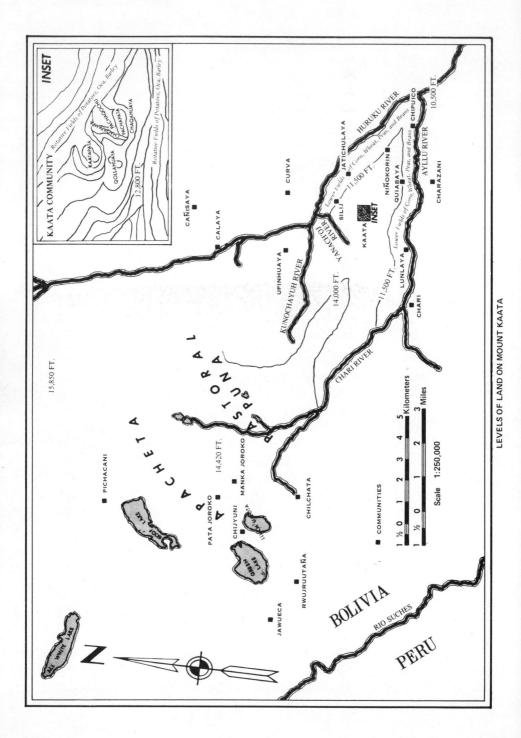

INSET

KAATA COMMUNITY

Rotative Fields of Potatoes, Oca, Barley

NINOKAINA
CHAQAPAMPA
KAATAPATA
CHOQOYO
PACHAPA
CHAQAHUAYA
QOLLAHUAYA

Rotative Fields of Potatoes, Oca, Barley

12,800 FT.

CAÑISAYA

CALAYA

CURVA

HURUKU RIVER

JATICHULAYA

SILIJ

Lower Fields of Corn, Wheat, Peas, and Beans

11,500 FT.

NIÑOKORIN

QUIABAYA

CHIPUICO

10,500 FT.

AYLLU RIVER

CHARAZANI

KAATA INSET

UPINHUAYA

KUNOCHAYUH RIVER

YANCHOJ RIVER

Lower Fields of Corn, Wheat, Peas, and Beans

LUNLAYA

11,500 FT.

CHARI

14,000 FT.

CHARI RIVER

15,850 FT.

PASTORAL

PACHETA

14,420 FT.

PICHACANI

PATA JOROKO

CHIJYUNI

MANKA JOROKO

CHILCHATA

RWUJRUUTAÑA

JAWUECA

BOLIVIA

RIO SUCHES

PERU

N

COMMUNITIES

Kilometers

5 4 3 2 1 0 1 ½

Miles

3 2 1 0 1 ½

Scale   1:250,000

LEVELS OF LAND ON MOUNT KAATA

and Apacheta. The community of Kaata is nestled on the central slopes (11,500-14,000 feet) of Mount Kaata, above the community of Niñokorin (10,500-11,500 feet) and below the community of Apacheta (14,000-17,000 feet). The people of Niñokorin and Kaata speak Quechua, and those of Apacheta speak Aymara. The communities differ in settlement and subsistence patterns and are quite far apart; from Niñokorin to Kaata takes a two-hour climb and from Kaata to Apacheta takes a full day. Nonetheless, social principles and the cultural understanding of the mountain unite these different and distant communities into one ayllu.

Near the base of Mount Kaata, Niñokorin (11,000 feet) rests on the lower fields of the mountain. The northern and southern slopes of Mount Kaata ascend abruptly from the gorges of the Ayllu and Huruku rivers (10,500 feet), and between these altitudes narrow riparian strips produce corn, wheat, barley, peas, and beans. These fields lie within the upper zone of corn cultivation entwining about the Andes from eight to eleven thousand five hundred feet. During the frost-free rainy season from December until March, the moist ashy loam of these fields permits yearly wheat and corn rotations, the vegetables growing around the corn and wheat. Lunlaya, Quiabaya, Chipuico, and Jatichulaya, each with about ten families, are also scattered along both river banks. The four settlements are economically and politically independent of each other, yet they comprise a single cultural part of Mount Kaata. They all speak Quechua. Moreover, they are agriculturally, socially, and symbolically the lower people of Mount Kaata as the term Niñokorin means "Lower son."

The highlands of Mount Kaata are called Apacheta, and one hundred and twenty Aymara-speaking families live there. These herders graze alpacas, llamas, sheep, and pigs on Mount Kaata's high level. The high level is between the upper limits of potatoes at about 14,000 feet and of vegetation at about 16,000 feet (Troll 1968:35). Animals graze on clumps of tough strawy bunchgrass (*Festuca scirpifolia*), which grows in this freezing zone. Apachetans go with herds and as a result live far apart. Although these herders are spread apart in dispersed settlements, they are culturally united by language and by living on the high level of Mount Kaata. As part of ayllu Kaata, furthermore, Apacheta is culturally united to the communities of Niñokorin and Kaata.

Apachetans farm an occasional plot of bitter potatoes and the grain called quinoa (*Chenopodium quinoa*) in places protected from the frost and cold. An astute folklore enables them to discern the place and time to plant hybrid seeds specifically developed for an area where there is frost more than 250 days of the year. Because of the altitude and proximity to the equator (17°S), the highland pastures are warm, bright, and comfortable during the day when temperatures soar into the eighties; but once the sun sets, icy winds sweep down from glaciers bringing frost and lowering the temperature to below freezing. In the northern United States, the contrast of a cold winter and a warm summer affects the ecological activity of all organisms, while in the central Andes the daily fluctuations of a warm day and cold night not only curtail plant life but also influence cultural themes of reciprocal exchange between contrasts.

The Andeans are an ingenious people. They use frost and sun to dehydrate potatoes (*ch'uño*) and oca (*khaya*), for example, so that these tubers can be preserved and transported. The Indians freeze potatoes at night, crush them with their feet in the early morning, and then dry them in the sun. This process of preserving food allowed Andeans to settle permanently in the high mountain country (Troll 1968:33).

Every day, Kaatans are able to see mountains miles away, be enclosed within a cloud, hear the whistle of the wind, perceive a stillness, and feel intense heat during the day and severe cold at night. Even greater than the contrast between day and night in the Andes is that between the rainy and dry seasons, which corresponds to winter and summer in North America. From about November until March, clouds climb the Carabaya valleys, bring rain to the slopes, then dissipate over the mountains. The eastern side of the Andes of Bolivia and Peru draw rain from southeast tradewinds, and the Qollahuaya region receives an estimated thirty inches yearly (Sauer 1963:339). The valleys are also enormous windgaps through which dry and moist air are exchanged between the moist tropical forest of the Amazon basin and dry puna highlands. A gale-like wind, capable of carrying small stones, begins suddenly each morning and blows along the valley floor and up the mountain slopes, often leaving the Qollahuayas in fog.

The central fields also follow a cycle every eight years. Extensive tracts of land (*qhapanas*) produce potatoes, oca, and barley during each rainy season for three years, and then lie fallow for five years. As Kaatans say, the fields are put to sleep. The fields slowly replenish their nutrients by the fertilization of the droppings of grazing sheep. Night frost decreases as the rainy season advances, and tuberous plants are able to grow in the upper region of the mountain's temperate zone above thirteen thousand five hundred feet. On the lower fields where there is less frost, from about eleven to twelve thousand feet, barley grows.

These central fields nestle around Kaata community like swatches of a patchwork quilt: the white and yellow flowers of potatoes and oca, the green stems of barley, and the tan grass of those fields resting for the year. The people of Kaata farm these rotative fields, supplying the potatoes and oca for the peoples of the highland and lowlands, who exchange their own produce with the people of the central lands.

Until recently, the communities of Niñokorin, Kaata, and Apacheta exchanged produce from level to level and provided each other with the necessary carbohydrates, minerals, and proteins for their balanced subsistence. Exchange of produce, however, has become less a uniting factor on Mount Kaata since the Bolivian Agrarian Reform of 1953. The administrators of the reform insisted that Apacheta, Kaata, and Niñokorin become autonomous communities, each with political leaders subordinated to Charazani, the provincial capital, and to La Paz. In 1956, the Bolivian government surveyed Mount Kaata, defined the boundaries of the three levels, and generated endless border disputes between them. Roads to each of the three levels encouraged horizontal selling and buying in Charazani and La Paz in preference to altitudinal exchange between levels. The reformists looked to the external diversity of Mount Kaata without considering its territorial, social, and symbolic integrity. They divided Mount Kaata into three separate zones: lower corn and wheat fields; central rotative fields of potatoes, oca, and barley; pastoral highlands with alpacas, llamas, and sheep. There were notable differences among the human groups who lived at each of these altitudes. Apachetans spoke Aymara, lived apart from one another, and herded llamas. Kaatans spoke Quechua and lived together in a large community. The peoples of Niñokorin spoke Quechua and lived in smaller communities along the river. The reformers, therefore, concluded that the three communities were independent of each other and that they should compete with one another as autonomous societies.

Yet for Kaatans, there is a wholeness in their mountain, which is an ayllu. In their context, ayllu refers to a mountain with thirteen earth shrines and with communities on low, middle, and high levels. And if history is an indicator, then ayllu Kaata will remain intact for years to come. The Indians of Mount Kaata, nonetheless, remained united to each other by social and cultural principles. Kaatans argued in 1598 against the Conquistadores and in 1953 against the agrarian reformists that like a human body, the mountain is composed of parts organically united to each other. The lands of Mount Kaata belong together because they are parts of a social and human mountain.

The social principles of ayllu Kaata not only distinguish the three levels on Mount Kaata but also integrate the communities on each level into one ayllu. Patrilineal claim to land provides continuity and permanence on each level because male descendants remain on their ancestors' land. Moreover, the communities are linked together by marriage ties across levels as well as by the woman's access to land in her community.

Throughout ayllu Kaata, men remain on the land inherited from their male ancestors. The settlement of male descendants on the same plot of land guarantees continuity on each level. Men do not customarily marry women from the same level, but rather marry women from either of two levels adjacent to their levels. The settlement of Yanahuayas in Qollahuaya hamlet illustrates patrilineal claim to land: half of the thirty families in this hamlet are Yanahuayas and descendants of Marcelino's male ancestors. Although Marcelino Yanahuaya married Carmen Quispe from Niñokorin, a low community, he could have chosen someone from Apacheta, a high community. The custom of the men selecting wives from adjacent communities unites the vertical communities by marriage ties.

A corollary to exogamous levels and patrilineal claim to land in ayllu Kaata is virilocality, which means that the wife moves to her husband's community. After Carmen married Marcelino, for example, she moved from Niñokorin to Kaata. Because men remain on their ancestors' land and marry women from other levels, their wives must live on the men's levels. Women, however, inherit *access* to land from both parents according to bilineal inheritance customs found throughout ayllu Kaata. On the one hand, women marry and move to another level where, because of distance, they have limited access to their inherited land. But, on the other hand, these women's daughters return to their mothers' level if they marry someone from that community, and they work their mothers' land. The gaining of access to land is one guarantee that women will return to levels from which women departed in the preceding generation.

HUMAN MOUNTAIN

Kaatans look to their own bodies for an understanding of the mountain. How they see themselves is how they see their mountain. For a long time, Andeans have personified their land, and Kaatans still do. They name the places of the mountain according to their positions within the human body, and these places, set far apart on Mount Kaata, are organically united.

The anatomical paradigm for ayllu Kaata does not correspond entirely to geography, ecological zones, and communities. The metaphor involves imagination, ability to understand meaning of three languages, embellishment by oral tradition, and, most of all, the external application of the metaphor in ritual.

The organic wholeness projected on the communities originates from Kaatans' understanding of their physical bodies. The body (*uqhuntin*) is all the parts and only those parts which form one inner self. Kaatans do not conceptualize interior faculties for emotions and thoughts as distinct from corporal organs. Rather, they refer to their bodies as within or inside (*uqhu*). The body includes the inner self, and experiences are not dualistically perceived as those of the psyche and those of the body.

Without this dualism of material and spiritual or corporeal and interior, then, Kaatan ritual does not intercede with the spiritual in behalf of the material; rather, ritual composes both terms into one. Kaatan religion is not conceptual nor does it contain a world of spirits, but is a metaphorical relationship with their land. Kaatans do not pray to the mountain to appease its spirit; rather, they feed the

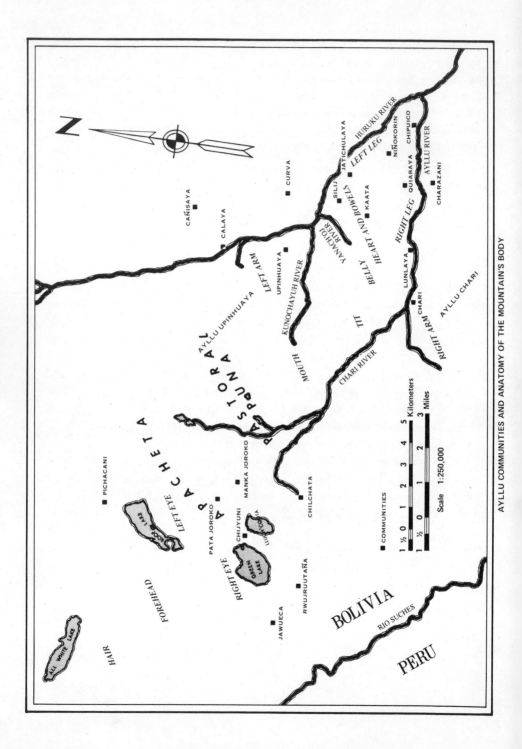

AYLLU COMMUNITIES AND ANATOMY OF THE MOUNTAIN'S BODY

mountain blood and fat to vitalize and empower it. Ritual involves them physically with the mountain. The mountain is their land and their divinity.

Andeans understand their body as a gestalt, and the suffix *ntin* of uqhuntin expresses this completeness. When Andeans add *ntin* to a word, it means transformed wholeness. *Tawantinsuyo* was the Andean name for the Inca empire. It meant the four (*tawa*) places (*suyo*) in so much as they were distinct yet united (*ntin*). The solidarity of the Inca empire was its similarity to a human body, as Garcilaso de la Vega, an early part-Inca chronicler wrote:

> The Inca Kings divided the Empire into four districts, according to the cardinal points, the whole of which they called Tawantinsuyo, which means the four parts of the world. The center was Cuzco, which, in the Peruvian language, means the navel of the world. This name was well chosen, since Peru is long and narrow like the human body, and Cuzco is situated in the middle of its belly. (Ed. 1961:57) . . . the inhabitants of Upper-Cuzco were to be considered as the elder, and those of Lower-Cuzco as the younger brothers. Indeed, it was as in the case of a living body, in which there always exists a difference between the right and left hands.
>
> All the cities and all the villages in our Empire were subsequently divided in this way into upper and lower lineages, as well as into upper and lower districts (ed. 1961:45).

The communities and land compose the parts of Mount Kaata's body, and they form the mountain's inner self, which is like a center whose axis simultaneously touches every point. The points suspend the axis and yet are always in touch with the center. Apacheta, Kaata, and Niñokorin are different levels on the mountain body, and their position is what constitutes the mountain's inner self. The inner self then gives its life to the parts.

Blood and fat empower the body: blood (*yawar*) is the life principle and fat (*wira*) is the energy principle. There are different bloods—strong, weak, frightened, and exhausted. Qollahuaya medicine men always feel the sick person's pulse to determine the type of blood. Juan Wilka, a Kaatan curer, said that Elsa Yanahuaya's blood was weak because a landslide had taken it and replaced it with water. Landslides, floods, and turbulent streams wash the land away; and water, instead of blood, flowing through the body is associated with loss of land—as well as with death. The association is that Kaatans refer to their ancestral line as blood neighbors (*yawar masikuna*) and that blood is a symbol of claim to land. An important gesture of the agricultural ritual is to sprinkle the earth with blood, vitalizing the land with the animal's principle of life as well as ratifying a kinship relationship with the mountain body (Urioste 1976).

The most important part is the heart (*sonqo*) which pumps the blood through the body. The heart is thought, intentions, and emotions. Sonqos are sad, happy, and sick; and to determine the heart of another person, the diviner places a guinea pig's mouth next to the person's heart to read its content. The person's heart is symbolically transferred to the pig's heart, which is then read, revealing the type of heart in the person.

Fat (*wira*) empowers the body, and is produced in the bowels. *Wiraqocha* (Sea of Fat) was the name of an important divinity and emperor. The powerful Spaniards were called Wiraqocha, and today Kaatans call white people by the same name. The bowels include the liver, pancreas, kidneys, stomach, and intestines. At New Earth, Sarito reads the llama's heart and bowels to determine the agricultural life (blood) and political authority (fat) of the ayllu.

Kaata is the viscera of the mountain body. Its central lands yield potatoes and oca, root plants grown inside the earth, just as the viscera gives vitality and power to the person. The hamlets are joined together as are the vital organs surrounding the heart: Kaatapata, the oldest and highest of these hamlets, forms the liver where the ayllu's central chapel is located, and the secretaries (the dominant political leaders for the entire ayllu) constitute the heart. The eight large rotative fields fold like thick layers of fat around Kaata community.

Kaata's place on the mountain geographically qualifies its people to be the major ritualists for the ayllu body, the Qollahuaya area, and the Andes. These ritualists can best circulate blood and fat, because they live where the vital organs of the mountain produce these charged symbols of life and energy. Kaata's symbolic position does not mean, however, that communities outside of ayllu Kaata conceive of it as being the center of the universe, but that Kaatans' conception of their ayllu, according to three levels and a human anatomical paradigm, places Kaata community at the center and the inside of the whole.

From the center of the mountain, the slopes slant up to form the mountain's chest (*kinre*). The right breast is called Tit Hill (*Nuño Orqo*) with its knob shaped like a nipple. Sophia, Carmen and Marcelino's fourteen year old daughter, was born on Nuño Orqo, which became her place on the mountain. It will make her fertile, if she feeds it blood, fat, and coca.

The highlands are the head (*uma*). Bunchgrass grows near the summit of the mountain, as hair on the head. The wool of llamas that graze on this grass resembles human hair. As new hair grows after cutting, so do llama wool and bunchgrass continually grow in the highlands. Similar to the regeneration of human hair, llamas originate in the highland lakes, or its eyes (*ñawi*), according to Kaatans' belief. The sun dies into these eyes of the highlands, but from the reflections within the lake come all living creatures. The lake's reflections (*illa*) are the animals and people returning from inside the earth.

Animals and people originate from and return to the head of the mountain. It is the place of origin and return, like the human head which is the point of entry and exit for the inner self. The dead travel by underground waterways to the mountain's head (*uma pacha*) from which they can arise to the land of the living. The living emerge from the eyes of the mountain, journey across its head, chest, trunk, and legs, and die in the lowlands. They are buried and return with the sun to the uma pacha, point of origin and return.

Apachetans' home near the summit of the mountain qualifies them to be the ritualists of the lakes and the dead. These highland herders travel to Kaata and Niñokorin for the Feast with the Dead. After praying for the dead and receiving bread, they carry the dead's food to the highlands. A highland herder feeds Lake Pachaqota a llama fetus during the major herding ritual of All Colors. Kaatan diviners assist Apachetans in this ritual by prophesying from guinea pigs, and Niñokorins bring *chicha* (corn beer) to the highlands.

The dispersed settlement pattern of pastoral Apachetans resembles the differentiated face; Jawueca is the hair; Ch'uyuni (four families) is the right eye; and Zaqtalaya (six families) is the left eye. Ch'uyuni and Zaqtalaya resemble eyes since each has large lakes. Water holes are necessary for livestock, and alpacas need the softer marsh areas to keep their hooves from cracking.

Wayra Wisqhani (Door of the Wind), a cavity within the earth from which air arises, is the mouth. Whenever it rains too much, mountain ritualists feed a llama heart into Wayra Wisqhani so that its breath will blow the rain clouds away.

Flowing from the summit, the Chari and Kunochayuh rivers form the *maki* (hand to elbow) of Mount Kaata. The right arm is ayllu Chari and the left arm is ayllu Upinhuaya. Although Chari and Upinhuaya have formed ayllus, Kaatans still consider them as parts of their ayllu, and they participate in Mount Kaata's rituals. Upinhuayan women are the major ritualists for dispelling misfortune and inflicting curses. During the Misfortune Mass, Rosinta Garcia washed a rat fetus into the Kunochayuh River so as to remove sickness from the Yanahuaya family. Upinhuayans are ritualists of the river who can remove, as well as cause, misfortune.

Mount Kaata's lower fields are the *chaqi* (foot to knee) and the indentations on the river are the *sillu* (toenails). The long narrow fields run parallel to the rivers descending to the jungle, and the mountain appears to be standing on them. The left leg is Niñokorin (eighty families) and the right is Quiabaya (fifteen families). The sillu are at the periphery of Mount Kaata where it joins at its lowest points with ayllus Chari and Upinhuaya. The two small settlements of Silij (four families) and Jatichulaya (three families) are the left toenails, and Lunlaya (fifteen families) forms the right toenails. Many more sillus, however, naturally arise every time the rivers subside after flooding.

The lower fields produce corn, which is fermented into *chicha*. Chicha is the sacred drink of the Andes, although it has more recently been replaced by sugarcane alcohol. The mountain and its people drink chicha during all ritual occasions. Niñokorin's people take care of the lower fields, not only by agriculture, but also by ritual to guarantee abundant corn for the mountain. The lower peoples annually feed their shrines at the feast of Corn Planting, which is similar to New Earth. Apachetans contribute a llama and Kaatans bring blood and fat to the corn planting ritual at Niñokorin.

Kaatans perceive of their ayllu as an identity between the mountain and a human body. They love metaphors between people and nature, and the association may be a resemblance of parts, similar use, or identical words. Uma, for example, means head in Quechua and water in Aymara. This double meaning fits their symbolic understanding of Apacheta. Kaatans are alive to the multiple interpretations of behavior, words, and natural phenomenon. They compared my beard to the rays of the sun, but they also associated it with heart, because I always confused heart (*sonqo*) for beard (*sonk'a*). They later explained, however, that I had spoken correctly, since Kaatan pictographs depict the sun with a beard for its rays and a heart for its center.

Several villages near Tiahuanaco, for example, understand their ayllu as organically united according to the metaphor of a cougar (Albo 1972). Andean legends personify the mountain; it has toenails, legs, a trunk, and head (see Urioste 1973). *Pariya Qaqa* (Igneous Rock), for example, is a major Andean divinity, and the account of his birth illustrates Andeans' cultural conceptions of the mountain. Pariya Qaqa was born unnoticed as five eggs, hawks, and humans on the summit, and Baked Potato Eater (*Watiya Uquri*), the son of Igneous Rock, was the first to worship him as the divinity of the mountain.

Andeans associate five with the completeness (*ntin*) of the four parts of the Inca empire as well as the organic body (Urioste 1971). Pariya Qaqa is the mountain made up of fired rock and people. Potato Eater is both his son and worshipper; the central and highlands were united by kinship and divinity.

According to legend, the lowlands were joined to the highlands in an infectious union. Red, Yellow, and Blue Llama (*T'anta Nanka*) was the most powerful man on the mountain. Parrot, rhea, and eagle feathers covered his house. He married a corn woman and went to live in the lowland, where he became Corn Leader of those people. His penis (ayllu) became infected from his wife, and he suspected her of adultery. Marriage between highlanders and lowlanders at first resulted in a feuding mountain, that is, an infected penis. Corn Leader also claimed to be a diviner (*amaut'a*), but was unable to cure himself.

One day humble Potato Eater arrived at the sick man's house to ask for his daughter in marriage. Powerful Corn Leader laughed at his outrageous request. But before Potato Eater left, Corn Leader bargained to give him his daughter if he could cure his penis. Knowing the cause of the infection, Potato Eater agreed.

"A corn kernel popped out of your wife's skillet and into her vagina," he explained.

"Cure me, then!"

"Two snakes and two toads live beneath the grinding stone," Potato Eater advised. "Take them and throw them into a deep well." Corn Leader did this and was cured. Potato Eater became the diviner of the mountain and married Corn Leader's daughter. And it came about when Corn Leader had been cured and he had traveled with Potato Eater to Lake of the Condor that Pariya Qaqa, main divinity of the ayllu, was born in the form of five eggs, five hawks, and five humans on *Kuntur Qutu* (Mountain of the Condor). "A wind blew, but there was no wind," the legend ends (ms. 3169, Ch. V).

Pariya Qaqa is born again when the llama, corn, and potato people come together in kinship and ritual. Pariya Qaqa is the mountain, but he is also a body. He is formed by the parts of the mountain.

The mountain is healed when the peoples of two different communities join in marriage, when they believe the divinations of the potato people, and when they worship Pariya Qaqa (Igneous Rock) together.

4

New Earth

Pariya Qaqa, the personified mountain and divinity of the ayllus, was born again when the herders and the corn and potato farmers arrived at the summit of Mountain of the Condor to worship him. He appeared as five eggs, five hawks, and five humans, which symbolized the unity of the levels and communities on the mountain. New Earth, an important agricultural ritual, effects a similar rebirth for the body of the mountain. Apachetans, Kaatans, and Niñokorins come together during New Earth to recreate the mountain's body. The lower and upper communities send leaders to Kaata for this rite, each bringing his zone's characteristic product, a llama and chicha. The llama's heart and bowels are buried in the center fields, and blood and fat are sent by emissaries to feed the earth shrines of the mountain. The body awakes to become the new earth.

New Earth is the second of three rites dedicated to the rotative field of the year. The earth, however, is gradually awakened by three ayllu rituals. One year before planting, the community leaders study the fertility of the fields lying fallow to see which one is ready to begin another growth cycle of potatoes, oca, and barley. The Lord of the Seasons, Sarito, observes nature's omens and asks the neighboring mountains for their assistance. Once a field is picked, Kaatans celebrate the rite of Chosen Field (*Chacrata Qukuy*), in the middle of the rainy season. Holding high their rhea feather flags, the secretaries dance across the field's terraces to the music of flutes (*pinquillo*), and they offer an unborn llama fetus, which the Elder Guide places into the field's earth shrine.[1] The fetus brings new life to the soil, and it becomes the anointed land (*enoqa qhapana*) for the year. Kaatans later fertilize their plots by spreading sheep dung along the grooves where they will plant potatoes.

The rains continue to soak the anointed field, and near the end of the rainy season, in April, Kaatans prepare to plow. But before the earth can be entered, it must be nurtured by the sacrifice of a grown llama during the rite of New Earth. With New Earth the land is vitalized; it is opened for water, air, dung, and blood, until Potato Planting, when it is covered over again. Potato Planting (*Khallay Papa Tarpuna*) is the field's final ritual, celebrated after the Feast with the Dead, who push the potatoes up from the inside of the earth, according to Aymara legends. Also in November, Niñokorins celebrate Corn Planting (*Khallay Sara Tarpuna*) and at Christmas

Feeding the Mountain a Llama Fetus

time Apachetans sponsor their herding ritual, All Colors (*Chajru Khallay*). Although each rite is concerned with the animal and plant life of its zone, collectively, the rites influence the corporate life of the ayllu, and leaders from the three communities participate in all of the ayllu's rituals.

Ayllu rites correspond to fertilization, plowing, and planting, which Kaatans understand as movements toward life. The upswing to life culminates with the harvest, to which are dedicated the man and woman saint fiestas, rites of distributing and sharing the goods of the earth. Death and life are a pair of contrasting experiences for Kaatans, and they are found in their agricultural and ritual cycles. The movement towards death is also associated with the head of the body or place where the sun dies, and the movement towards life with the legs of the body where the sun rises.

Death and life, according to Marcelino, are also found in the societal cycles when a community moves its site from one place to another as, for example, in the decline of the population of Kaatapata and the increase of Chaqahuaya. Kaatapata still has the great shrine which is an abandoned patio in the midst of ruins, but Chaqahuaya has another shrine, Phesqa Pata, which is now associated with political authority of the community. Andeans' sense of time reflects this life and death cycle. Time is not a set point, but a cycle between two strokes always circulating within the mountain's agricultural, ritual, social, and corporeal bodies. Like the swing of a pendulum, each stroke can go only so far, and then it starts back again. Furthermore, each stroke propels the other. The death of the llama, for instance, is the life of the ayllu's agricultural body. New Earth is part of a ritual cycle which corresponds to the life and death of plants, and it is fitting that when the earth comes alive Kaatans celebrate its rebirth.

THE LORD OF THE SEASONS

Sarito, also called Lord of the Seasons, influences the life and growth of the people, animals, and crops by circulating blood and fat to the earth shrines of Mount Kaata during the ritual of New

Earth. According to Andean belief, blood is associated with life and comes from the heart, and fat is associated with energy and comes from the bowels. Since Sarito lives in Kaata, the heart and bowels of the mountain/body metaphor, he can circulate life and energy throughout the parts of the mountain. Moreover, the leaders and commoners of ayllu Kaata not only supply him with large chunks of llama fat to give energy to the mountain body, but they also anoint his heart and forehead with llama fat. In rites of anointing and fertility, Kaatans rub the person and object with llama fat. For the feast of San Juan, for example, Carmen Yanahuaya burned llama fat before the statue of San Juan, charging it to increase her sheep; at other times, she mixed fat with cow and sheep dung, which she then buried in the ground for abundant crops. If, on the contrary, fat is stolen from Carmen by the legendary *Qhariciri*, who slices layers of fat from sleeping people, then her strength slips away into the hands of this fat-cutter.

Fat and blood, fluid and systemic symbols, are external to the ritualist whose role is to circulate life and energy throughout the social and ecological levels. He sets in motion vital principles which unite the mountain into a social and metaphorical whole. On the other hand, if Sarito is unable to bring it together, then he has lost his ability to circulate the blood and fat. Shortly thereafter, the leaders will rub another diviner with fat to make him the Lord of the Seasons.

Sarito, however, is a charismatic leader who has his own fat. Before he was anointed to be chief ritualist, he had successfully manipulated the blood, fat, and coca for many people, and his divinations were fulfilled. The influential mestizos of Charazani, moreover, always call on Sarito to perform their rituals in exchange for a month's salary.[2] Kaata has 100 ritualists to choose from, and few Bolivians would pay such a high price unless Sarito had power.

Sarito has no doubt of his own skills independent of the official anointing, and he often complains about the drudgery of performing the long agricultural rituals for only a llama skin as pay. The drunks constantly pester him and complain about his advice concerning the agricultural cycle. Fights between communities vitiate his ritual attempts to create a solidified ayllu. Sarito once threatened to resign before Potato Planting, but the community gave him more cloths containing llama fat and persuaded him to continue for another year.

Sarito's expertise resulted from years of apprenticeship to his father, Ambrosio Quispe. Ambrosio had been crippled by lightning, the Lord of the Air, who swings hail in his sling and pours rain from his pitcher. According to Andean tradition, Lightning Flash (*Intuillapa*) gave Ambrosio its ability to control rain and hail. Whenever there is an impending hailstorm, Sarito waves his staff and shouts at Intuillapa to sling his hail at Kaata's enemies. Accompanying his father during such a ritual, Sarito was grazed by lightning, but fortunately it only singed his hair. Sarito, then, became a descendant of a metaphorical lineage which claims its origin from a god-like construct whose works are carried on year after year by human beings who possess divinelike powers.

Ambrosio taught Sarito to read the coca leaves and manipulate the blood, fat, and coca for the masses. When he became ill, Sarito continued his father's practice, and after Ambrosio's death, Sarito inherited his valuable scallop shells (*mullu*), the sacred dishes from which the lords of the season and ayllu could be fed.

Kaatans attribute magical properties to objects which combine, or are combined with, different elements. Coca from the eastern tropics and shellfish from the Pacific Ocean, both from the peripheries of the central Andes, are considered exotic foods, fruit of the gods, and fine offerings for the earth. Kaatans, however, do not feed the mountain the meat of the shellfish, but use this fish's home as a serving dish for their divinities. Coca and shellfish might not be magical individually; rather, it is the gesture of combining coca with seashells, then placing these offerings inside the earth shrine that is magical. The snail, which combines within itself different elements, is an important Kaatan symbol. Magical properties are attributed to the snail because not only does it live on land and in the water, but also carries its home up and down the mountain.

Coca, an oracle of the earth and a divine remedy for curing, is the most extensive Andean symbol. Qollahuayas always distinguish between the religious specialists who cure with plants (*curanderos*) and those who heal by reading coca and feeding the earth shrines (*yachaj*). Although some curers prophesy outside of the province, the Qollahuayas discredit them and say they are incompetent.

Andeans realize that to cure effectively with herbs, the curer must know the symptoms of sickness and the pharmaceutical properties of many plants. The curer, then, has very little time to specialize as a diviner, which involves just as much apprenticeship in learning the liturgy of the rituals and the folklore of the land.

Kaatans are attuned to their environment with the wholeness of an intuitive knowledge which is grounded in lore and wisdom. Sarito is very skilled in this knowledge which assists him in reading the coca leaves, and his rites of divination are often communal sessions for discussing the signs of nature. Sarito realizes that he will be put to the test of having his prophecy come true, and a few bad calls would be a sign to the people that he had lost his fat.

Sarito also knows by reading the coca leaves, and Kaatans say this about coca:

> The leaves are like God. They have wisdom. We don't know how Sarito is able to prophesy from the leaves, but one day he appeared saying, *"Yachaniy nispa,"* ("I know, saying"). Before him, Ambrosio Quispe was the prophet, but he died and his son Sarito began prophesying. When Sarito dies another person will appear saying, "I know." Sarito knows all the names of the saints, the lords of the ayllu, the passes, the mountains, and the volcanoes.

Yachay is "to know," and ritualists are called *qari yachaj* (man knower) and *warmi yachaj* (woman knower). To "know" is not an interior faculty reflecting upon an outside world as we might understand it; but it is the ability to intuit one's heart which is at the inner center of the body. It is the omniscience to understand the secrets of the mountain body in terms of the corporeal body. Earth and humans no longer exist as dichotomies but rather as endless reflections of differently shaped mirrors. There is no need to look for the distinctions between earth and humans since they are essentially identical. To "know," then, is to be associated symbolically with the heart, and it is a bodily unity with everything around oneself, in so far as the body is understood as inner self. By participating in the drug effects of coca, the body is united spiritually to the earth. This communion, furthermore, reveals the nature of the earth to Andeans. People come together with the mountain by chewing coca.[3]

Sarito knows the names and location of the earth shrines on

Mount Kaata, and the life and death of the ayllu depends on how well he feeds them. Earth shrines are natural openings or small holes dug into the ground. They are covered with rocks, except during ritual feedings. Alongside the hole is usually a rock pile, where Indians place their coca quids before fresh leaves are put inside the hole. Earth shrines are found near passes, waterholes, knobs, and rocks. The shrine's many names express history, humor, geography, and social relationships. The eastern leg's site, for example, is called Jilakata's Recourse, because it was once a rest stop for Kaata's mayors on their journey to pay tribute to Charazani officials. The shrine's knob suggests its other names: Goat Corral, Bachelor's Haven, Coitus, and Chicha Bubble. Each name has a long explanation, and it is Sarito's role to recall these during rituals.

Mount Kaata has thirteen earth shrines, each of which is interpreted according to its association with an ecological level and the body metaphor. The three community shrines are Chaqamita, Pachaqota, and Jatun Junch'a. Chaqamita, located to the east near the legs, is related to the sun's birth, fertility and corn, making it a suitable shrine for Niñokorin and Quiabaya, whose Corn Planting rite reverences this site. This lower lake is also a shrine for Curva and Chullina, neighboring ayllus. Earth shrines, when shared by several ayllus, religiously unite separated mountains, and so Qollahuayas claim that they are one people because they worship the same shrines. Pachaqota, a large lake on the head, is the "eye" into which the sun sinks; it symbolizes death, fertilization, and llamas. Apachetan herders celebrate All Colors on the shores of Pachaqota.

The Great Shrine (*Jatun Junch'a*), associated with the liver and Kaata, lies in the hamlet of Kaatapata. This is also the major shrine of the mountain, because of its central location and physiography. Kaatapata rests on a spur, which rises from the slopes and resembles a small mountain. The Great Shrine is nourished at the rite of Chosen Field and is also the site of a mock battle (*tinku*) between the elders and clowns of Carnival. The clowns, who sprinkle people with water, are symbolically put to death by the elders slinging ripe fruit at them. Usually the youth join the clowns in open conflict with the adults, and sometimes both groups rally against the women, who invade the courtyard with cornstalks, beating the males to the ground. Marcelino proudly displays a scar above his eye from a tinku.

Similar ritual battles are fought in other places; the Aymaras of the Bolivian Altiplano, for example, wage theatrical warfare between the upper and lower divisions of the community. Tinku emphasizes the importance of contrasting pairs, and in the Andes almost everything is understood in juxtaposition to its opposite (Duviols 1974). Earth shrines are also interpreted according to binary opposition. Chaqamita and Pachaqota, for instance, correspond to life and death, and each term explains the other; moreover, each leads to the other.

The high, central, and low lands have community shrines reflecting their ecological zones; but from the viewpoint of the ayllu, the community shrine is only one part of the body metaphor. In some way every level must feed all the mountain's shrines during the ayllu rites, such as New Earth. Apachetans, for example, contribute a llama fetus to the lower eastern shrine, just as Niñokorins supply chicha to feed the highland shrine. Although the shrines are located on specific levels of the mountain, they are part of the total religion of the mountain.

In addition to holistic considerations, earth shrines have specific meanings. Earth shrines are stratified according to levels of land, social groupings, time, and historical epochs. The patrilineage has its household shrines dug into the inside and outside of the house; the community has its shrine corresponding to its level on the mountain; and the ayllu has its thirteen shrines on the whole mountain. Ayllu Kaata has thirteen ayllu shrines, twelve on Mount Kaata and one on nearby Chaqamita lake. Ayllu shrines are ritual sites for the annual and major rituals of Apacheta, Kaata, and Niñokorin. The community of Kaata also has eight field shrines, one on each of the rotative fields. A field shrine is fed only when its rotative field is first being worked on, or every eight years.

Corresponding to these stratified shrines are distinct, yet similar, rituals. Moreover, there are certain times when these shrines are fed by specific rites and specialized ritualists, carefully skilled in such matters. At other times and places, the Catholic and saints' rituals are performed by catechists and priests. Catholic services are held in the chapel with a procession around the plaza. By time and place, therefore, Kaatans distinguish between the earth shrines for the saints and those for the mountain. They never mix the two classes of shrines and their specific rituals.

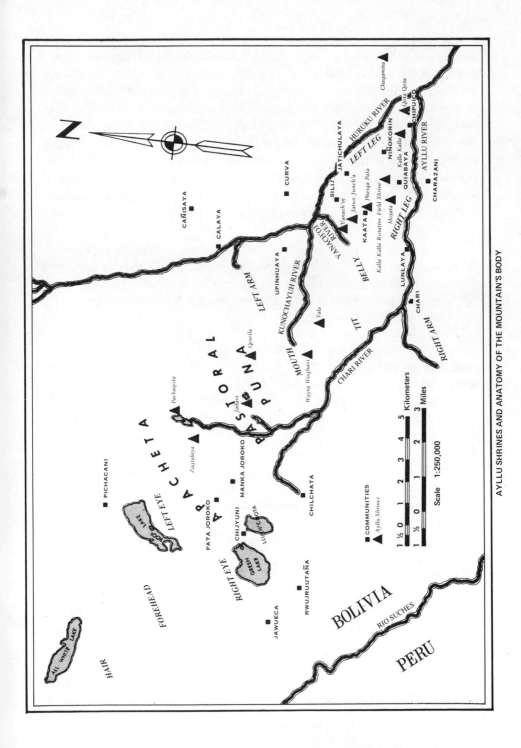

AYLLU SHRINES AND ANATOMY OF THE MOUNTAIN'S BODY

Kaatan diviners service the earth shrines of Mount Kaata as well as those of other Andean mountains. Earth shrines are found throughout the Andes, and they follow a long Andean tradition. Early Andean religion focused on earth shrines and fetishes to places.[4] Missionaries in the sixteenth century attempted to exterminate Andean religion by destroying earth shrines. In a Jesuit manual of extirpation of idolatry, the following questions were asked of the Indian communities: "Name of the huaca? Is it a rock, hill, or crag?" (Arriaga 1621:118) which reveal that the extirpators associated the Indians' shrines with a specific geographical place. The community and province had distinct shrines, as Polo de Ondegardo (1571:*ex capite* 98) writes:

> Each province has a temple or *huaca principal* where the entire population adores and sacrifices. Each central community has another temple, or *huaca minor*, where they also gather. Each of these shrines maintains ministers as well as the necessary items for such superstitions.

Ayllus also claimed their descent from prominent landmarks, and they maintained a ritual relationship with that place as their totem (see Bandelier 1910:145).

Two important pre-Columbian temples on the Altiplano were on the islands Titicaca and Koati, and their principal shrine was the puma rock, which was oriented to the sun. "Nevertheless, that rock," Bandelier (1910:237) says, "and not the sun, was the principal fetish of the island."

The arrangement of shrines according to geography and the sun added a sacred dimension to people associated with these places. The ruins of the ancient city of Tiahuanaco (circa 900 A.D.) illustrate this. Andeans, at a time when Europe was still barbaric, transported mammoth rocks along Lake Titicaca and across fourteen miles of the Altiplano to construct shrines to the sacred earth. Tiahuanaco's major shrines were built on different levels of the earth. Akapana was a large hill with staircases. The top of the hill held a cistern of water, suggesting a similarity to the head of the mountain, where the water originated. Kalasasaya, with its erect monoliths and sun gate, was a courtyard shrine raised slightly above the surface of the earth. Excavated into the earth was a subterranean courtyard about the size of a suburban swimming pool. Carved heads of totemic animals and ancestors emerged from the sides of the walls. Shrines on the hill, at ground level, and below the surface symbolized the high, central, and low lands. The sun gate in Kalasasaya was used for solar observations, harmonizing the agricultural cycle with the celestial cycle. Inside these "Standing Rocks" (Kalasasaya) was the door, Gateway of the Sun, through which the sun would shine, marking off four fiestas corresponding to the azimuths of the sun and pivotal points on the frieze of the gateway. The Tiahuanaco priest-astronomers had to determine the different seasons of the year exactly, in order to know the precise dates of the different agricultural periods, which also marked the principal religious fiestas of the time.[5]

The geography of Cuzco is another pre-Columbian example of sacredly organizing space by earth shrines. Cuzco was planned according to imaginary lines (*ceques*), which radiated from the central temple to earth shrines around the city (Zuidema 1964). The ceques separated Cuzco into four divisions, which corresponded to four matrilineal, exogamous moieties linked by asymmetrical cross-cousin marriages. Each division was again separated into locations corresponding to full-blooded (*Qollana*) and half-blooded (*Payan*) Incas, and others (*Cayoa*). The arrangement of the shrines were related to the journey of the sun and to the three hierarchical social units living in places that were sacredly ranked. The place of the Inca was the sacred space.

Sarito and the secretaries lead the mountain's people through the agricultural and ritual cycle of life and death. This cycle is a traditional characteristic of Andean religion; Cuzco and Tiahuanaco synchronized social, agricultural, and ritual behavior with the celestial cycle during pre-Columbian times. Moreover, contemporaneous Altiplano Aymaras continue to celebrate rituals which correspond to harvesting (autumn equinox), ch'uño-making (winter solstice), first planting (spring equinox), and second planting (summer solstice).

Sarito and the secretaries send emissaries to the ayllu's shrines for the first half of New Earth. Before this rite, secretaries and emissaries are elected by Sarito and commoners. The mountain's people contribute coca, llama fat, guinea pigs, and chicha. Receiving these gifts, Sarito prepares and dispatches these empowered symbols with the emissaries to the ayllu's shrines.

Kaatans name the secretaries after the Feast with the Dead. The incumbent secretaries make up a secret list of the candidates, selecting commoners who have arrived at the specific burden (*cargo*) which needs to be filled. Women are encouraged to become secretaries, although they are not obliged, and Kaata has two female leaders. Every Kaatan male climbs a ladder of consecutive posts, which he is required to hold regardless of his leadership qualities or charisma. At sixteen, he is expected to be host of a flute band for one of the saint fiestas. He next becomes an assistant to the Secretary General or Secretary of Relations. Military service can substitute for these burdens. After this, he is ready to fill one of the minor secretary roles, such as that of press and propaganda, sports, roads, treasury, agriculture, notes, justice, social welfare, and education. He must be minor secretary twice, after which he can be sponsor for any of the two major or minor saint fiestas. He is then called on to be a major secretary, by which time he is in his forties. He is still further required to be sponsor for a major fiesta, and he finally ends his burdens by being *corregidor* for Kaata. Women do not perform all the minor secretary roles before they are nominated sponsors for the female saint fiestas. They can then be major secretaries, but this is rare in Kaata because women shun these costly roles. The Kaatan adult has then finished his communal responsibilities, and he is a whole person (*pasado runa*) who has been empowered so many times by his community to lead it. The whole persons are the elders of Kaata, who decide important community matters and who hold places of honor at rituals and fiestas.

These secretary roles were legislated for every Indian community by the Bolivian Agrarian Reform in 1954. The Agrarian Reform legislated yearly elections and insisted upon leadership qualities for the elected officials rather than automatic and consecutive appointments. After the abolition of feudalism, the secretaries were to govern their communities as directors of peasant syndicates. Each secretary's role was to foment the specific item for which he was named, for instance, the secretary of sports might introduce soccer. Although Kaata's officials were called secretaries, their roles still corresponded to those of the cargo system.[6] The community leaders continued to concentrate on their ritual responsibilities, disregarding their proposed roles as rural and community developers.

However, Kaatans are not anxious to assume these responsibilities, which are very time consuming and require large expenditures. In 1972 the newly appointed secretaries refused to take office, until the subprefect in Charazani officially forced them to assume the roles under threat of a heavy fine if they did not. Other Kaatans realize the advantage of filling the posts quickly, while one is young and able, and then profiting from the advantages of being a whole person. Posts are held for only one-year terms, and a man is usually required to wait several years between each post. The secretaries' major task is to sponsor and organize the agricultural rituals with Sarito.

On a Tuesday night in March, 1972, the major secretaries visited Sarito. A rocky path wound upward through eucalyptus trees to Sarito's hut in Chaqahuaya. Sarito met them where the path entered a tiny courtyard, which was scattered with broken boxes, chickens, dung, and dogs. The barking dogs stopped the visitors until Sarito tied the dogs. They entered the kitchen, where Maria, Sarito's wife, served them soup. Everyone ate and chewed coca. About an hour later, the leaders asked the Elder Guide, "*Tatay*, would you be so kind and generous to feed the *mallkus* for us?" Condor (mallku) is a sacred name for earth shrines. The condor (*Vultur gryphus*) symbolizes the mountain in several ways. Young condors are born from eggs on the summit, where their mothers nest. The condor is a metaphor of Andeans who, according to legend, also originate and return to the uma pacha. When the condor sits, its natural shape resembles the three levels. The toes branch out similar to the lower fields protruding onto the river. The condor's black back slants like the trunk of the mountain, and a white collar sets off a crested head, which parallels the snow around the summit. Kaatans also call Sarito "Mallku," because he is charged with the task of feeding the mountain to make it alive like the condor. After Sarito was requested to perform New Earth, he reviewed his own schedule for a moment and said that he had time Wednesday and Thursday, April 12 and 13. Wednesday and Thursday are the days for the agricultural rites and health masses; Tuesdays and Fridays are days for performing sorcery and dispelling misfortune; and Saturday and Sunday are for Catholic rituals.

Once Sarito had set the date, the Secretary General handed him coca and fat, which he had collected from the people. Sarito stacked them into piles for the lords of the season, patrons of the kitchen and patio, and for Phesqa Pata shrine, located next to the Secretary General's house. Sarito's assistant burned these bundles in the fire pot, spreading the ashes in the shrine to the patron of his patio. The secretaries handed coca to Sarito, and he threw the leaves to determine the emissary for each secretary.

The secretaries began preparations a week before New Earth. Each major secretary slaughtered a llama and the minor secretaries either baked bread or contributed alcohol. The herders scrutinized their llamas for a fortuitous offering to the mountain, and the corn planters brewed chicha. The Secretary General commissioned the other secretaries to collect the quotas (suk'anas) from each family, which were one guinea pig, one pound each of llama fat and coca, and a pint of alcohol. After the commoner had contributed, the secretary invited him, saying, "Come to the banquet of New Earth on Wednesday."

Political leaders, as well as the Elder Guide, manipulate blood, fat, and coca, presented to them by the communities. When authority is bestowed upon them they must use it for the growth of the agricultural and social body. Religious and political leadership is not personal power nor should it accrue to the holder's gain. On the contrary, to have the power is to carry the weight (cargo) or fat to the metaphorical body.

In other words, blood and fat are symbols that have both ideological and physiological referents (see Turner 1967:28). They are physiologically rooted in the body, pertaining to the life and energy of the organism. They also connote the community's life and energy, when they are entrusted to the secretaries and Elder Guide.

DISPATCHING THE BLOOD AND FAT

New Earth began after midnight on Wednesday. The Secretary General welcomed Marcelino and me into his meeting room. Smoke crept through the sooted straw roof, making it difficult to see the secretaries and the emissaries asleep on a platform. As we began sharing coca and alcohol, they awoke and chatted about a frost which had set in the night before. Sarito arrived hours later, and everyone greeted him solemnly, beginning with the highest, and ending with the lowest official. He assigned Chaqamita to the secretaries of education and sports, and Pachaqota to the secretary of treasury. The benches were in a rectangular arrangement, and the secretaries sat on them, whereas their wives were seated in a circle on the dirt floor. The women were busy preparing soup. The Elder Guide had appointed one assistant, Julian Ticona, to spread the ritual cloth in the eastern corner and to untie cloths of coca and fat for the mass. The secretary of education gave Sarito fat and coca, and Sarito prepared six plates for Chaqamita, naming them: Chaqamita's ayllu shrine, the shrine's servant, lords of the season, patrons of the kitchen and patio, secretary of education, and his wife. He also chose Concepción Quispe, the second best ritualist in Kaata, to be the emissary for this important fertility shrine. The Elder Guide served the lords of the mountain and the secretary the foods of knowledge, life, and power, and the secretary's wife brought soup and drink to Sarito and the emissary. Sarito slurped the soup, pushing large chunks of llama meat into his mouth. By morning, he had eaten thirteen such servings. Thirteen servings symbolize the earth shrines and leaders of Mount Kaata. Like the condor, Sarito is an embodiment of the mountain, and once he eats thirteen servings, then the mountain has symbolically been fed. The mountain will consequently reciprocate by an abundant harvest.

Sarito and Julian put thirteen coca leaves, llama fat, and guinea pig blood on wads of cotton, praying for the success of the harvest, the secretaries, and the community. The thirteen servings expressed the coming together of the shrines, secretaries, and societies on the mountain.

Once the plates had been prepared, Sarito wrapped the cotton around the coca, fat, and incense by crossing east, west, south, then north corners. He next set the five plates on one corner of the coca cloth, which was folded over coca leaves. The complementary corner was likewise folded over the cotton bundle, and the sixth bundle placed on top for Chaqamita. Everything was then tied to a large llama fetus. The wrapping of the four corners around the coca and fat into cotton balls, and then sorting them into groups of five, symbolizes the Inca empire, Pariya Qaqa, and the mountain body. The llama fetus would symbolically carry these ritual gifts to the center of the mountain.

The first rays of dawn sent streaks of red, pink, and white over Chaqamita as several roosters loudly and persistently announced the birth of the sun. Some of the secretaries had fallen asleep and were snoring in the corner of the room. Sarito shook them from their sleep as he announced, "Companions, secretaries, emissaries, it's time to feed the earth shrines." Everyone arose, staggering from tiredness, food and drink, and entered the courtyard. The Chaqamita emissaries and their secretaries turned towards the birth of the sun, while the Pachaqota emissaries with their secretary and his wife looked towards the death of the sun. Sarito gave each of the secretaries one of the thirteen cotton bundles, which they held close to their hearts. While they prayed to the lords and the shrines, they slowly revolved from east to west and back again.

Sarito gathered the thirteen gifts from the secretaries. After he had put five of them in the coca cloth, he tied the corners around the fetus and the bottle. He put another five with the llama fat. Sarito held the coca cloth with the fetus on the secretary of education's head. Sarito prayed for his good fortune and for his leadership of the community. He did similarly for the secretary of sports and his wife, and then handed the bundles to the second emissary to Chaqamita. The same was done for the Pachaqota emissary and his sponsoring secretary of treasury.

The community, the secretary, and his wife sent blood to the mountain's body by giving guinea pigs to their emissary. Sarito held a large male guinea pig on the secretary's chest and forehead. When the guinea pig touched the forehead, it received the secretary's sweat, which symbolized his labor. Sarito marked out this pig for Concepción, saying that its viscera would reveal the secretary of education's heart. Sarito did the same with a female guinea pig, placing it on the secretary's wife, and then a smaller one was assigned to the community. The emissaries would open the stomachs of these guinea pigs at the place shrines, first pouring some blood into a cup for libation of the places. The emissaries would then decide what information could be revealed from the guinea pig's heart, pancreas, and liver concerning the person or community whose forehead and chest had been touched.

Kaatan diviners look for certain indicators in the heart and bowels of the guinea pig. A beating heart and large pancreas and liver predict good fortune. If the heart is not beating and the other organs are withered, then bad luck will come to the person or community. Twin organs of any of the bowels indicate fertility for women, animals, and crops. White spots on the bowels are signs of frost or snow. The diviner reads these organs in the presence of the person seeking the information, and he thoroughly explains the signs and the consequences to the seeker. Often the person disagrees with his interpretations, but the diviner merely replies, "We will see." The emissary is unable to display the organs to the secretary, but he shows his assistant, so that his interpretations can be verified. The Elder Guide always selects emissaries who prophesy accurately, such as Concepción, who was sent to Chaqamita.

The emissaries fastened firewood across their backs and filled their medicine bags with coca, fat, and other ritual items. Anxious to go, they paraded between two rows of secretaries, who cheered them on. Two of them headed to the birth of the sun, and the other two went to where the sun is buried. These Andean emissaries were returning to the highlands and lowlands to circulate the blood and the fat. Until late that morning, emissaries traveled to other earth shrines on the parts of the mountain body. Sarito similarly prepared meals for shrines Qowila and Kalla Kalla.

Qowila and Kalla Kalla correspond to the arms and legs of the body. Qowila lies on a knoll west of Kaata near the source of the Kunochayuh River, which forms a boundary between ayllus Kaata and Upinhuaya. Both ayllus dispatch emissaries to feed this shrine, and its common religious value to both communities links them in spite of their hostilities. Kalla Kalla shrine protrudes from the land mass which forms the crotch of the two legs, Niñokorin and Quiabaya. As Qowila is an interayllu ritual site, Kalla Kalla is similarly an inter-ayllu market site for exchange of produce and specialized ayllu products among the Qollahuayas during the fiesta of the Virgin's Birth. Ayllu Amarete trades its pots and wooden farm instruments for the fruit from ayllu Chullina, and ayllu Kaata trades bread with ayllu Chari for dried llama meat (*charqui*). Kalla Kalla's chapel and plaza are the ritual site for Niñokorin's male and female saints' fiestas.

Sarito and Julian next prepared meals for Zaqtalaya and Tala. Zaqtalaya is associated with the left eye, and Tala is near Tit Hill. The Tala emissary would also travel to the Door of the Wind, where he would feed blood, fat, and coca into the mouth of the mountain's head. Zaqtalaya, a lake, would be supplicated for rain. Sarito dispatched these emissaries and began preparing meals for the last three ayllu shrines located at the trunk of the body.

Mojata, Yanach'oj, and Phesqa Pata are the viscera shrines. Mojata shrine lies between the rotative fields and Llach'alaya. In

Rhea-Feather Flags and Qollahuaya Mountains

addition to being an ayllu shrine, Mojata is an *apacheta* for ayllu Kaata. This shrine should not be confused with the community and place of Apacheta, found in the head of Mount Kaata. Throughout the Andes, the apacheta is the highest place on a road, where the Indian rests from his ascending journey, discards his coca quid, and throws several stones into a large pile, consciously symbolizing the removal of his load and the restoration of strength. Apacheta is derived from *apachiy*, meaning to have something or someone carry the load away. Annually, in memory of Jesus carrying a cross, Kaatans carry a large wooden cross to Mojata apacheta, where it is placed on top of the rock pile. The multivocality of the cross and the apacheta allows the possibility of many meanings, and so the apacheta is associated with the unloading of the cross, its sins, their sufferings, and, perhaps, the historical burden of Christianity. In this way the symbol allows one symbolic system, Qollahuaya religion, to be expressed by, and to express, another symbolic system, Catholicism. The symbol affords a continuity of Kaatan culture in that its "polysemic" property (Turner 1967:50) can tokenly satisfy the conquering people with one meaning (the cross that Jesus died on) on one hand, while on the other it can also refer to another meaning of the culture (a burden to be unloaded). The polysemic property of which Turner writes has the quality of allowing an impositional symbol to take on the meaning of an indigenous symbol, as well as the reverse. These are the layers of history to which the symbol may refer. Kaatans, however, usually structure their symbols according to those for their indigenous beliefs and those for the Catholic beliefs; yet to them it is one whole system of religious beliefs and practices.

Yanach'oj shrine is near the Yanach'oj River, which divides the rotative fields of Nak'a and Qolla, northwest of the hamlet of Qollahuaya.

Toward the middle of the morning, Sarito prepared the ritual items for the last shrine of Phesqa Pata, which was recently established in Chaqahuaya. Lightning had struck Phesqa Pata in 1965, and constituted it a shrine for the hamlet and ayllu, much to the consternation of the other communities of the ayllu.

After the secretaries and Elder Guide had sent the emissaries to the thirteen shrines, they relaxed by drinking alcohol, chewing coca, and chatting about the weather. It was close to noon, and they deserved a rest, for they had meticulously prepared symbols of an ancient liturgy since the middle of the night. Everyone was mildly intoxicated. Throughout the ritual, the attitude was relaxed and humorous, yet, at the same time, serious and sacred. Jokes and clever remarks were appreciated and heartily enjoyed. Sarito never demanded solemnity nor deference, which he emanated naturally, but he chatted amiably while he worked, occasionally being the wit of the group. Julian, quite intoxicated, talked loudly and shouted jokes for everyone to enjoy. He was not only the ritual's assistant but also the jester, providing the comic relief for the solemn and lengthy rituals.

The Elder Guide and secretaries concretely classified the ayllu according to the metaphor of the body, which divides the highlands into the head, the central lands into the belly, and the lowlands into the legs.

The sending of the emissaries is, however, more than a conceptual ordering of the parts within the whole in that it symbolizes the sending of life and energy to the parts of the ayllu body. Blood and fat have physiological reference to the heart and bowels of the corporeal body as well as ideological references to the life and energy of the cultural body. The very fluidity of these concrete symbols adds another dimension to the ideological referents of life and energy. Life and energy of the ayllu is fluid, as is blood and fat. At every point the ritual suggests that the blood and fat are passed on and circulated by the commoners, the secretaries, and the ritualists. The secretaries and their emissaries circulate the fat and blood from the center to the parts. Political authority, the handling of the fat and blood, is not inherited, nor innately present, nor endowed by the Bolivian state, nor dependent upon personal charisma. Ayllu life and energy are found in all the parts but are circulated during important rituals from the Kaata community, whose Elder Guide and secretaries send fat and blood to the mountain's parts. The ritual emphasizes to some degree that the commoners, secretaries, and ritualists all handle blood, fat, and knowledge. They are entrusted with these vital principles of another body, which is just as complete as their own, yet geographically, socially, and historically beyond their corporeal body.

BLOOD AND FAT FOR THE CENTER

For the second part of New Earth, the leaders fed the shrine of the field chosen for the year. Kalla Kalla was selected as the rotative field for 1972. The secretaries from the head, heart, and legs gathered at the field shrine to nurture it with coca, fat, and blood. The movement of the second half was the reverse of the first, for now the peoples from the peripheries would come to the center.

At noon the Secretary of Relations and four minor secretaries marched with rhea flags to the Kalla Kalla field shrine, while the Secretary General, four minor secretaries, and a flute band remained near Kaatapata and Phesqa Pata shrines with four similar flags. The Elder Guide, his assistant, two children, and some commoners followed the Kaatan flags of rhea feathers plummeting from the top and a white cloth from the side of the pole.[7] Victor and Erminia Quispe, the children, would first plow the earth for the community. Victor was dressed in a red poncho, with the steel-tipped wooden plow (*tajlla*) strapped across his back. His young female companion wore a soft red felt skirt underneath another snail-motif skirt with woven stripes of animals and birds. These children had been selected because they were the offspring of hard workers. In the morning Victor and Erminia had been the guests of honor at the Secretary General's house, where they were served plates of soup and several orange drinks.

Another band of a dozen flutists silently joined the secretaries at the earth shrine. Sarito explained their silence by saying that, because the shrine had not yet been fed, it was in an irritable mood. The field shrine was nestled on the hillside of a small grass terrace, which Kaatans cultivated for the Elder Guide. Sarito would be given the fruits of this field in payment for his service. Sarito and Julian carefully removed the rocks covering the shrine's opening, about the size of a basketball. Inside the cavity were decayed coca leaves, fat, and ashes reddened by blood, which had been fed to the field in 1966, when it had begun another three-year cycle of work. Everyone looked away as Sarito touched three leaves to his heart; then looking towards Aqhamani and praying silently to the lords of the season and of the ayllu, he gently placed the leaves into the shrine. Silently, as if by eternal coincidence, six herders descended upon the field shrine. Following them in their own independent way was a llama herd, which was accompanying the *qochu*.

The qochu is the gift of the sacrificial llama from the highlands, and the word is derived from *qochuy*, which means getting great pleasure from something. The earth shrine enjoys the llama's blood and fat. The llama, which symbolizes the highlands, has a great exchange value to all levels of the ayllu: its hair is necessary for weaving; it transports goods between levels; and its meat is dried for charqui. The llama, furthermore, provides Andeans with dairy products, leather, and fertilizer. Large llama herds signify wealth for ayllu Kaata.

Andean legends consider the llama to be a prophetic being, as the following sixteenth century oral tradition illustrates:

> Now we will return to the traditions of the very early ancestors. The story is as follows: a long time ago, this world was about to be destroyed. A male llama knew that the ocean was ready to flood the earth. Although the llama herder was having it rest in a very good pasture, the llama refused to eat and looked very sad. It wept, saying, *"In, in."* Very angry, the llama herder threw a cob of corn that he had just eaten at the llama and said, "Eat dog! Look, I'm letting you rest in so big a pasture!" Then the llama beginning to speak as a human being said, "You are silly! What things are you capable of thinking? Five days from today, the ocean will overflow as a giant waterfall. Thus the world will come to an end."
>
> "How will we be? Where could we go to save ourselves?" spoke the herder.
>
> "Let us go to the Huillcacoto Mountain. There we will be spared. Bring food to last five days," the llama said. Then, departing very hastily, the herder carried the llama and all its load. When they arrived at Mount Huillcacoto, there were already all kinds of animals: a mountain lion, a fox, a *guanaco*, and a condor. As soon as that man got there the ocean began to overflow. All stayed very close to each other there.
>
> As the waters buried all the mountains, only Huillcacoto, or rather its very summit, was not reached by the water. The fox had its tail wet by the water. They say that this is why it turned black. Five days later the water went down and it began to get dry. As it was getting dry, the ocean receded all the way down after having exterminated all mankind. Afterwards, man began again to multiply. This is why there are still men today.

We Christians believe that this tradition speaks of the time of the flood, while they believe that it was Huillcacoto that saved them (Huarochiri ms. 3169:F. 66).

The qochu again saves man by coming from the place of origin, shedding his blood for all the parts, and returning to the mountain.

The Apachetan herders were called ayllu men (*llahtaruna*) because they were political leaders from Apacheta as well as leaders of the ayllu. The lower ayllu men also arrived from the communities representing the legs and toenails of the body. They arrived with chicha, with which they would sprinkle the earth throughout the ritual. This white fluid from the legs of the ayllu body would be served to all. The ayllu men exchanged coca with the Kaatan secretaries, and they gave Sarito coca and fat to be used ritually during the feeding of the shrine. They all assisted the Elder Guide in preparing a banquet for the lords of the season, the lords of the ayllu, and the field shrine. On each shell, Sarito placed coca, llama fat, carna-

Children Plowing the Fields

tions, incense, and blood. He served twenty-six shells to the old and new lords of the season, the lord of the community, the lord of the rotative field, the lord of the llama, and the lord of the lower fields.

While the ritual table was being prepared, the children began plowing the terrace in front of the shrine. The flute band played to the field, blowing a repetitious pattern of four notes (ré fa mi dó re re) while the drum loudly beat a thudding 6/8 time. Victor forced the curved plow's iron blade into the earth, then pushed down on the arched handle to uproot clods of turf, which his female companion, kneeling on the earth, held close to her belly and gently turned over, forming straight rows. Together they made the furrows and rows neither too far apart nor too close together. Kaatans plant seeds the same way: the man opens the earth with a plow blade and the woman takes the seed from her lap and deposits it into the earth. The man with his plow symbolizes the vertical opening of the earth, and the vertical claim of his patrilineage to land, while the woman spread out on the earth buries her seeds across it.

Sarito finished preparing the ritual foods and began dissecting guinea pigs to foretell the fate of the crops and to sprinkle their blood onto the earth. The flutists stopped playing and everyone froze, quite literally, for several seconds. Sarito held out the insides of a guinea pig to show that its liver was covered with white spots, a sign he forecast as frost and snow coming to destroy the harvest. Sarito called two elders, Juan Ticona and Marcelino Yanahuaya, to discuss the ill omen. They decided that they would give more blood and fat to the field shrine.

While Sarito was prophesying, an Apachetan ayllu man climbed the hill behind the shrine, carrying a long rope and whistling to the qochu. The seven llamas stopped grazing and looked at their herder, who approached them tenderly and tied the rope around the neck of a large white one with a brown patch on his back. The qochu quietly followed him to the center of the terrace which was being freshly plowed by the children. The Elder Guide and his assistant were distributing the shells to the participants standing in a large circle around the qochu. For an instant the qochu showed a little resistance as they persuaded him to lie down by turning his ears and coaxing him to the ground. His thighs were hobbled, and for a moment he tried to rise, but as soon as his ears were released, he lay quietly in the center of the circle.

Meanwhile, flames arose from the shrine's mouth. Everybody held their plates to the shrine of the birth of the sun, and they prayed with the Elder Guide:

> Earth shrine receive this meal and invite the lords of the old season, the lords of the new season—Sillaqa, Aqhamani, and Sunchuli. Earth shrine receive this meal and invite the lords of the ayllu, Chaqamita, Pachaqota, Qowila, Jailani, Zaqtalaya, Tala, Mojata, Qota Qota, Kalla Kalla, Yanach'oj, and Phesqa Pata.

The Elder Guide led them in a spiral path going around the llama from east to west in a counterclockwise movement, to face Aqhamani and Sunchuli in the north, Zaqtalaya and Tala in the southwest, and Mojata in the south. The dancers' spiral path decreased in size to face the nearby east ayllu shrine, Qota Qota, the closer east shrine, Kalla Kalla, the center east shrine, Phesqa Pata, the center west shrine, Yanach'oj, and finally the major shrine in Kaatapata, Jatun Junch'a. When they came to the llama, they reversed their direction and retraced their steps.

The Elder Guide led them four-by-four to the mouth of the earth shrine, telling them, "Ayllu men and only ayllu men, in so much as you constitute one ayllu (*llahtantin runa*), feed this field shrine." In groups of four, the ayllu men from the high, central, and low lands together poured the ritual foods into the fire and, as the smoke curled around it, they said, "Serve yourself, field shrine. With all our heart and sweat receive this and serve yourself."

The highland herders carried the qochu to the terraced edge of the plowed field. The qochu knelt facing across the verdant valleys towards Chaqamita, off in the distant clouds. The Secretary of Relations and his wife knelt alongside of the qochu. Tears were in their eyes as they embraced the llama's neck, kissed him, and bid him a final farewell for his journey to the uma pacha. The Elder Guide prayed:

> Ayllu shrines, lords of the ayllu and seasons, Isqani Tuana, Mallku Tuana, Mallku Ik'ituana, these Apachetans invite you to eat this llama and to drink his blood. Small and large valleys grant us abundant food. This we ask of you, Mother Earth, and we give you blood with all our heart. Today the children break the earth for potato planting, and as fine children we will work and we will break the earth.

While some were embracing and kissing the qochu, others were drinking alcohol and sprinkling his head and back with a few drops of alcohol.

They tied a cloth with coca around the llama's neck to be taken with him on his journey to the uma pacha. The herder led him to the western side of the field, so that his body faced the place of origin and return. The qochu's head was twisted back to face the place of the sun's birth. Two Kaatan secretaries cut deeply into his throat, then into his breast, immediately removing his heart, which was given to the Elder Guide. One woman secretary from the legs of the ayllu body caught the qochu's blood in a basin. Everyone filled small cups with blood and quickly sprayed it over the ground in all directions while the heart was still beating. They called out:

Lord of the qochu, lords of the ayllu, lords of the season, receive this blood from the qochu. Give us an abundant harvest, grant increase to our flocks, and grant us good fortune in all. Mother Earth, drink of this blood.

Embracing the Llama before its Death

The blood from the ayllu's most esteemed animal flowed to all parts of the ayllu body and vitalized its geographical layers to produce more life.

Sarito read the qochu's heart. It revealed that the rains would come early as they had the preceding year, and so the commoners should plant early. This year would also have a plentiful harvest because the ayllu and the field shrines had been completely served. The lords and shrines were content.

After Sarito had cut the qochu's heart into small pieces, he gave each shell a chunk, which Julian fed into the field shrine's mouth. Several cups of blood were poured into the shrine, while Sarito prayed for a good harvest. The ayllu leaders butchered the llama by first skinning the hide, which was awarded to Sarito, and then cutting out chunks of fat for the secretaries of the highlands and the lowlands. They passed on this fluid energy from the center to the upper and lower levels. Sarito fingered the qochu's viscera to read what they revealed and then was silent. Afterwards, he then fed these organs into the shrine.

Once the earth shrine had eaten and the children had plowed the field, the lowland secretaries poured chicha for everyone and the flutists danced around the new earth. They danced in their slow east-to-west spiral, which every so often reversed its direction and retraced its steps, until finally at the point of completion, the dancers turned and marched from the small field toward Kaata. Everyone else followed. The Secretary General and Secretary of Relations from Apacheta held two flags, and the secretaries from the lower communities held the other two flags. As mysteriously as a sun being constantly reborn or a circle revolving in upon itself, the chain of musicians moved toward Kaata to the staccato beat of the drum and the four recurring notes of the flute.

THE DANCE OF THE FLOWERS

The procession from the field shrine wound slowly along the rocky path to Kaata. The emissaries, who had returned from the distant ayllu shrines, joined the flute players and secretaries. In Kaata,

Dance of the Flute Players

at the far-off sound of the other band, the Secretary General's flute
band began to play.

Carrying abreast the four rhea flags, the Secretary General and
accompanying secretaries marched to the plaza of Chaqahuaya. With
the flutes, the women arrived with pots of soup and bundles of corn,
potatoes, and bread. The Secretary General's group danced around
the plaza in a concentric circle, while those from the field shrine
wound down the ridge above the plaza. The music became louder as
both groups came closer together.

They met in the plaza. Music and people blended to form one
large circle of brilliant colors and rhea feathers, of upper, central,
and lower secretaries, and of two bands of flute players. Women ran
back and forth, and then danced with the others. The emissaries
were seated in places of honor alongside Sarito and Julian. The music
became faster and louder. Symbols, gestures, and events blended
together for one sacred moment in time, yet out of time—in culture
and society, yet beyond it.

The music stopped and everyone ate from common servings.
The men sat along the benches surrounding the plaza, and the women

crowded in a circle on the ground. Corn on the cob, boiled potatoes and oca, and baked bread were placed in large piles parallel to the men and in the center of the women. The guests served themselves from these hills of food, while they were being brought plates of soup. The guests of honor were the upper and lower secretaries, the emissaries, and the ritualists. Each of them soon had as many as twenty plates of food in front of them, from which they could either serve themselves or give to someone else. In many instances, they would give some of the plates to friends, relatives, and elders, subtly renewing ties of reciprocal exchange. Food is to be shared, and abundance belongs to everyone. Midway through the meal, the lord of each household gave a gift (*abjjata*) of bread and fruit to each secretary, who graciously received it and returned the plate with food from his wife's pot.

According to Qollahuaya tradition, bread is a ritual gift for many Kaatan fiestas. For Carnival, *limbrillos* (baked breads with cheese and hot sauce in four corners and a hole in the center) are strung on a rock sling and given to the sponsors of the feast. Bread birds and babies are given to the groom and bride, respectively, for marriage. For the Feast with the Dead, assorted breads in the shape of llamas, babies, trout, ladders, and birds are given to the dead and to those who pray for the deceased.

When everyone had finished eating, each person expressed thanks to those sitting nearby and paraded to the Secretary General's house.

The ritual ended with the dance of the flowers, which the emissaries had gathered from the ayllu shrines. The emissaries had fed blood, fat, and coca into the mouths of the shrines, vitalizing and empowering these places; in a gesture of reciprocity so basic to Andean exchange, the shrines had given them flowers, which the emissaries carried back to their communities as symbols of life within the earth. Each emissary carried two bouquets wrapped in the same coca cloth in which he had carried the blood, fat, and coca. Two-by-two, the emissaries presented the bouquets to the secretaries who had sent them. They placed the flowers on a table around which the leaders of the ayllu were seated, and as they set them down they explained to the Elder Guide what the guinea pig's heart and bowels had revealed.

"Four men will die!" ("*Tawa chacha runakunas wanuqachej!*"), Concepción said. The ill omen came from the guinea pigs designated for the secretaries of education and sports, implying that the deaths might involve them. Concepción also told the secretaries of the white spots on the community guinea pig, which predicted snow. Everyone knew that Sarito had foretold a similar destruction of crops. These top ritualists cast a spell of fear upon everyone present. The other emissaries brought good luck to all concerned. Sarito and the Secretary General decided that the next day they would sacrifice twice as many guinea pigs and fat to the Phesqa Pata shrine.[8]

The table was covered with a large assortment of flowers from the distinct parts of the ayllu body. Lilies, roses, and carnations had been gathered from the loamy soils and warmer areas near Kalla Kalla and Qota Qota. *Qantutas*, (red, trumpet-shaped flowers), buttercups, and snapdragons had come from the central shrines of Mojata, Phesqa Pata, and Yanach'oj. From the scrubs (*helichrysum* type) of the regions surrounding the shrine of the head, the emissaries had brought woolly leaves. These same clothlike leaves were sprinkled on people and animals for Carnival. The highland emissaries had scooped an edible water plant from Lake Pachaqota called the ch'uño from the lake, which if eaten, would bring an abundant supply of ch'uño for the next year, because potatoes originated in the highland lakes.

Sarito called the secretaries to receive their bouquets. They grasped the flowers in their left hands, held them close to their hearts and carried the rhea flags with their right hands, as they danced to the flute music. The flutists wore red ponchos, and the secretaries were dressed in brown ponchos. The rhea feathers waved with the movement. The courtyard became a field of people and flowers, both in harmony with the flutes. The flowers danced up and down the paths winding around the houses. Once they had completed a circle, they returned to the Secretary General's courtyard. "The flowers have danced," they told Sarito.

After the dance, the secretaries presented half of the bouquets to their wives and the rhea flags to their emissaries. They placed the flowers in the hatbands of all the men and poured them cups of chicha. Their wives did the same for the community's women. The commoners thanked the secretaries, poured libations to Mother Earth (*Pachamama*), and gulped down the remaining chicha. The hats were covered with red, orange, yellow, and blue flowers. These flowers danced through their wearers' courtyards.

New Earth's liturgy had ended once the commoners returned to their homes with the flowers. The festive atmosphere, however, continued for three days of drinking, dancing, and eating. Kaatans were assured that, just as the parts of the mountain's body had been amply fed, so too the parts of their body would be fed.

New Earth expressed how levels of land were understood in terms of a body with a head, heart and bowels, and legs, through which blood and fat circulated. Kaatans experienced the solidarity of their mountain similarly to the way they experienced the organic unity of their corporeal bodies. The individual's corporeal life was dependent on environmental life. The ritual symbolically circulated the blood to the ecological parts of the ayllu body. This gesture, in turn, assured their organic life by awakening the earth to a good harvest. The people inserted themselves by ritual into a cycle of the environment, not to control it, but to experience and be in exchange with it. Time was corporeal and environmental, circulating and cyclical.

New Earth showed the organic relationship of the three distinct communities of the ayllu body. As the symbols of blood and fat suggested, these societies were held together by a life and force external to the particular leaders, which was pumped from the center to the parts, but also returned from the parts to the center. The handing on of the fat and blood underlied political and ritual authority.

The mountain metaphor pervades the political and economic dimensions of the ayllu. It is as basic as the circulation of blood through the body.

NOTES

1.   During the rite of Chosen Field, a man is dressed as earth and another as plants. Earth and Plant interact with the wives of the leaders, only to be abandoned by the women when they are drunk. These wives are castigated by the sheriff, who dances with them and trips them to the ground. Earth and Plant next dance with the secretaries around the Great Shrine at

Kaatapata. Earth is carrying fertile soil on his back and Plant is loaded with potatoes and oca. The male secretaries lead Earth and Plant to the house of the Secretary General, who throws them in the direction of the chosen field. They lie unconscious as the leaders from the lowlands and highlands take earth and plants from them to nurture their levels of land.

2.   Rituals performed outside of ayllu Kaata feed the shrines of the particular place where the ritual is staged, such as Ilimani and Mururata for La Paz. The *mallkus* served at the banquet are those of the participants. Pazeños particularly prefer divinatory rituals, such as throwing coca leaves. Once the divinations are made, then they choose either a lineage ritual or misfortune ritual.

3.   Sarito had his own way of teaching me about knowing.
    "At what place is the sun now?" he asked me after we had chewed coca for several hours in Marcelino's house.
    "Four o'clock," I said, glancing at my wrist watch.
    "The watch knows?"
    "Yes, the watch knows!" I told Sarito. Everyone laughed.
    "How can the watch know at what place of the mountain the sun is, where it is born, and where it dies?" Sarito questioned. It seemed ludicrous to them that the watch could know about the sun dying and being born again, the crows of the cock announcing the time to rise and work, and when the sun is overhead indicating the midday rest. In comparison, then, the watch is to time what the mind is to knowing, mediators in a dualistic universe.

4.   The importance of places in Andean religious beliefs and practices has also been discussed by Tschopik (1946:558), Morúa (1922:236-238), and Monast (1966:101).

5.   Posnansky (1945) hypothesizes that Tiahuanaco was the cradle of the original American inhabitants, and for this reason his works are somewhat discredited. His four-volume study remains, however, a documentary masterpiece of the archaeological findings of Tiahuanaco.

6.   The cargo system has also been explained as the community's equilibrium mechanism for distributing excesses within the closed corporate peasant community. Eric Wolf (1955:452-455) typologizes the peasant community as a small social enclave, strongly integral, and with access to limited resources. Whatever upsets this equilibrium is rejected from the system. Alfred Métraux's study of Andean ritual (1967: Ch. VIII) says that being

sponsor of the fiesta is one such equilibriating mechanism of the wealthy distributing excessive resources to the poor.

This explanation does not seem suitable for Kaata's cargo system. The economic function of their fiestas is not so much a leveling of resources as it is an exchange between ecological levels. Every adult, whether rich or poor, is expected to fill all the roles. The poorest peasant often goes into debt for many years by sponsoring an expensive fiesta. Although Kaatans communally hold land, there is a rotative hierarchy inherent in their authority and ritual.

7.   The rhea (*suri* in Quechua and *Rhea macrorhichus* in Latin) were found near Oruro, and are now near extinction. Kaatans classify the rhea between the llama and the condor, because it is similar to the llama in color, neck size, and speed, and resembles the condor in size and feathers. It also symbolizes the anomaly of Andean man who cannot fly.

8.   By the time the rite was over, more than seventy guinea pigs had been sacrificed to nurture the earth with their blood. Their meat is never eaten after they have been sacrificed to the shrine, as is the meat of the qochu.

*

5

Birth Rituals

Birth rituals, marking the end of one condition in life and the beginning of another, are rites of passage in many different religions. At baptism, for example, a minister pours water on the baby's forehead which, according to Christian theology, washes away original sin and bestows God's grace. The baby passes from paganism to Christianity. At a briest, a rabbi circumcises a male child which, according to Jewish theology, makes the boy a descendant of Abraham, who was chosen by God. The boy passes from heathenism to Judaism. At *Mallkuta Qukuy*, an Andean ritual, a diviner gives the baby an earth shrine. At this rite of passage, the Indian passes from the inside to the outside of Mount Kaata. According to Andean cosmology, the infant originates from the summit of Mount Kaata and travels on its slopes during life. In all three rites, the infants pass into different theological states which corresponds to religious beliefs; consequently, if we want to understand Andean rites of passage, we must begin with their understanding of the universe.

Andeans view the universe and their relation to it differently than we do. Although we still say that the sun rises and sets, we realize that the earth rotates and revolves around the sun. Kaatans learn about their universe from legends and observations of nature, rather than from formal education which was only introduced to Kaata within this generation. At dawn, according to Andean tradition, the sun rises from Chaqamita Lake near the eastern base of Mount Kaata; it ascends over the lower slopes during the morning, rests above the central slopes at noon, and climbs to the summit of the mountain, where it dies in Pachaqota Lake at dusk. Pachaqota swallows the sun, extinguishes its fire, and shrinks it to the size of a shriveled orange. On its rebirth, the sun sinks to the bottom of the lake and swims down the springs beneath the three levels until it reaches Chaqamita Lake where it emerges as the young sun.

The sun is regenerated during its daily journey. The young sun (*wayna inti*) has fewer (twenty-eight) rays than the old sun which has forty-four rays on its woven pictographs; and Kaatans say that the old sun has a beard. The old sun also contains a miniature sun (*uña inti*) with a heart. When the old sun dies in Pachaqota Lake, the miniature sun grows to become a young sun and finally arises from Chaqamita. In other words, the sun contains within itself regenerative principles which grow into new suns. Kaatans use analogies from human and plant life to explain the daily birth and death of the sun.

Andeans also explain their life cycle in terms of the birth and death of the sun on Mount Kaata with the difference, however, that the Indian's journey reverses the path of the sun. Although babies (*wawakuna*) are born all over Mount Kaata, they originate as miniature babies (*uña wawakuna*) near the summit of Kaata in Pachaqota Lake. During life, the young Indian (*wayna*) walks on top of Mount Kaata, often crossing its levels while herding animals and cultivating its soil. When Indians are old (*machu*), they die and are buried in the mountain where they undergo a regenerative cycle. First, they decay until only the bones are left, then they swim as a miniature person to the summit. From Pachaqota Lake, the point of origin and return for all life, the miniature person becomes a baby which is born on top of the mountain.

Nonetheless, the origin of the baby's sex is decided by human sources: the sex of the child is determined by whether the husband or wife "wins" in intercourse. Each sex contains its embryo which is directly passed from mother to daughter for females and indirectly passed through the wife along the male line. They believe that if the man climaxes before the woman, then he injects his male embryo into her and she conceives a boy. But if the woman climaxes before the man, then she "wins" and conceives a girl. Consequently, Andeans have very earthy, as well as metaphysical, concepts about their origins; both types of belief underpin Kaatan birth rituals.

Essentially, then, Andean birth rituals prepare an infant for a journey upon Mount Kaata. The first ritual, Mallkuta Qukuy, vows the infant to an earth shrine on Mount Kaata. This rite symbolizes the mountain's ownership of the person who comes from it and returns to it. Immediately after birth, a diviner determines the baby's earth shrine. Moreover, Mallkuta differentiates male and female shrines for boys and girls which emphasizes the distinction of sex roles within Andean society. After the earth shrine is selected, the diviner feeds coca from the same pile to both the shrine and the baby: sharing coca ratifies a relationship between the infant and the mountain.

Dedicating the baby to Mount Kaata, Celia, daughter of Carmen and Marcelino, gave birth to a baby girl at 4 a.m. on Saturday, June 30. Carmen and another midwife assisted Celia, who lay upon thick furs which covered the floor of the cooking room—the only place with a fire. Without washing the baby, Carmen wrapped her in swaddling clothes and brought her to Martin, who was waiting in the courtyard with Marcelino; delivery is a female activity from which men are excluded in Kaata. Martin, somewhat disappointed by the birth of another girl, stared into the baby's face, wrinkled and screaming. The infant weighed four pounds, the average weight of newborn babies in Kaata, where four out of ten babies die. Martin immediately summoned Juan Barrera, a diviner, to decide his new daughter's earth shrine.

"Then, at least," said Carmen, "if she dies, the mountain will claim her." The Yanahuayas and the Mejias believed that an earth shrine was necessary to assist the baby in her climb up and down Mount Kaata. In comparison, Christian missionaries taught Kaatans that baptism was necessary in order to get to heaven. Kaatans, however, had little interest in going to heaven; rather, they wished to remain forever on their mountain. So it was important that the infant have a place, an earth shrine, on Mount Kaata.

The rays of the rising sun were illuminating the snows of Aqhamani and Sunchuli mountains when Juan Barrera arrived in the patio of Martin's house to begin Mallkuta Qukuy. A lanky figure, Juan bent over the baby as he placed Celia's *ist'alla* of coca leaves on the baby's head and heart. Opening the ist'alla, Juan selected thirteen leaves. Carmen, Marcelino, Martin, and his parents watched as Juan neatly bit marks into the edges of the leaves. He marked and named each leaf according to one of the thirteen ayllu shrines on Mount Kaata, namely, Chaqamita, Qota Qota, Kalla Kalla, Mojata, Phesqa Pata, Jatun Junch'a, Yanach'oj, Tala, Wayra Wisqhani, Qowila, Jailani, Zaqtalaya, and Pachaqota (see map of ayllu shrines). An ayllu shrine (junch'a), usually a hole in the earth, is a ritual site where coca, llama blood, and fat are deposited to feed Mount Kaata. After Juan had named each leaf, he put it on the ist'alla in an east-to-west order; thereby, he followed the path of the sun over the earth shrines. Finally, Juan marked a leaf for the infant.

Theoretically, the baby's earth shrine would be selected as soon as her leaf fell upon the leaf of an earth shrine. Nevertheless, social considerations influenced their decision; divination rituals include not only chance but also choices within the options provided by social principles. The selection of a shrine for the infant included a careful review of the earth shrines and their social significance. Essentially, rituals were arenas for debates about social organization. For this reason, Juan, eager to receive potatoes for his pay, had to throw the leaves many times until a suitable shrine had been picked for the baby girl.

Early in the ritual, when the baby's leaf had landed on top of the leaf for Jatun Junch'a, the group discussed the social significance of this earth shrine. "How could Jatun Junch'a, a community shrine, be a Yanahuaya's earth shrine?" they asked each other. They added that Jatun Junch'a did not have the time to protect their daughter because it was too busy watching over the community of Kaata. In other words, whatever is common property of the community does not belong to any individual.

Community shrines protect all the people on each level and provide abundant harvests for everyone. The community shrines of Chaqamita, Jatun Junch'a, and Pachaqota are patrons of the respective villages of Niñokorin (lowlands), Kaata (central lands), and Apacheta (highlands). In return, each community dedicates an annual rite to its shrine: highland herders celebrate All Colors at Pachaqota for the increase of llama herds; potato and oca farmers of Kaata celebrate Selection of the Field at Jatun Junch'a, and corn farmers around Niñokorin feed Chaqamita at the rite of First Corn Planting.

Community shrines, like food, are not the exclusive rites of the community, but rather they are to be shared by all three communities on Mount Kaata.

After the Yanahuayas had dismissed Jatun Junch'a, Juan again cast the leaves, and the tip of the baby's leaf rested on Zaqtalaya, a hill on Mount Kaata. This time, Carmen protested that Zaqtalaya, was a male shrine and it could not be her granddaughter's earth shrine.

Carmen realized the importance of male and female earth shrines in Kaatan society which distinguishes sex roles. Male earth shrines, on the one hand, are rocks, hills, and high places because men are thought to be permanent like the mountain: they settle on the land of their male ancestors. Qualities of erectness and permanence are associated with Kaatan men. This is also manifested in daily behavior; for example, these men sit upright on benches, cut the earth with bladed plows, and chew coca from individual coca bags. Female earth shrines, on the other hand, are lakes and low places because women are considered fertile and cross levels. An underlying principle of exogamy in Kaata necessitates that men and women marry someone from a level adjacent to their own level. After marriage, the woman leaves her community to live with her husband on his level of land, according to virilocal residence patterns also practiced on Mount Kaata. When she bears children, her sons will remain on her husband's land and her daughters, after they marry, will return to either their mother's level or to another level.

Moreover, Kaatan women's behavior ideally corresponds to qualities of fertility and sharing symbolized by female earth shrines. Women sit on the earth in a circle where they chew coca from a common pile. They share the food they cook with their family, similar to the sharing of resources between the people of ayllu Kaata. By weaving, women clothe their husbands and children with garments, similar to the covers of vegetation crossing Mount Kaata. For this reason, the river is often a metaphor for women because it not only crosses the levels but also binds levels together. Rivers, however, are not earth shrines, whereas lakes, the sources of rivers, are. Consequently, Juan kept throwing the coca until the baby's leaf paired with a lake.

Juan's eyes were dilated from coca and lack of sleep when he threw the leaves for the final reading. Although the others could read the leaves, only Juan, a diviner, would choose the earth shrine for the baby.

"The coca says that Qota Qota is the baby's earth shrine," Juan said after he had scanned the leaves. "She will have many children." Carmen immediately approved and said that this was a suitable shrine for the infant. Of great significance to Carmen, Qota Qota is a female shrine which bestows abundance of food for the kitchen and fertility to the womb of the woman who feeds it. In addition, Kaatans think of Qota Qota as a feminine symbol because of its location on the lower slopes of Mount Kaata where two rivers converge. According to the body metaphor, Qota Qota is located between the crotch of the mountain's legs, which are formed by the divergence of the rivers Llahta and Huruku. The shrine is a dried-out lake, another place of fecundation associated with women. Qota Qota is also the ayllu shrine that overlooks the fertile lower fields (10,500-11,500 feet) of corn, wheat, peas, and beans surrounding the ayllu's lower communities of Niñokorin, Lunlaya, Quiabaya, and Chipuico (see map of levels on page 38). Carmen grew up in Niñokorin and her parents still live there. Carmen's maternal grandparents, moreover, are buried near Qota Qota in the cemetery of Niñokorin and would also assist their granddaughter. Consequently, Carmen was pleased to hear that the ayllu shrine from her village and of her ancestors was to be her granddaughter's earth shrine.

Juan dedicated the infant to Qota Qota when the sun, climbing up Mount Kaata, was directly above this earth shrine. The ritual moment was the crossing of the paths of the sun and the baby over Qota Qota; at this coincidence, Juan symbolically brought together the infant and Qota Qota, as well as mountain and sun. The coming together (*tinka*) of the person and shrine may be accomplished in other ways, as for example, when Carmen gave birth to Valentina on the highland pastures near the shrine of Tala which *de facto* became her earth shrine. The essence of Mallkuta Qukuy, then, is the bringing together of the person and the earth shrine.

Juan led the group into the courtyard where they faced the sun and Qota Qota. Marcelino held the baby while Carmen stood alongside. Stretching his arms to the sun, Juan offered the leaves of the baby, Qota Qota, and community Kaata to Qota Qota earth shrine. Next he placed these leaves on the baby's forehead and heart, praying that her labor and love be united to the mountain. Finally

Juan sprinkled the infant with incense, saying, *"Qota Qota mallkuyki qanyuh!"* ("Qota Qota, your earth shrine, claims you!") The baby was surrounded by puffs of smoke which slowly disappeared into the sky and ratified the relationship between the infant and Mount Kaata. Like the sun resting in the mountain, the baby was carried in Carmen's arms to Celia who began breast-feeding her. The baby had begun her journey across the mountains.

When Juan spoke the words *"qanyuh"* over the baby, a relationship of metaphorical kinship was established between her and Qota Qota, a bond similar to the kinship relationship between parents and children, as well as between siblings. Consequently, Celia and Martin did not participate at the tinka for fear that the natural relationship with their daughter would impair her metaphorical relationship with Qota Qota. "Qanyuh" means "claiming you," "lord over you," or, as translated into Spanish, *"tu dueño"* ("your owner"). Kaatans employ classificatory kin terms: their kinship terminology blurs the distinction between lineal and collateral relatives, so that all uncles are fathers, all aunts are mothers, all male cousins are brothers, and all female cousins are sisters. Moreover, they transfer the biological ties with lineal relatives to the classificatory ties with collateral relatives so that relationships learned in the family are projected to classificatory parents and siblings within the community. Qollahuaya hamlet, for example, is composed of many fathers and mothers, brothers and sisters of the baby. However, when Kaatans want to distinguish lineal relatives from collateral, they add *dueño* to the kin term: for example, a boy can call his sibling brother *"dueño wawqui"* to distinguish him from his cousin, *wawqui;* parents call their natural children *"dueño wawakuna"* which distinguishes their offspring from nieces and nephews, called *wawakuna*. Dueño, a Spanish word, emphasizes the proximity of kinship ties among lineal relatives and is a metaphor for familial rather than community ties. When Qota Qota became a dueño for the baby, then the earth shrine was metaphorically united to her as a mother to a daughter. Celia's absence, however, expressed that her daughter's relationship to Qota Qota precedes and perdures family ties. Before birth, the baby originated from the mountain, and after death, she would return to it.

The participants reviewed cosmological truths and social principles during the selection of a shrine for the baby. The infant originated from the summit of Mount Kaata, and she travels across it during life. Analogously, she follows the sun, but in the opposite direction. She received a female earth shrine, emphasizing the distinct roles of men and women in a society with patrilineal claim to land, exchange of women and resources between levels, and virilocality. Finally, the baby was joined to the earth shrine with ties similar to kinship relations between lineal relatives. Essentially, ritual provided cultural and social continuity for Kaatans, who have few written laws and schools. At rituals, they arranged symbols according to patterns and conceptualized truths of their society.

Later that morning, the daughters of Carmen and Marcelino— Elsa, Sophia, and Valentina—visited Celia and the baby. These classificatory mothers would provide companionship to the infant because loneliness is the worst tragedy of life in the Andes. Elsa, the older sister of Celia, was *paya mama* (elder mother) to the child and if Celia died, Elsa would raise her, as well as cook for Martin until he remarried. Sophia and Valentina, younger sisters of Celia, were *chana mamakuna* (younger mothers), who shared in motherly responsibilities, such as carrying the baby on their backs, washing her in the river, and running alongside her in the fields. This morning, however, the younger mothers would babysit for Erminia, two year-old sister of the infant, while the elder mother, Elsa, carried the infant to a catechist for name giving.

A catechist named the baby after the saint for the day on which she was born. Qollahuaya hamlet had two catechists, Venancio Yanahuaya and Damaso Yanahuaya, who performed *jich'a suti* (name giving). Father Connors, O.F.M., had trained them to be catechists in a two-week course on Catholic dogma. Father Connors also encouraged them to baptize sick babies, guaranteeing the child's entry into heaven if it died, and to conduct Bible services, substituting for priests, who were scarce in this region. Every Sunday evening, Damaso and Venancio joined with twenty Indians to study scripture and praise the Lord. Venancio and Damaso were diviners who practiced Andean rituals. Although Father Connors did not approve, Venancio and Damaso, as well as other Qollahuayas, saw no conflict in being catechists and diviners because each role required distinct rituals performed in different places and times. In other words, they did not mix the symbols of Andean and Catholic religions.

Marcelino chose Venancio to name the baby. Marcelino and his family were ostracizing Damaso because the grandfather of Damaso, Romualdo Yanahuaya, had usurped Marcelino's land fifty years earlier. When Andeans select a ritualist, they review their social relations with all the candidates. Social relations express events of the past and their interpretation in the future. Venancio and Damaso were classificatory sons of Marcelino and grandsons of Marcelino's father's brothers, Mariano and Romualdo, respectively (see *Genealogy*). Marcelino's mother died shortly after his birth, and his father, Bonifacio, died in 1929, leaving the family's weavings and four gardens to Marcelino, then seven years old. After the funeral, Marcelino set out on a curing trip with Pedro Yanahuaya, his elder father. Riding horseback, Pedro and Marcelino crossed the central Andes and coastal desert to Lima, Peru (700 miles) stopping to heal sick people along the way; however, they increased the distance and time to several thousand miles and a year and a half. On the circuit back, Pedro, tired of traveling, remained in Arequipa to practice medicine. Marcelino, also disenchanted by the travels of an herbalist, continued on to Kaata where he could farm.

Begging, Marcelino wended his way from Arequipa, Peru to Kaata, a distance of 250 miles. Several times he almost froze to death crossing the mountain passes, but herders, finding the sleeping boy, carried him to their shelters. Assuming that Marcelino was dead, Romualdo, his classificatory father, had taken Marcelino's weavings and land. One cold, rainy night, Marcelino came home. Romualdo resented his return, but Mariano, a younger father, warmly welcomed him with clothing and food. Marcelino tried to regain his property, but Romualdo refused to restore the cloth and gardens to him; so Marcelino settled on the smallest garden plot which Romualdo had abandoned.

Since then, Marcelino quadrupled his land, yet it remains incomplete. Even though the younger father, Romualdo, took land from his son, Marcelino, forty years ago, the situation is now reversed, as Marcelino is the younger father for Damaso, grandson of Romualdo. Damaso later became my friend, but he was always afraid of Marcelino and only visited me when Marcelino was away. This event shows that the time of the family is not marked by years nor by a past tense, which somehow buries events as actors and circumstances change. The family's classificatory nature guarantees an extension of social relations, whether they are good or bad, so

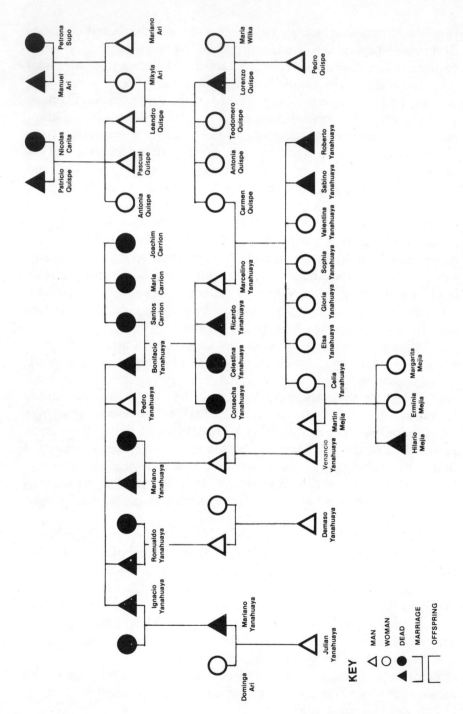

Genealogy of Carmen Quispe and Marcelino Yanahuaya

KEY

△ MAN
○ WOMAN
● DEAD
▲ DEAD

⊔ MARRIAGE
⊓ OFFSPRING

that an event initiated fifty years ago persists today when the baby is brought to Venancio's house and not to Damaso's house.

At noon, Elsa fastened the baby to her back and climbed a hill to Venancio's house in Qollahuaya. Elsa, slowly recovering from sickness, had recently returned to Kaata after selling bread in La Paz for two years. She could no longer endure the long trips across the Altiplano, riding in the back of trucks and stopping to sell bread at the villages along the way. An infection had caused her ankles to swell; yet, in spite of her weakened condition, Elsa, always thoughtful and conscientious, shared fully in the responsibilities of the family. When Elsa arrived at Venancio's home, she greeted him with coca and asked him to name the infant. Honored with the request, Venancio removed coca from her ist'alla and put it into his ch'uspa, a gesture of compliance. Elsa and Venancio talked about the baby, for whom they were classificatory parents. But Elsa never told Venancio the name of the baby's earth shrine. The earth shrine was her dueño and only people who shared the same kinship tie as dueño (brothers, sisters, parents, and grandparents in the lineal line) could know which place shared a similar relationship to her. The name of the saint, however, would be shared with the community.

Once Venancio learned that the infant was born that same day, he studied the *1972 Almanaque Patriótico*, an astrological, Catholic and civic calendar, posted on his wall. He carefully calculated the day of the birth, counting back from Sunday when he was in Charazani; Monday, Tuesday, and Wednesday he had worked in the fields; Thursday it rained and he rested; and Friday was *qayna* (yesterday).

"*Kunan punchay Sabado*" ("Today is Saturday"), he announced. "It is the tenth of June. Margarita will be her name." The almanac listed only one other saint, a man, Zacarias, for that day.

Venancio immersed the baby's head in a washbasin of water and prayed in Spanish, "I baptize you, Margarita, in the name of the Father, Son, and Holy Ghost." Repeating the baptismal formula, he put a pinch of salt on Margarita's tongue, anointed her breast with olive oil, and dressed her in a white garment. Elsa thanked Venancio, handed him three eggs, and returned home to tell everyone Margarita's name.

BAPTISM

Margarita remained unbaptized even though Venancio had poured water over her head and had pronounced the baptismal formula. Only the priest in Charazani baptizes babies, and until then, babies are potentially dangerous creatures in the universe of the Qollahuayas. If an unbaptized baby dies in Kaata, for example, its soul goes to limbo, the celestial source of hail. Whenever hail destroys the crop, Andeans punish the parents of unbaptized babies, often by beating them. From fear of punishment, Kaatans secretly bury unbaptized dead babies in the cemetery without the secretaries, who customarily attend all funerals. The secretaries have to pay a fine to the sheriff of Charazani every time a baby dies without baptism. Utilizing this destructive power to their advantage, Qollahuayas sometimes bury unbaptized babies in their enemies' fields so that hail will destroy their harvest.

Historically, Qollahuayas first associated unbaptized babies with hail and limbo during the late sixteenth century when Catholic missionaries taught these Indians the necessity of baptism by negative conditioning. The missionaries said that when unbaptized babies die, they do not go to heaven nor to hell, but to limbo, a place in between heaven and hell, where souls without grace and mortal sin live. God sends hail on the communities where an unbaptized baby dies. As a result, Qollahuayas still refer to unbaptized babies as "limbos," and one reason why they baptize babies is to prevent hail. By baptism, the baby is no longer a "limbo."

Missionaries also taught the Indians that baptism is a rite of passage during which the baby passes from being an heir to limbo to being an heir to heaven. Although the Yanahuayas, like most Andeans, have a token appreciation of heaven and its glory, they do not see heaven as a desirable goal. Most Andeans don't want to fly in heaven, which they experience as wind, sun, rain, and clouds. Where would they farm and herd in heaven? They want to remain on the mountain when they die. Qollahuayas, therefore, have reinterpreted baptism as a rite of passage which separates babies from *chunchos*, uncivilized jungle Indians, and incorporates them with Qollahuayas, civilized mountain people. Qollahuayas call unbaptized persons "limbos" when they are small, and "chunchos" when they are adults.

According to Qollahuayas, chunchos are uncivilized lowland Indians who are naked, don't eat salt, and hunt with the bow and arrow which Qollahuayas consider inferior to agriculture and herding. The Yanahuayas, for example, interpret the putting of salt on the baby's tongue at baptism and the dressing with the baptismal robe to mean that the baby is no longer a chuncho but a Qollahuaya who eats salt and wears clothes.

The Yanahuayas' belief about chunchos is embedded in legends rather than personal contact with these jungle people. The legend of Matias Akarapi, grandfather of all Qollahuayas, refers to a battle between Qollahuayas and chunchos. Kaata's storyteller, Juan Wilka, narrated this legend the day after the naming ritual when he came to cure Elsa. Juan arrived a little intoxicated after a few rounds of drinks with the secretaries. Trying to be professional, Juan, also an herbalist, took Elsa's wrist, crossed himself with the sign of the cross, said *"Por Jesus,"* and read her pulse.

"Your blood does not flow well," he told Elsa. "It is frightened." He put his ear to her wrist, listening to its beat. "You've been wet and cold. The sun hasn't warmed you." He gave Elsa a tea made from *luriwichu (Salvia opositiflora)*; this relaxed her and she began to recover. Juan then told the legend:

> A long time ago when Jesus began the fight with devils and Jews, the Qollahuayas fought against the chunchos and won with their medicine bags (*kapachus*).[1] They came from the Yungas (*yunka*); they had never heard of salt. They shot arrows and didn't wear shirts.
>
> One day the chunchos traveled from their hills (*montañas*) to an apacheta near Chinchata.[2] When they arrived, they snatched the headband (*winch'a*)[3] from our grandmother, the wife of Matias Akarapi. The chunchos said that they had come to steal headbands from all the women.
>
> When Matias Akarapi, the grandfather of all Qollahuayas, learned of this, he became very angry and went to the apacheta. The chunchos shot arrows at him. The only thing to protect Akarapi was his medicine bag with amulets, herbs, and coca. With all these things, Matias made it snow.
>
> The shirtless chunchos yelled, *"Alalay*, why has only white fallen?" The chunchos ran to the jungle, but one chuncho died from the cold and he is buried near Apacheta. For this reason, today Apacheta is called Chuncho Apacheta.

The legend classifies Qollahuayas and chunchos. Qollahuayas originate from the summit and live on three levels of the mountain (8,000 to 17,000 feet). The founder of the Qollahuayas resembles Christ who fought the devils and Jews. Qollahuaya men carry medicine bags because they are herbalists and ritualists who control the weather, and women wear headbands, because they are fertile, a quality which chunchos covet. Unlike Qollahuayas, chunchos live in the jungle (below 3,000 feet) and Yungas (3,000 to 8,000 feet). They are sided with devils and Jews, do not wear shirts or eat salt, and use bows and arrows. Moreover, even though they desire Qollahuaya women, they cannot live on the levels of Mount Kaata where it snows.

Baptism is a rite of passage from being a limbo and chuncho to being a Qollahuaya. Unbaptized babies are structurally in categories peripheral to Mount Kaata and are associated with an inferior-anterior group. Limbos live in the sky and chunchos live in the jungle. According to Qollahuaya belief, extremes of high and low are undesirable places, usually symbolized by hail, lightning, and snakes. After baptism, the baby is no longer a chuncho, but a Qollahuaya, a civilized mountain Indian.

The social aspects of baptism are also important to Qollahuayas. Baptism, as well as marriage, provides the baby with godparents, and these ritual ties unite families from different ecological zones and societies. Because Qollahuayas have adapted the ritual kinship of Spanish-Catholic origin to their classificatory kinship system, baptism creates a set of relationships similar to those received at birth. Godparents and godchildren form ties not only with each other but also with all the lineage. Godparents are ritual brothers, sisters, sons, and daughters to the relatives of their godchild. In turn, a godson is a son, brother, or father to the natural relatives of the godparents, and a goddaughter is a daughter, sister, or mother to them. If the godparents die, their siblings assume responsibilities for their god-child, and if the godchild dies, then his or her sibling receives the benefits. Baptism creates a sacred set of relationships which meta-phorically reflect the ties of natural kinship. The social relationships of natural kinship influence ritual kinship, and ritual kinship supports the ties of natural kinship.

Baptism, moreover, extends relations beyond natural kinship which is necessary for the larger social and cultural Kaatan units,

Carmen, Elsa, Margarita, Celia, and Marcelino Yanahuaya

such as the ayllu and province. The Yanahuayas, for example, have Indian godparents in Apacheta and Niñokorin with whom they exchange potatoes, llama meat, and corn. When Marcelino sponsored the saint fiesta for 1965 in Kaata, his ritual kin assisted him by contributing corn beer and llama meat. Qollahuaya rituals involve a complex network of reciprocal ritual obligations between natural and ritual kin. As a result, ritual unites the communities of ayllu Kaata. The Yanahuayas also have mestizo godparents, Eulogio and Aurora Oblitas, in Charazani. The Oblitas family, politically prominent, assist the Yanahuayas in civic and legal concerns; in return, the Yanahuayas and their relatives purchase supplies from Eulogio. Marcelino and Carmen also select godparents because they wish to secure a friendship with someone they like. For this reason, perhaps, Marcelino asked Judy and me to be godparents for Margarita. After we accepted, Carmen said, "Now we have relatives in Gringoland."

Padre Carlos Steen, O.F.M., baptized Margarita in Charazani

on Sunday, August 20, 1972. Padre Carlos visited the mission of Charazani monthly to baptize and marry the Indians, and catechists prepared the Indians for the reception of these sacraments. Marcelino, Carmen, Martin, Celia, Margarita, Judy, and I walked the four-hour trip to Charazani early Sunday morning. After a notary registered the names of Margarita, her parents and godparents, and her birth-date in the provincial birth book, he gave us a baptismal permit necessary for the priest. Padre Carlos listed similar information in the parish register. From these legal records, Margarita can later receive a *Fe de Bautismo* (baptismal certificate) essential for legal proof of her age and identity.

Padre Carlos baptized Margarita the same way that Venancio had performed name giving. Judy and I held Margarita as he put salt on her tongue, anointed her with oil, poured water over her forehead, and placed a white robe upon her. Waiting outside the church, Celia and Martin relegated their natural offspring to her ritual parents.

After we left the church, Celia and Martin embraced Judy and me, calling us *compadre* and *comadre*, while Carmen and Marcelino sprinkled confetti, flowers, and candy over us. According to Qolla-huayas, these gestures reinforced the bonds between natural and ritual kinsfolk. Judy and I next placed a banana, orange, and bun on Margarita's forehead, saying, "This is your head." For the rest of the afternoon, we exchanged alcohol, coca, and cooked potatoes, until everyone was satiated. We walked back to Kaata, arriving just before sunset.

Godparents often intervene for their godchild in family affairs. Once a year during Carnival, natural and ritual parents gather to discuss the development of the godchild. The natural parents give a bottle of alcohol, a cloth filled with coca, and sheep to their ritual kin. The godparents suggest improvement for the child's welfare, and if the natural parents have mistreated their child, the godparents can beat them. Although I have never witnessed this concerning the godparents of baptism. I have twice witnessed in the Altiplano matrimonial godparents bitterly reproaching husbands for beating their wives. For this reason, mistreatment of children and spouses is less frequent in the Andes than in other places. Andeans have godparents to whom they can reveal domestic injustices. The god-parents, moreover, can be relatively unbiased in resolving the dispute because they are not natural kin of either husband or wife, parents or child.

Judy and I intervened once in the family affairs of the Yana-huayas when Erminia was dying of typhoid fever. Erminia, two-year old sister of Margarita, was our classificatory godchild. After a month of herbal treatment, Erminia still suffered from persistent vomiting and diarrhea. Celia and Martin said she was recovering, but Judy and I wanted to take her to a doctor in La Paz. Marcelino agreed, but Carmen refused: she feared the death of Erminia on the long trip because she would then have to be buried in a place other than Mount Kaata.

Erminia, nevertheless, died in Kaata after the coca predicted it. Losing my temper, I yelled at Marcelino for not letting me take Erminia to a doctor. They listened to my reprimand, and later, when Martin broke his collarbone, they sent him to a doctor. The Yana-huayas would have been dismayed if I had reflected their views on Erminia's curing. They would have thought it inconsistent with our behavior, and they were comforted to know that we cared and would do for our godchild what we would do for ourselves. Because ritual kinship incorporates people of a different area, class, culture, and society into a relationship with natural kin, this provides other layers of ideas, involvement, and intervention. Ritual kinship is a means by which Indians establish links with upper-class members of Bolivian society. Although the members of the upperclass use these ritual networks to influence Qollahuaya society, Qollahuayas use them to protect their own rights. The Qollahuayas have also adapted ritual kinship to strengthen their classificatory system and to solidify ties between communities on Mount Kaata.

Margarita became a Qollahuaya not only by her birth but also by rituals. At the earth shrine ritual, Margarita began her journey across Mount Kaata from which she originated and to which she will return; at name giving she received a name and saint, and at baptism, Margarita became an Andean who eats salt and wears clothes. By birth and its accompaning rituals, Margarita entered Qollahuaya society with male and female distinctions, and classificatory and ritual kinship. These rituals taught, and still teach, Qollahuayas essential cosmological and social premises of their society. Ritual, therefore, is an essential process by which we can understand the underlying premises of Andean society.

NOTES

1.   *Kapachu* is a woven shoulder bag, in which men carry food, money, and herbs. Qollahuayas weave pictographs into kapachus which have religious meanings.

2.   *Chinchata*, now called Chuncho Apacheta, is located in the higher pastoral region of Mount Kaata. This small village is a stopping place on trade routes between Charazani and Apolo, a Yungas center for coca, quinine, and gold.

3.   *Winch'as* vary in width from one to three inches, have bands of woven designs (animals, people, snails, mountains, and suns), and are worn exclusively by women.

6

First Haircutting

Qollahuaya girls learn to herd and weave at an early age, because children assume adult responsibilities soon in the Andes. By herding and weaving, girls produce cloth which serves physical, spiritual, and social needs of the Andeans. Fuel is scarce above 8,000 feet and glacial winds chill Andeans during the day and especially at night. Clothes, the major means of warmth, break the wind and pocket body heat. On a spiritual level, clothes refer to cosmological truths through the pictographs woven into them. Finally, clothes represent roles in society: men and women wear distinct clothing; and as Qollahuayas progress in social status, they wear more elaborate clothing. A child who is beginning to walk receives an adult set of clothes at the ritual of First Haircutting. During this ritual, the godparents cut the hair of their godchild, give the child clothes and a ewe to begin a flock. Both girls and boys then begin herding, and at about six or seven years, girls learn to weave.

Valentina, a young shepherdess, had herded the Yanahuaya flock since she was three years old. Dimpled and pretty, Valentina was the ten-year-old daughter of Marcelino and Carmen. Valentina loved to frolic around the fields, free from her parents and the cares of school. One Saturday, Valentina asked me to herd with her. She began with a breakfast of hot soup and boiled potatoes. Carmen strapped Margarita on the back of Valentina with a cloth. Because Valentina was the younger mother of Margarita, she had to teach her to herd. Martin and Celia's nine sheep accompanied Marcelino and Carmen's flock of thirty-seven; so Margarita was already working for her parents and providing companionship for Valentina.

Qollahuayas seldom permit a child to herd alone, not only because companionship dispels loneliness, but also because the complementarity between pairs is important to Andean society. Lineages, for example, are distinguished between the man's and the woman's kin group; siblings are classified into youngest and oldest; and communities have upper and lower sections. Ritualists always serve two plates to each earth shrine. For example, if a shrine is male, then a plate is also set for its female companion. Shrines are usually served in pairs, such as young and old, mountain and lake, and helper and owner. Ritual teaches Andeans the complementarity between contrasting pairs, and activities such as herding provide lessons in the sharing of wisdom and love between older and younger children.

At about 7:30, Valentina opened the corrals and forty-six sheep, nine pigs, two burros, two dogs, and one horse rushed across the patio and through the gate. Valentina tried to separate the squealing pigs from the bleating and excitable sheep, but the congestion at the door forced the sheep against the jambs. Pushing from the rear, the pigs tried to get under the sheep, while T'inti, a large black dog, climbed over the sheep and jumped the fence. T'inti caught the lead sheep and nipped him in line, as Valentina, enjoying it all, swung back and forth behind the flock, moving them along with the words, *"Ch', Ch'uy, Ch'uy!"*

Outside Marcelino's courtyard, the animals calmed down after the pigs left. The pigs roamed freely, scavenging garbage, digging for worms, and eating fecal waste. As the grazing animals walked along with neighboring herds, several hungry sheep strayed into potato patches, but Valentina stopped them shortly with a stone from her sling. Valentina guided the sheep to Naka, a large rotative field two miles west of the hamlet of Qollahuaya.

Eight rotative fields surround the community of Kaata. Each field produces potatoes, oca, and barley for three consecutive years, then rests for five years. When dormant, the field recovers its topsoil by grass and fertilizer: sheep clip the grass and, in return, spread their dung around the field. An astute observer of this recycling process, Valentina grazed her sheep on different fields daily, which enabled the grass to grow and the manure to be evenly spread across the field. Valentina also knew where her family had grazing rights in Naka and the other rotative fields. The Yanahuayas, as well as other Qollahuayas, grazed sheep on plots which they inherited or gained access to by exchange of either work or resources. Leaders of Kaata also allocated pasturelands to families. The Yanahuayas had grazing rights on eleven plots of Naka; if they had the same number of plots in the other seven fields, then Valentina herded sheep in about eighty-eight different places of Mount Kaata. As a herder, Valentina already knew a lot about ecology and land use on Mount Kaata.

Throughout the morning, Valentina grazed the sheep, wandering up and down the Yanahuaya plots in Naka. Occasionally she stopped a lamb from either wandering off or getting too close to a precipice. She called each by its name: "Black Eyes" because of its dirty eyes, "Rascal" from its efforts to stray away from the flock, and "Creeper" because it was always last in line. Valentina knew her flock and felt for them as no modern farmer did. The flock was not just a number of animals to be herded, sheared, and slaughtered; it was the lineage of each lamb, and myths about how and when it was born. The flock was the pasture and mountain where Valentina and the animals played together.

T'inti, named after a grasshopper, patrolled the area, perceptive to the strange sounds of a bleating sheep and to the smells of a stranger. T'inti guarded the sheep at night. He walked along the wall of the corral, ready to spring upon predators.

While T'inti herded the sheep, Valentina and Margarita rested and played in their vast Andean playground. They dressed a bread doll which Marcelino had baked. Then Valentina hid behind some rocks, playing hide-and-go-seek with the travelers winding along the valley paths. Surprising them, Celia, who came with food, found Valentina and Margarita hiding in the rocks. Celia embraced them and gave Valentina ch'uño and corn before she breast-fed Margarita. Celia took Margarita back early in the afternoon, and Valentina returned shortly before sunset, herding the sheep into a corral alongside the house. After playing with our dog Boo for awhile, Valentina packed cargo saddles on the burros and horse, and led them to the eastern side of the hamlet where Carmen and Marcelino were harvesting oca.

A different stage of Valentina's life began the morning she started school. She wore a pink blouse and blue skirt typical of La Paz and carried a small metal lunch bucket and a notebook. I barely recognized her, and Carmen cried. Another layer of history with a different form of dress was being imposed upon Valentina, as so many levels of land or encrustments of earth, with its sense of stratified geological time, yet continuity.

The director of schools had previously fined Marcelino ten dollars for refusing to send Valentina to school. A Bolivian law required children to attend four years of primary school. Kaata had only a primary school (first to sixth grade), and Charazani had a secondary school, where only a few Indians attended because of the distance. Most Qollahuaya children, however, attended school for only four years. Bolivian education belittled Qollahuaya culture and the teachers taught them to speak Spanish, to dress like Westerners, and to value modern ways. The educated children laughed at the traditions of the old folks and moved to cities, where life was easier, or so they thought. In La Paz, many migrants settled in squatter settlements where they barely survived on depletion allowances from servial tasks. They cleaned houses, gardened, and carried garbage. Education had introduced the Indians to urban life, but did not qualify them for it. Marcelino and Carmen knew that the primary school taught their daughters to work in other places, such as La Paz, where their daughter Gloria worked as a maid. Schooling caused a labor shortage for the Yanahuayas; since Valentina had to go to school, Carmen had to herd, taking an adult from a more skilled role.

Carmen and Marcelino realized both the richness and sadness of the Qollahuaya way of life and that each year—bit by bit—slipped beyond memory and was gone. They tried to educate their children in the ways of the Yanahuaya ancestors. Carmen, for example, taught Sophia, Valentina, and Judy how to weave, which involved learning many things about Andean society. Carmen first had the girls observe for several hours without any verbal instruction. Then, letting the girls practice, Carmen told them which threads to pull for the different designs. Finally, when they knew how to pick the threads, Carmen watched each of her pupils, encouraging them with an occasional *"Alliñapuni!"* ("Excellent!"), or chiding them with *"Manan alliñchu"* ("Not so good"). She patiently assisted when a design had to be redone.

After two weeks, Judy could copy pictographs from other garments by counting the threads and working very slowly. Carmen and Elsa, who wove the designs frequently, had memorized the patterns so that they could weave in a day what Judy wove in a week. Carmen taught Valentina with heavy threads and simple designs. Valentina disliked weaving and preferred to play with the animals. Gently encouraging her, however, Carmen frequently pulled out Valentina's uncompleted loom to see if she showed a little more interest, but Carmen never forced her. The complicated designs and the necessity of great finger strength made it difficult to learn. Carmen did not demand perfection at first. Sophia's first belt (*ch'ompi*) had many mistakes, but Carmen praised her. When Sophia ran off to play, Carmen told Judy that the pictograph of the horse on Sophia's belt looked like a jackass.

The Yanahuayas weave most from the time after harvest, in late August, until first planting toward the end of November, as well as during any other free time. They weave in the hot sun which stretches the yarn, resulting in a tighter weave, but when it rains they weave inside. They first pound four pegs into the ground relative to the corners of the garment; next, they tie a stick crosswise to two poles on the end where they will weave, and on the opposite poles, they lay crosswise another stick set on rocks. A person at each end winds the threads so that they cross in the center. Although colors are mixed throughout, Qollahuayas employ the following principles: a symmetrical pattern which begins and ends with six red threads and has a white thread between every two colored threads. Next, the threads are selected and tied into groups with white string (*illawa*). There are four string groups: a white and a colored group at the top, and the same at the bottom. The weavers pull threads to make a design first from the top yarns and then from the bottom. After each selection, the pulled threads are brought to the working end, pushed down six times with a wooden blade, and a separate brown thread is brought through, thus sewing it. Because the weavers cross the two groups from the bottom with the two from the top, the separated white threads become pictographs on a colored background.

Qollahuayas judge a person's weaving ability by the number of finely woven *cortes* in a day. A corte is a measure of weaving from the beginning to the end of a pictograph. For a mantle, the width of a towel, two cortes per day are usually expected of *ayni* and *minc'a* weavers, who come to the house for work exchange (ayni) or a salary (minc'a) of coca, food, and produce. Hired women, however, weave only work cloth for the Yanahuayas, such as brown or grey ponchos, mantles, and carrying sacks, because the Yanahuayas weave the finer garments.

Artists in their profession, Carmen, Celia, and Elsa weave into cloth not only geometric designs of trapezoids, parallelograms, and stairs, which represent the mountain and levels, but also pictographs of nature, which represent animals, plants, and people. For example,

Carmen Teaching Sophia to Weave a Belt

when Judy asked Elsa to weave a mantle, which we would later give to Margarita at First Haircutting, Elsa called in her aged maternal aunt from Apacheta (twenty-six miles by foot) to teach her a very old method of weaving. After six months, Elsa wove an elaborate red mantle, which traditionally represented her maternal lineage. Woven from dyed sheep and alpaca wool, the mantle had parades of people, horses, condors, frogs, snails, and dogs marching across it. The nature of the weaving represented these figures with linear emphasis; for example, the rays of the sun and the mane of the horse were woven with lines of white thread. Squares and triangles added geometric form to the pictographs of nature. Complementing the linear and geometric, intertwining and overlapping threads provided an organic unity and shape to the figures. Indeed, the red mantle matched some of the tapestries of the sixteenth century Flemish.

Cloth is an important symbol to the Qollahuayas and other Andeans. Carmen spent four days explaining to Judy the associations of the classes of wool, colors, designs, and styles to Qollahuaya cosmology, resources, and society. The pictographs formed meaningful patterns which could only be explained by reference to their land and society. The weavings of each ayllu, for example, had different styles with unique color combinations and divisions into bands which represented the levels of land and resources on that mountain. The weaving style of each ayllu had a certain flexibility so that its communities and lineages could represent themselves in weavings.

Generally speaking, the designs and types of cloth represent clearly defined meanings in the Andes. Cloth's symbolic property of multivocality neither condenses nor polarizes a disparity of meanings, but rather, cloth, with its style of weaving, pictographs, and shapes, restricts and defines the interpretation of symbols. In this respect, Andean symbols differ from African symbols. The symbols of the Ndembu have the properties of multivocality, unifying diverse meanings, and polarizing ideological and physiological referents (Turner 1967:27-30). The milk tree, for example, is the dominant symbol of the *Nkang'a* ritual for the Ndembu. The milk tree stands for women's breasts, motherhood, a novice at a girl's puberty rite, the principle of matriliny, learning, and the unity and persistence of Ndembu society; the milk tree contains diffuse meanings. In contrast, Andean symbols have specific meanings. The generic symbol of cloth becomes a definite vehicle of meaning by the type of garment, form of weaving, and the style. For example, the *ch'uspa*, a small bag, has pictographs and can only be used by men to carry coca; the *ist'alla*, napkin-sized cloth, has pictographs and can only be used by women to carry coca; but the *inkhuña*, similar to an *ist'alla* but without designs, can be used by both men and women to carry food. Cloth's meaning is permanently set into it by the design and form given it by the weaver.

The importance of clothing for reflecting social status in Kaata can be seen clearly in the clothes worn for political and ritual roles. When Marcelino became Secretary General of Kaata in 1965, for example, Carmen wove a snail-motif poncho for him. She wove it in a year, and the eye strain was so great that she feared she would go blind if she wove another. Carmen's finest weaving, the poncho, had long rows of curlicues which, according to Qollahuayas, represented snails. Andeans attribute magical powers to snails because they carry their homes (shells) with them up and down the mountain and live on land and in water (Urioste 1976), somewhat similar to the Qolla-huaya's journey on top of and inside Mount Kaata. Marcelino wore the snail-motif poncho during the year when he was Secretary General and when he was sponsor (*preste*) for the fiesta of Santa Rita. After this, Marcelino wore his poncho on other occasions because he had fulfilled his major adult responsibilities in Kaata and was entitled to the respect due the wearer of the snail-motif poncho.

Signifying lesser statuses, the red poncho was woven of wide red bands and bordering yellow, green, orange, and black stripes and represented the colors of the earth and sky blending together. Laborio Yanahuaya, a seventy-year-old neighbor, wove exceptional red ponchos. He was the only Yanahuaya male who wove, although men knit sweaters and wove tweed pants with upright looms. Participants of secondary importance dressed in red ponchos for the agricultural and saint fiestas, and participants of still lesser importance dressed in brown and grey ponchos which were woven in solid colors with no designs. Qollahuayas, however, wore the different classes of ponchos at times other then during rituals; this indicated to the community that the wearer had attained a certain ceremonial and social status in the community.

Judy and I experienced the social growth into clothes when we arrived in Kaata. The Secretary General asked me to wear a red poncho and Judy to dress in a red mantle. He said the foreigners who dressed in jackets never became Qollahuayas. I wore a red poncho and Judy dressed in a red mantle (which were appreciated in the cool mountain air) all year, until the last week. As we were preparing to leave Kaata, Carmen and Marcelino presented us with a snail-motif poncho and mantle. We were entitled to wear the snail-motif garments because we had participated in all the minor and major ritual roles.

In a metaphorical way, the woof and warp of wool on a weaving is analogous to vertical and horizontal ties between people on Mount Kaata. For this reason, perhaps, cloth symbolizes the bonds between friends and relatives and between the living and the dead. A young Andean woman, for example, presents her husband with a dowry of weavings, and as they mature in marriage she weaves gray, brown, red, and snail-motif ponchos for him and for their children. The Yanahuayas communicate with their dead relatives through cloth: Marcelino daily sticks coca beneath the hat and poncho of Sabino, his dead son, and asks him to return soon.

Moreover, godparents from other levels and lands strengthen their ties with godchildren when they clothe them for the first time. The godparents assume the first responsibility of natural parents to clothe their child. This emphasizes the necessity of ritual kinship in addition to natural kinship.

Margarita was less than a year old when Celia and Martin asked Judy and me, "Would you cut the hair of your godchild?" I replied that Margarita had not yet begun to speak and that perhaps, we should wait another year. Martin knew that we were leaving for the United States, so he insisted that it would be all right to perform First Haircutting before Margarita could walk or talk. We agreed and exchanged coca. Discussing the appropriate day for the ritual, I suggested Friday, but Martin said that only sorcery rituals to the river were performed on Tuesdays and Fridays. The various classes of rituals are assigned to different weekdays in Kaata: meals are offered to the earth shrines on Wednesdays and Thursdays; Catholic and community rituals for the household, chapel, and plaza are performed on Saturdays and Sundays. Therefore, First Haircutting was scheduled for Sunday, December 17, 1972, and we began inviting friends and relatives, natural and ritual kin.

First Haircutting began Sunday afternoon with a meal at which everyone shared food. The men served the guests plates of soup which Martin distributed to his guests, and the women placed cooked potatoes, oca, and corn on the cob on common inkhuñas, which were in the center of the encircled women and in front of the line of men. As the First Haircutting specialty, Celia had prepared a pig's head soup. Although many of the guests had already eaten eleven plates of food, they were still delighted to see Celia's soup which, like dessert, meant the end of the meal.

Sharing of alcohol and coca followed the meal which in its ritualized exchange suggested unity and solidarity between the participants of First Haircutting.

"Chew coca, please, co-father," Martin said as he gave me his ch'uspa. I thanked Martin and gave him my ch'uspa with coca. The rest of the men also exchanged coca with each other until everyone had chewed coca from the others' ch'uspas. Judy and the women chewed coca from a pile in the center of their circle, to which supply they had originally contributed. Then twice Martin gave me a bottle of alcohol and an ist'alla of coca to serve the guests. We chewed coca for about an hour.

Margarita was sleeping in another room during the meal and exchange of coca, and when we had finished, Celia woke her, cuddled her for awhile, and then breast-fed her. Taking Margarita in her arms, Judy fondled her and gave her a candy before dressing her. She placed a red skirt and a green blouse, woven from dyed sheep's wool around Margarita. Next, Judy fastened the open shoulders of an axso, a jumper-like dress, by pinning them together with tupus, engraved spoons with spike handles. Andeans traditionally used tupus to measure food; the needle was inserted into a sack of cereal or other produce to measure a standard quantity (one tupu). The spoon served everyday household uses from dispensing medicine to sipping alcohol. Now restricting the use of tupus to jewelry, Qolla-huaya women wear these ornate silver spoons with settings of jewels and coins over each breast. Judy finally placed gray and red mantles over the axso. She secured the axso around Margarita's waist with a red, white, and black belt, then covered her back and shoulders with gray and red mantles, also fastened at the neck with a tupu.

Gregorio Yanahuaya, Marcelino's classificatory brother, was cashier (cajero), who would collect gifts in exchange for clipping locks of hair. Gregorio grabbed a tuft of Margarita's hair and handed me the scissors. I clipped it telling everyone that I was replacing Margarita's hair with a sheep whose wool would clothe her. I put the hair into a plate with three coca leaves, praying, as Marcelino had instructed me, *"Kaypi tejjsi Margaritapah!"* ("This is the cement of Margarita.") Tejjsi, the foundation of Andean houses, are cemented rocks upon which the walls, two layers of adobe, are set. The first set of clothing and sheep are like the foundation and walls of a house. The ewe will grow wool and reproduce, forming the foundation of clothes and flock. The clothes circumscribe the person like the walls surround a house.

More significantly, tejjsi also means "origin." The person's head is associated with the summit of the mountain where pastoral grass grows and llamas graze. Grass and hair share the quality of regrowth. The cycled quality of grass and hair metaphorically applies to Andean cosmology, which teaches that people come out of highland lakes, journey down the slopes, die, and return to the highlands where they "grow back" once again.

Gregorio invited each person to cut a lock of hair, also trying to shame them into being more generous. "You can't cut a lock for that pittance," he reprimanded. Each time the donor put the money, hair, and coca on a plate set on a sacred cloth, *wayllasa*. Then Martin thanked the giver and poured him a drink. This continued until the hair had been removed. From the scissors' cuts, Margarita's head literally looked like an irregularly terraced field.

Judy, as is customary of the godmother, put a woven headband (*winch'a*) around Margarita's head. The headband had columns of snail-motifs and pictographs set off by glass beads; the snails, animals, and plants impart their power to those who wear the headband. This power is not a sharing of the object's vital nature, but a representational magic which provides the wearer with fertility. This fertility results in children, animals, and crops.

Jesus and the earth also charge headbands with reproductive power. At Ascension, for example, Qollahuaya women hang their headbands around the neck of the statue of Jesus which is carried in procession. The women, drunk and permissive, prostrate themselves on the ground before the statue. They grasp for Jesus, as he is carried on a litter above them. When the statue rests in the chapel, they snatch their headbands back. This gesture is similar to the one at the Field Selection rite (Chacrata Qukuy) when women dance on the field until they collapse upon it in an embrace. In both instances, according to informants, the women symbolically join in a reproductive union: at Ascension they unite with Jesus, and at Chacrata Qukuy, with the earth. This reproductive union should be understood not only as a sexual union, but also as a sharing of fertility.

The headbands of Margarita, moreover, were those of her great-grandmother, grandmother, and mother; headbands represent female lineage. Mikyla Ari, great-grandmother, gave Margarita the widest headband with precious dark blue beads, which she had inherited from her mother. Women carry the female embryo of their lineage from one generation to the next, similarly as they inherit headbands.

The cashier and his assistant, the treasurer, sprinkled alcohol and coca on the elegantly dressed Margarita. They petitioned Pacha-mama and huacas to provide Margarita with clothes and sheep. Finally, the treasurer listed the donors and their gifts in a notebook which he would keep until Margarita married, at which time he would read her the names and gifts. This will guarantee that Margarita receives these gifts and that they will not be consumed by her parents. Margarita has rights to her property.

Margarita possesses distinct rights within her family from early childhood, and she has godparents who can assure these rights. If Celia and Martin take Margarita's sheep and cloth, she can appeal to Judy and me. Moreover, if they mistreat her, we must beat Martin and Celia, or at least, severely reprimand them. Beyond the social relations of the family is another ideal and ritual set of relations, which, in a sense, idealize natural kin patterns, but also set limits upon them.

Margarita was given her first set of clothing at First Haircutting, and as she progresses through life she will accumulate more cloth. Becoming a young woman, Margarita will weave additional mantles, headbands, and belts, making herself attractive to some man who will marry her. At her wedding, she will be attired in a snail-motif skirt and mantle with a canopy headset. For every fiesta, especially when her husband is sponsor (*preste*), she will appear with an expensive felt cloth (*bayeta*) beneath her woven mantle and belt. When she dies, Margarita will be buried in some of her weavings. She came naked from the earth, but will return to it dressed in fine clothes.

7

Marriage and Mountain

The mountain metaphor symbolically consolidates Apacheta, Kaata, and Niñokorin at New Earth. The metaphor expresses a cultural corporateness for the mountain communities, and also serves as the basis for the ayllu's social structure. Statistical evidence shows that the selection of spouses is restricted to the three levels. The woman moves to her husband's level, yet she inherits land from her mother. The woman's inheritance is never claim to but rather access to the land. When the daughter marries and returns to her mother's level, she inherits access to her mother's parcel.

Marriage patterns indicate, then, that the mountain is the symbolic parameter of a social structure which is based on even exchange between high, central, and low levels. The metaphor which is the basis of the social structure in that society becomes the mountain symbolically understood as a body possessing three levels.

But the metaphor goes beyond its landmark either to incorporate new high and low areas, such as La Paz and the Yungas, or to bring the mountain to the city. Kaatans, for example, live in La Paz and continue to exchange spouses between the three levels of that city. They have carried with them the mountain metaphor, and it still influences their social structure. Consequently, the wedding ritual expresses this metaphor by making visible the exchange between groups living on different levels of land.

Four informants knew the origin and settlement of all 205 families in the community of Kaata. And Kaatans are just as aware of the exchange of persons as they are of goods—they know to the gram what they gave to and received from anyone ten years ago. From this information, percentages of endogamy, exogamy, virilocality, and matrilocality were arrived at, as indicated in Table 1.

Table 1. Marriage Patterns: Percentage of Endogamy, Exogamy, Virilocality, and Matrilocality Within the Hamlet, Community, and Ayllu

	Hamlet Kaatapata	Hamlet Chaqahuaya	Hamlet Qollahuaya	Community Kaata	Ayllu Kaata
Endogamy	13/36:36%	109/139:78%	8/30:27%	174/205:85%	193/205:94%
Exogamy	23/36:64%	24/139:22%	22/30:73%	31/205:15%	12/205: 6%
Virilocality	26/36:72%	133/139:96%	29/30:97%	188/205:92%	188/205:92%
Matrilocality	10/36:28%	6/139: 4%	1/30: 3%	17/205: 8%	17/205: 8%

Patterns of endogamy and exogamy seem confusing; men from two of the hamlets, for example, marry women from outside, and those from the other hamlet marry from within. Endogamy increases from the hamlet, to the community, to the ayllu; yet within each of these social and geographical units there is also exogamy.

The confusion vanishes, however, when one realizes how Kaatans consider endogamy and exogamy. Manifesting Kaatans' viewpoint, the wedding ritual emphasizes the exchange of persons in marriage; this exchange always takes place betwen people from two levels of land, either symbolically or actually. The ritual symbolically associates the woman's access to land with the lowlands and the man's claim to land with the highlands. When they marry, the two levels are symbolically interrelated, even though the partners live only one hundred yards apart in the same hamlet and in the same ecological zone.

The corporate nature of the mountain discourages the selection of spouses between similar levels, just as subsistence encourages the exchange of resources between ecological zones. The levels, moreover, are composed of classificatory relatives among whom marriage is taboo. Ayllu Kaata employs classificatory kinship terminology, which blurs the distinction between lineal and collateral relatives. Hence, there is ambiguity between biological and classificatory relatives. Male and female cousins, for example, are classificatory brothers and sisters. The young child has many classificatory mothers and fathers, brothers and sisters living on his level. The classificatory nature of Kaatan kinship extends the social relations learned and experienced within the immediate family to the other classificatory mothers, fathers, sisters, and brothers of the larger social units of the hamlet and community. Kaatans say a person who marries a classificatory relative is condemned (*condenado*), and the community of Kaata has only one such condemned person.

As population and settlement patterns change, Kaatans apply the mountain's division of three ecological zones to other elevations of high, center, and low, between which spouses are exchanged in marriage. In the eighteenth and nineteenth centuries, Kaatapata was the only settlement of the Kaata community with about forty families.[1] Kaatan men did not marry women from their own area but rather those from the higher and lower communities of Apacheta and Niñokorin, as well as from the higher and lower ayllus of Chajaya and Curva.[2] In the twentieth century, Kaatan men selected spouses from their own area, but only after that community had divided into three levels of high, center, and low. After their wells had run dry and lightning had devastated several of their homes on this rooftop site, some Kaatapatans moved to Qollahuaya, the saddle between the hill and the basin. By 1928, twenty Peruvian families settled below Qollahuaya in Chaqahuaya,[3] which is a basin left from a dried-out lake. Land laws enforced property ownership for members of the community only; this restriction created problems for the woman who moved outside of her community in marriage yet held inherited land in her parents' community. Traditionally, she had access to her inherited land, descending to work it, but legal titles to land became more important than concepts of access. High, center, and low levels, similar to those of the mountain, were applied to

Kaatapata, Qollahuaya, and Chaqahuaya, and the people from these areas also inter-married.

More recently, Chaqahuaya has quadrupled in size, with 139 families compared to Kaatapata's 36 and Qollahuaya's 30. Although Chaqahuaya still selects spouses from Qollahuaya and Kaatapata, it too has divided into three levels, exchanging spouses between Pachapata on the hill, Chaqapampa on the lower slope, and Pachaqochu at the bottom of the basin.

Exogamous and endogamous categories have no objective existence as independent entities for Kaatans (see Lévi-Strauss 1969:49). They represent "viewpoints" of structural triads and guide Kaatans in exchanging persons with other levels of land and social groups. Their solidary perspective refers to any unit with a high, center, and low level, among which people are exchanged in marriage. Mount Kaata's three levels are reflected in its subdivisions, as illustrated below.

Mount Kaata's Three Levels

AYLLU

Communities

High - Apacheta

Hamlets

MOUNT KAATA: *Center* - Kaata: *High* - Kaatapata

Center - Qollahuaya   Barrios

Low - Chaqahuaya: *High* - Pachapata

Center - Chaqapampa

Low - Pachaqochu

Low - Niñokorin

Quiabaya

Changes in virilocality have occurred in Kaatapata, where one-fourth of the marriages are matrilocal. Matrilocality, however, is looked down on by Kaatans, who call the male settlers "boarders without land." Settlement patterns, migration of men, and available land can explain Kaatapata's increasing matrilocality. Some of the men returning in marriage to Kaatapata are the sons of men who moved from this land, yet these sons have a patrilineal claim to land at this site.

The shortage of men in Kaatapata, and in other parts of the mountain as well, is mainly the result of urbanization and colonization. Once Kaatans are educated in schools, they travel to La Paz to serve the city's increasing tourist business as bellhops and servants, or they descend to the lowlands to labor in the coca fields, orchards, and mines. Some Kaatapatan men have moved their ritual practices to more productive economic centers, giving their land to their daughters, who attract men from another high level, Apacheta; thus, five Apachetan men have moved to Kaatapata.

The ayllu's people prefer that the man stay on his inherited land and that the wife move to his level. Marrying a woman on the same level would disturb the husband's claim to land by having affinal relatives with land holdings close to his own. The two patrilineal groups would be geographically merged and united in the offspring, who then would bilineally inherit land. Each lineage's ancestors would become very angy about this, perhaps striking the male offenders with ancestor sickness (*machula onqosqa*).

According to statistics, moreover, the exchange of spouses between levels is balanced,[4] which indicates that the levels of high, center, and low are not hierarchically ordered, such as would be the case in a system of asymmetrical exchange. The communities do not understand their relationship to each other in terms of subordinate to superior, but rather in terms of parts of an organic whole, which necessitates specialization and integration.

In summary, then, the mountain metaphor expresses the levels' organic solidarity on a cultural level, but it is also embedded within the social structure. The balanced exchange results from the following principles of Kaatan social structure: exchange of women between high, center, and low levels, matrilineal inheritance of land, and virilocality. The woman moves away from her inheritance in the first generation, but her daughter moves back to renew access to her mother's land.

Ayllu Kaata has a balanced exchange of women with its neighboring ayllus and establishes solidary links within the Qollahuaya area. Spouses often meet at inter-ayllu markets and fiestas, where the

marriageable women come dressed in their finest weavings. Their
dress reveals their availability and whether they are from ayllus with
which there is an exchange of women.

Ayllu Kaata's exchanges of women have been limited to two
other ayllus during different periods of history. The viewpoint of
high, center, and low has shifted over time: toward the end of the
eighteenth century, for example, ayllu Kaata exchanged women with
ayllus Chajaya and Chari; at present it exchanges with ayllus
Upinhuaya and Curva.[5] Furthermore, the ayllus have similar ecological levels, and so Kaatans apply another metaphor to low and high
by associating low with east, where the sun leaves the earth, and high
with west, where the sun enters the earth. Ayllu Curva is east of
Kaata and is the low ayllu; ayllu Upinhuaya is west of Kaata and is
the high ayllu. Similarly, two centuries ago Chajaya was to the east
and Chari to the west of ayllu Kaata. But Mount Kaata always
remains at the center.

MAKING VISIBLE THE EXCHANGE BETWEEN LEVELS

Mount Kaata, with its distinct crops, geographical levels, and
relation to the sun, is a cultural perspective for exchanging women in
marriage. These cultural patterns of exchange emphasize a continual
mechanism of reciprocal exchange between high, center, and low
levels. Andean cultural patterns are explicated in ritual, which makes
visible these unstated facts. The wedding ritual, for example, is a
sacred and visible moment when both levels come together to cere-
monially express a bond of unity, distinction, and reciprocity.

Kaatan marriages haven't changed since the union of Carmen
Quispe and Marcelino Yanahuaya twenty-five years ago. Carmen's
parents are Mikyla Ari and Leandro Quispe of Niñokorin, and
Mikyla's parents are Petrona Supo and Manuel Ari of Qollahuaya
hamlet of Kaata. After Mikyla married Leandro, she moved to the
lower community. Before Carmen was married, her maternal grandmother gave her access to a large garden plot with a shed in
Qollahuaya. Petrona Supo knew her granddaughter would be able
to utilize the land if she married a man from Qollahuaya and settled
in that area.

Marcelino Yanahuaya had been out of touch with exchange patterns. As a boy, he had traveled throughout Peru with his herbalist uncle, and later served with the military in Potosí. Because Antonia Quispe, Carmen's older sister, had married a man from Kaatapata and wanted her sister nearby, she introduced Carmen to Marcelino at the fiesta of San Juan in Charazani. Carmen and Marcelino danced throughout the day and went to the fields together that evening. Some months later, Carmen climbed to Qollahuaya to tell Marcelino that they should get married. Marcelino was pleased to know that Carmen would bear him offspring and they agreed upon marriage.

The exchange is repeated when one of Carmen's daughters marries a man from Niñokorin to gain access to the vast properties which their grandmother has accumulated. Elsa Yanahuaya, Carmen's daughter, is now courting a man from Niñokorin. As in the instance of Carmen and Elsa, the woman's tie to her inherited land guarantees a return of the exchange to gain access to the land in a society of virilocal residence, yet matrilineal property.[6]

The meeting of Carmen's people and Marcelino's people was the coming together of the *masi ayllu* and *jatun ayllu*.[7] These terms are used by Kaatans to refer to the wife's relatives and level of land (masi ayllu), and to those of the husband (jatun ayllu).

The kinship basis for the distinction between jatun and masi is that, from the man's viewpoint, jatun (erect) would symbolize the vertical generations, especially his male ancestors. Masi means neighbor and people not related by common ancestors but by horizontal links. Kaatan women, for example, called me *masi turay* (neighboring brother) and Marcelino refers to Carmen's brothers and sisters as masi.[8] Jatun ayllu is the viewpoint of ego as he considers the ancestral claim to his land, and masi ayllu refers to the place and to all people related to his wife.

TINKA: THE RITUAL MEETING OF THE HORIZONTAL AND VERTICAL AYLLUS

The joining of the vertical with the horizontal is expressed by *tinka*. Tinka is the important ritual action of bringing together separated or contrasting parts, such as the meeting during ritual of the highlands and lowlands, the vertical kin group and the horizontal kin group, and the living and the dead.[9] Kaatans' roof-thatching ritual is called tinka, where the vertical and the horizontal or the highlands and lowlands are symbolically brought together by joining the poles from the lowlands with the straw from the highlands. Tinka can best be expressed by the more encapsulating idea of completeness, which Kaatans understand as the bringing together of all the parts and only these parts insomuch as they constitute one whole.

Marcelino asked two friends from Kaatapata to be vertical sponsors (*jatun padrinos*) for his marriage, and Carmen asked two friends from Niñokorin to be horizontal sponsors (*ara padrinos*).[10] The people from the vertical ayllu of Marcelino brought a llama, soup, potatoes, oca, alcohol, and a five-piece flute band, while those from the horizontal ayllu of Carmen contributed mantles, chicha, bread, and another flute band.

The vertical bridesmaid prepared most of the banquet, which would be held at the house of Pedro Yanahuaya, Marcelino's classificatory father, since his natural father was dead. The horizontal bridesmaid, Philomena Yupanqui, accompanied Carmen from Niño-korin to Charazani early Sunday morning, and when they arrived at the church, Philomena began dressing Carmen in layers of skirts and mantles. Two fine red and green skirts of soft felt were placed over a tightly woven pinafore. Another snail-motif skirt was placed on top and blended with a large mantle of a similar design covering her back, along with six other mantles. Engraved silver spoons fastened the mantles in front. A canopy of black lace covered her head and face, so that she could neither see nor be seen—she was a mountain of cloth. Each skirt symbolized a pregnancy, and Carmen literally appeared to be carrying a child with so much cloth around her. Her wedding dress expressed that her lineage was giving to Marcelino's patrilineage layers of cloth, or fertility to his land and patriliny. She would bear Marcelino many sons to carry on his ancestors' claim to land.

Marcelino's clothing was also of the snail-motif design, but he wore only one set: a simple poncho, a multi-colored stocking cap beneath a white felt hat, a medicine bag, coca bag, and black pants over longer white pants. The vertical best man carried a two and a half-foot ebony staff (*wara*) and Marcelino wore an engraved silver cross. The staff referred to the mountain, the permanent claim to and authority over the land, and the cross symbolized the union of the vertical and horizontal lineages. The *alcaldes* and *jilakatas* (leaders of the community before 1954) always held this staff as a symbol of authority; for the household rituals the male head of the house held it; and for the saints' fiestas the sponsor carried it. The vertical best man symbolized, independently of the married couple, an ancestral claim to land, to which the man has direct right and in which the woman participates. The permanence of this claim was symbolized by the vertical best man accompanying Marcelino wherever he went, even when he relieved himself.

The vertical bridesmaid, however, did not always stay with the bride, but remained in Kaata to prepare an elaborate meal. The man's level would bring food to the bride, her family, and place, but the husband would not bring land. Going with Carmen to Charazani now, the horizontal bridesmaid from the lower community would always accompany her, symbolizing that Niñokorin and its people still had claim to her.

Carmen, Marcelino, and their sponsors participated in the Catholic marriage ritual, which consisted essentially of the exchange of promises to live with each other until death. The positioning of the bridal party also revealed the wife's ayllu as circular and on the periphery. Marcelino stood on the right side of Carmen and both were in the center; on the side of each were the vertical sponsors, encapsulating the bride into their ayllu. On the outside were the horizontal sponsors.

The bridal party's next ritual act was to "pay" the place of the man's ayllu. The night before the wedding the horizontal and vertical sponsors had offered coca and alcohol to their household shrines. They read the hearts and bowels of three guinea pigs: one to determine Marcelino's heart, another to determine Carmen's good or bad luck, and the third to foretell what effect this marriage would have on Carmen's place and people. The sponsors then offered tables of coca, fat, and blood to Carmen's and Marcelino's earth shrines. Marcelino's shrines were mountains Aqhamani and Sunchuli, representing his permanent and vertical control over land. Carmen's shrines of Tuana and Paya Tuana were near the place of the sun's birth, Chaqamita, and referred to plenitude of food and offspring.[11]

Ayllu Kaata has a shrine where every bridal party rests after the

Catholic liturgy and feeds coca and alcohol to the lord of marriage, who protects their married life. Feeding the lord of marriage is no less a gesture of exchange than that expressed in the chapel. Carmen, Marcelino, and the sponsors paused on this shrine's protruding knob, halfway up the steep slope, to feed coca and fat to Mount Kaata. This gesture ratified the union between the woman's and the man's levels. The two levels brought together in marriage were united in the mountain.

The panpipe band from Niñokorin began to play, leading the party up the second half of the slope to Mojata pass, where they were joined by another band from Kaata. Friends and relatives from Niñokorin and Kaata lined both sides of the path to Kaata. The best men gave Marcelino bread birds (*phesqo wawas*), which were baked in the shape of Xs; the best men tied them across his back, and the bridesmaids bundled bread babies (*t'ant'a wawas*) inside Carmen's mantles. She carried the breads on her back as though they were her own children. They say that Kaatan man dreams of being a condor, flying freely above the heights, and the woman longs for many babies which will spread her horizontally over the land. The villagers also gave Marcelino and Carmen more bread figurines, and by the time they arrived at Pedro's house, they had more than fifty each.

The reception was held in Pedro's patio, which was decorated with a large bamboo canopy and lined with ferns. At the head of the passageway was a long table, and near it were hundreds of cloth mantles spread over the ground. Marcelino sat on the throne with his best men on his right, and his classificatory mothers and fathers on his left. Kaata's leaders and elders sat in a rectangle around the table in front of Marcelino. Carmen with her bridesmaids and parents sat in a circle on the mantles. For the serving of the meal, the vertical bridesmaid gave the vertical best man a large pot of soup with llama meat; he, in turn, put the pot in front of Marcelino and served him a plate of soup. The same best man began pouring bowls of soup, which were then distributed to Carmen and her relatives, who brought cooked corn, bread, and chicha. The corn and bread were placed on the table before Marcelino by the horizontal best man. Another pile was placed in front of Carmen and her group. The exchange of drink followed a pattern of one group giving the other a bottle of alcohol or chicha, from which the recipient served his group and the donor group. Marcelino's group gave Carmen's a bottle of alcohol, from which the horizontal best man served both parties; and similarly, Carmen's ayllu gave chicha to Marcelino's ayllu.

The sponsors representing Marcelino's ayllu gave Carmen and Marcelino an ear of corn with each alternate row of kernels picked off. The sponsors told the spouses that the corn signified the field, and each row of kernels was a *wajchu* (row). Carmen was the furrow and Marcelino was the row, and as furrow and row were necessary for raising corn, so too the man and woman were necessary to bring children. The symbolism extended to the beneficial exchange of Niñokorin with Kaata. The lower fields were abundant in corn, wheat, and vegetables; and the central fields were fertile with potatoes, oca, and barley. Both communities needed the other's crops to live and reproduce, and as the exchange of resources between levels is necessary for the subsistence of all the mountain's people, so too is the exchange of partners in marriage.

Early in the evening, after the groups had danced and drunk together, the sponsors ushered Marcelino and Carmen off to bed. The bridal couple knelt before the bed and kissed the cross, as the sponsors advised, "Don't fight; work hard; respect your relatives and in-laws." The sponsors undressed the couple and locked them in the room.

The symbols of the marriage ritual make visible the unstated facts between levels, and the exchange between two social groups associated with different levels of land. These unstated facts of Kaatan society involve highly differentiated male and female roles which express the man's vertical claim to land and the woman's horizontal claim to cloth and children. The wedding makes visible these implicit assumptions between the contrasting levels of land and kinship groups by joining them within the same ritual. Low level is here juxtaposed with a high level, and a man's claim to land is seen in relation to a woman's claim to cloth. These two pairs become a complete set within the ritual.

Making visible these unstated facts between levels of land and society within the ceremonial occasion of the ritual adds the liturgical property of renewing all marriages, refurbishing old exchanges, and stimulating new ones. The statistics indicate that the exchange of women decreases as the geographical and social units become more comprehensive and extensive in size; for example, the exchange of women within Chaqahuaya and its three levels is much greater than within the province or inter-ayllu. From the decreasing exchange of spouses, however, one should not conclude that the exchange of goods is any less significant. The marriage establishes and perpetuates links beyond those which could be founded on exchange of economic goods. The wedding, then, symbolizes the interdependency of the lineages within the context of the mountain metaphor.

NOTES

1.   Estimated from the abandoned house sites.

2.   Twenty-four marriages of ayllu Kaata from 1786-1787 were entered in the parish register of Charazani. Twenty were an exchange between the high, center, and low communities of ayllu Kaata (i.e., Niñokorin, Quiabaya, Kaata, and Apacheta) and four were with women from ayllus Chajaya and Chari.

3.   A legal document of 1928 lists 500 Indians for ayllu Kaata, enumerating twenty native families and twenty settlers for community Kaata.

4.   The three hamlets exchanged spouses fairly evenly. Qollahuaya, for example, gave Chaqahuaya nine women and received eight; Kaatapata gave Chaqahuaya eight women, receiving four women and four men; and Qollahuaya exchanged four women with Kaatapata, which returned two women and one man. The exchange of women between the three communities is less balanced. Kaata gave Apacheta seven women and received eight women and five men in return; Niñokorin exchanged six women with Kaata and received ten in return; and informants said there was a balanced exchange between Apacheta and Niñokorin.

5.   Four women and one man came from Upinhuaya to Kaata, and one woman and one man came from Curva to Kaata. Informants said that five Kaatan women are married to Upinhuayan men, and live there, and that one Kaatan woman is married to a man from Curva and lives there.

6.   Carmen and Marcelino became wealthy, with many rooms and seven garden plots around their house. Carmen gave one of her plots to her brother's son, Pedro Quispe. Pedro's father died, leaving him with neither land nor income. Mikyla and Carmen agreed that part of the land which Petrona Supo had given Carmen in Qollahuaya should go to Pedro, who in return would give each of them half a llama. Marcelino did not approve of Carmen's gift to Pedro, but he did not interfere, completely aware of Carmen's right to relinquish her access to land and to give a male member of her patrilineage claim to that land.

7.   The term "ayllu" is multi-faceted and must be understood in context and according to the viewpoint of those using it. Mount Kaata's high, center, and low levels can be viewed as one ayllu or each level may be seen from the ego's perspective, according to which the person's place would be considered as the jatun ayllu and the other communities as *mitmaj ayllus*; for example, Marcelino would consider the community of Kaata as jatun ayllu and Niñokorin and Apacheta as two mitmaj ayllus. Although ayllu's meanings shift from different vantage points, they still are grounded in Mount Kaata and its land.

8.   The distinction between the vertical and horizontal ayllus is also found in lineage rituals when male and female members of the woman's lineage perform the feminine roles. In rituals of the Yanahuaya family, for example, Pedro Quispe's role will always be associated with womanly roles, because he represents the horizontal ayllu of Carmen.

9.   *Tinka* is different from *tinku*, which is a theatrical fight between two groups. Tinku emphasizes the constructive dialectic of diversity, whereas tinka stresses the montage of separations.

10.   *Ara* means altar or flat surface. The vertical and horizontal sponsors are two male and female couples. They do not remain with their respective spouses, but rather they "cross geographical levels" to form a continuity according to sex; that is, the vertical and horizontal best men serve the groom, and both bridesmaids serve the bride.

11.   Marcelino and Carmen each have two earth shrines. The second shrine accompanies the first as its companion. Aqhamani is paired with Sunchuli, an accompanying peak. Tuana is usually paired off with Paya Tuana, and both are manifestations of Chaqamita. Throughout the marriage ritual, binality of earth shrines reinforces the joining of two people in marriage, as well as the importance of pairs.

*

8

The Healing Mountain

Western medicine ascribes sickness to internal disorders of the body
or to the malfunctioning of organs within it, whereas Kaatan curing
looks outside the body to the malfunctioning of the social and
ecological order. In Kaata, bodily illnesses are signs of disorders
between the person and the land, or between the person's vertical
ayllu and Kaata ayllu. Diviners cure, not by isolating the individual
in a hospital, away from his land, but rather by gathering the
members of the sick person's social group in ritual, and together
feeding all the parts of Mount Kaata. The community and mountain
are inextricably bound to the physical body, and disintegration in
one is associated with disorder in the other. Sickness is usually linked
with either a social disturbance or a land dispute. The diviner's role is
to reveal this conflict and to redress it by ritual,[1] which resolves the
dispute and reorders the mountain.[2]

Erminia, two-year-old daughter of Celia and Martin, refused to
eat raisins, which she had always loved. Her round face had erupted
with boils, and I was asked to cure her. I diagnosed the boils as a skin
infection, perhaps an advanced stage of syphilis, and administered
lincocin, an antibiotic similar to penicillin. Marcelino, Celia's father,
placed thorny leaves against the boils to draw the pus. Erminia

129

refused to swallow the matés which Carmen had prepared; instead she spit them at her grandparents. The lincocin and herbs had little effect, and her chubby face remained covered with ugly protrusions.

Late one evening, shortly before midnight, Carmen slipped away to visit Sarito. A large cowhide basket swung from the ceiling of Sarito's cooking house, and next to it were strung the dried fetuses of llamas, sheep, and a pig. Carmen gave coca to Sarito and his wife, who was cooking over a dung fire inside a clay oven which was similar to three inverted swallows' nests. A young girl fed pellets of sheep dung into the fire and at the same time blew through a bamboo pipe to ignite the dung. Carmen gave Sarito twelve coca leaves, six of which she had placed under Erminia's hat and next to her face, and six of which she had secretly removed from Celia and Martin's household shrines. Sarito earmarked them for Celia, Martin, Carmen, Marcelino, and ancestors. Carmen prayed, and Sarito silently slid the leaves across his coca cloth. Martin's leaf paired with the ancestor's leaf. They chewed more coca and drank a little chicha for the decisive divination. Marcelino's, Martin's, and the ancestor's leaves paired together.

"*Onqosqa machula!*" ("Ancestor sickness!"), Sarito whispered.

"Tatay! Tatay!" Carmen exclaimed.

"Marcelino's ancestors are angry with Martin. They have sent ancestor sickness to Erminia."

The final throw revealed that Martin had dug near Marcelino's ancestors' grave west of Qollahuaya. The mummy site is a square rock building, the size of a small fish house, with tiny doors on four sides. Except for ritual use, these grave sites are no longer used by Kaatans, who now bury their ancestors in the Catholic cemetery.

Reaching into the cowhide basket, Sarito prepared three wads of coca, incense, and pig fat, and wrapped them in black llama wool. The ancestors were fed with symbols associated with death and decay, contrasting with llama fat and white cotton, associated with life and growth. He instructed Carmen to give these to Martin, who was to bury them near the ancestors' grave.[3]

Martin laughed when Carmen told him that Erminia's boils were caused by ancestor sickness. Having more schooling than Carmen, Martin had completed the third grade and doubted the tales of the ancestor mummies, often described as tiny people who ate, drank, danced, and played their flutes beneath the rock shrine. Carmen, in a whining voice, told Martin to bury the black wads next to the mummy site. She handed the wads to him. He handed them back to Carmen, saying, "Bury them yourself!"

"You're an ass!" Carmen shouted as she took the wads and returned to Qollahuaya.

Celia, Martin's wife, followed her mother to Qollahuaya, crying, and pleading with Carmen not to blame Martin. Marcelino met them both at the gate. After carefully weighing both sides of the argument, he agreed that Martin had been disturbing the mummy sites and that the ancestors were angry. What Marcelino failed to admit was that the ancestor mummies were angry with him.

Marcelino and Carmen had been married for twenty-five years. She had given birth to seven girls and two boys, but only five girls survived. Because she had reached menopause, there was no possibility of another male child. The Yanahuayas had become wealthy with seven garden plots and a large house. There would be no male offspring to continue Marcelino's vertical claim to the land. It was also unlikely that any of his daughters would marry a man from Qollahuaya, which was largely made up of their classificatory brothers and sisters, among whom marriage was prohibited. One of his daughters, Gloria, was living in La Paz, and she would probably marry a Pazeño and settle there. Some of Marcelino's daughters would marry men from the lower community of Niñokorin to regain access to the land inherited by Carmen from Leandro Quispe and Mikyla Ari. Marcelino and Carmen's dilemma was that they had property holdings in the high and low levels and, since their daughters would go to the lowlands to regain access to their mother's inheritance, there were no sons to remain attached to the highlands. Matrilocality would solve the land distribution problem of Qollahuaya land, but would not fulfull Marcelino's wishes to have a male descendant who would follow his ancestral line as the possessor of his property. Men were needed in his family, not only to perform agricultural tasks, but also to fill the roles of major secretary and corregidor, so necessary to secure the familial position in the community.

Erminia's sickness implied that Martin was its cause since he had dug near the ancestor mummy site. In effect, Martin had offended Marcelino's ancestors by failing to produce a male offspring. According to Kaatan ideas of conception it is the man who produces the

Carmen Holding Erminia

male child by being the first to reach a climax in intercourse, or, as they say, "winning" over the woman. The dead ancestors associated with the mummy sites greatly affect the living by causing sicknesses to those who do not provide offspring to work their land. The physical ailment of the boils added with other associational meanings indicated that Martin was the cause of offending the dead ancestors, and that Carmen and Marcelino wanted him to produce a boy. Moreover, Martin often avoided the Yanahuaya household and accepted little male responsibility in regard to it. In addition, Martin was very much concerned with his own claim to land in Chaqahuaya.

A first generation male offspring would be preferred to continue the patrilineage. But if there were no son, then a daughter's son could become a member of his maternal grandfather's lineage by moving to that land. The mountain metaphor influences patrilineage. The mountain is where the dead ancestors are buried, and their permanent presence is guaranteed by the immovable landmark and by the lineage. Blood is not entirely the lineage, but only one link with the ancestors. Living on the land of the ancestors constitutes another tie with them, if the settlers worship them by taking care of their land as the forbearers had done. The continuity of the lineage and mountain is the common factor of the metaphor. Marcelino knew he could perpetuate his ancestors' lineage by ritually incorporating Martin's son, if there were one, into that lineage. Marcelino's wished-for grandson would then move to Marcelino's land and continue his patrilineage.

Marcelino's ancestor mummies helped him through the years to maintain control of their land. After Marcelino's father died, his classificatory father, Romualdo, claimed the inheritance of Marcelino, whom they hoped had migrated to Peru (see Genealogy). Marcelino returned after two years in Arequipa and discovered that his inherited land and weavings had been usurped by relatives. He fought to regain his land, and the climax came when Mariano, his classificatory brother sided with Romualdo and accused Marcelino of beating a thief to death. Marcelino was imprisoned in Puerto Acosto for a month. He hired a lawyer and was released. Marcelino fought his classificatory father and brother with deep hatred, regained his land, and built the most prosperous household in the hamlet. In retaliation, Marcelino's ancestors struck Mariano with an early death, the blindness of his wife, Dominga Ari, and the impoverishment of his household. But Marcelino still fears reprisals from the descendants of Mariano and Romualdo, who compose many of the families now living in Qollahuaya, and considers these relatives just as eager to grasp his land as their ancestors once were.

Just as threatening to Marcelino's patrilineage was his son-in-law's behavior. Martin's refusal to feed the ancestor mummies not only insulted Marcelino, but also pointed the finger at him for not producing a son. Neither Marcelino nor Martin fed the mummies, rather Seferino, the village clown, did. Seferino had no relatives nor land; years ago, he had arrived in Kaata from the highlands as an orphan, and an old man had raised him. Seferino's clothes were ragged from doing rough and odd jobs for Kaatans, who then fed him. Seferino's mysterious origin gave him the flexibility of being sometimes a clown and at other times a skilled ritualist (see Turner 1969:95). His marginality to Kaata was similar to mine; we were both laughed at and listened to. This metaphorical role combining bum-like and god-like constructs which Seferino illustrates is also characteristic of other Andean villages.

Seferino put wads of black llama wool and fat inside the rock cubicle of the ancestor mummy. This rite did not cure Erminia's boils but Carmen claimed that the ancestors were pleased with the food when Celia informed everyone that she was pregnant. Both families were united once again, and Martin visited the Yanahuaya house regularly, especially to bake bread in Marcelino's oven. Marcelino helped Martin make the small breads, and they thoroughly enjoyed each other's company as they patted the small wafers and threw them into the igloo-shaped adobe oven.

Celia's pregnancy, therefore, symbolized that the ancestors had received the black llama wads as well as the possibility that there was a male offspring in her womb. Carmen and Marcelino were happy that Martin and Celia were doing everything possible to produce a son, and both families came together on the mountain.

In essence, then, ritual comes into play where conflicts have arisen between kinship groups as a result of structural contradictions (Turner 1957:330). The contradiction of the ritual was not between the principles of Kaatan social structure, but rather between a man who had no son to give his land, and a virilocal society with patrilineal claim to land and authority.

SYMBOLIC ORDERING OF THE LINEAGE RITUAL

Marcelino asked Sarito to perform a lineage ritual so that a grandson would be born, one who would carry on his claim to land. Sarito would do this by symbolically incorporating Martin into Marcelino's patrilineage and by feeding all the parts of the mountain. What is good for Mount Kaata is good for Marcelino's ayllu, and the feeding of one rebounds in the fortune of the other. That is to say, Sarito, by symbolically creating the mountain is also completing Marcelino's lineage.

Ritual is a symbolic medium, expressing the assumptions of a society, but these assumptions can be manipulated by the ritualist for the benefit of the actors. Concerning ritual in general, Mary Douglas (1966:153) writes:

> The analysis of ritual symbolism cannot begin until we recognize ritual as an attempt to create and maintain a particular culture, a particular set of assumptions by which experience is controlled. The rituals enact the form of social relations and in giving these relations visible expression they enable people to know their own society. The rituals work upon the body politic through the symbolic medium of the physical body.

The lineage ritual symbolically orders experiences in reference not only to conceptual principles of Kaatan society but also to a geographical and ecological ordering of the environment. The natural environment, rather than abstract ideas, is the paradigm of Kaatan cultural themes. The ritual brought a completeness to Marcelino's and Martin's families by symbolically combining all levels of land, kinship groups, night and day, dead and living, in a reciprocal exchange with the actors so that together these parts could be constituted as one whole. By so ordering, the lineage ritual unites the social with the geographical and ecological order of the mountain.

GATHERING OF RITUAL ITEMS FROM THREE LEVELS

The lineage ritual feeds the ancestors and the mountain shrines with food from the three levels of the ayllu as well as from the universe itself. The three levels are brought together by gathering ritual items from high, center, and low ecological zones. Ritual items symbolize a particular level of land either by being a product peculiar to the ecological zone or by resembling some aspect of the level, for instance, oranges are symbols of the sun, and cotton is a symbol of clouds, although both are grown in the lowlands. A llama fetus aborted on the high puna, a silver cross for the sky, and a staff for vertical authority and ancestral control also refer to the highlands. The central lands are symbolized by produce from inside, such as blood from the heart, llama fat from the bowels, coins from the mines, and eggs from the hens. Items symbolic of the lowlands are carnations and chicha from Niñokorin and Quiabaya, incense and coca from the lower Yungas, and seashells from the ocean.

Marcelino and Carmen spent a month gathering all the necessary ritual items from the different communities and ecological zones of their ayllu and province. Marcelino invited Martin to accompany him to Jawueca of Apacheta, a journey of about twenty-six miles.

Plates to Feed the Places for the Lineage Rituals

They arrived, tired, at the rock hut of José Blanco, whom Marcelino introduced to Martin as his godfather and as a very skilled ritualist for herding rites. The three of them visited awhile and then agreed to exchange three sacks of potatoes, oca, and beans for a live llama, which they butchered the next morning, quartered, and packed on a burro for the return trip to Kaata. They spent the night at José's home, and early the next morning José gave Marcelino a dried llama fetus (*sullu*). Marcelino admired the sullu with its leathery legs folded into its belly. The neck was disproportionately long, characteristic of this cameloid, with a rounded head and large nose from which protruded two bulging and blackened eyes. The fetus had been aborted during the months of August and September and had dried in the sun for several weeks before José found it. Since the fetus was the central symbol of the lineage ritual, it would be buried in the earth for its journey to the dead ancestors. "The sun purifies the sullu by drying it so that the worms will not eat it," Marcelino explained.

Carmen traveled six miles across ayllu Kaata to Upinhuaya, where she traded potatoes for incense from her sister's godmother.

Upinhuayans smell of incense, and the other communities call them the "incense carriers." Incense is a specialization of these one hundred fifty Aymaras, who walk for four days along the treacherous Ayllu River to the Yungas, where they harvest it. Their incense is the resin of a tree slashed the year before so that it cries and its tears harden for another harvester, who then slashes another tree to reciprocate (*ainirikusun*) the work done by the other man. Carrying two hundred pounds of incense on their backs, the Upinhuayans climb back to their village in five days. Upinhuaya is also famous for its women ritualists, who bewitch by hiding dog and cat hair underneath the roof. Any woman traveling to Upinhuaya is suspected of contracting a sorceress. For this reason Carmen traveled at night and without Celia, whose pregnancy made her vulnerable to an enemy's curse.

Carmen continued along the valley of Cañisaya of ayllu Kaalaya where she traded dried foods for a kilo of coca. Cañisaya is nestled in the foothills of snowcrested Aqhamani. Its sixty adults trade salt, charqui, and pots for coca with the Yungas village of Apolo. These people travel three times a year to Apolo, a journey of seven days by mule. Each mule carries thirty-two pots, for which these traders receive a twenty-two pound sack of coca; one pound of coca is exchangeable for five pots in Amarete. Relatives of the families of Cañisaya constitute many of the coca farmers of Apolo. Relatives in the Yungas and Qollahuaya area enable both settlements to have vertical control over two distinct ecological zones which provide not only produce but also distinct markets of exchange, as Murra's (1972:431) concept of verticality suggests.

The day before the lineage ritual, Carmen descended to Niño-korin to gather carnations. She asked her brother's son, Pedro Quispe, to represent her lineage. Pedro agreed to be the female assistant to Sarito Quispe, thereby representing a male leader from Carmen's place and people, and also assuming a female role with claims to food but not to land in relation to Marcelino.

Other ritual items were furnished by traveling neighbors. People from ayllu Amarete supplied the incense and firepots used only for ritual. A trader from distant Moro Karka exchanged for potatoes small figurines of stars, suns, moons, horses, llamas, fields, and houses, which only these people knew how to make from the soap-stone found in their area. The ritual items symbolically represent the levels of land experienced by Kaatans.

In the Andes, altitude is the great ecological variable, and as the mountain rises, the ecological bands decrease in width (Troll 1968). The Andean people live vertically on levels from 6,000 to 17,000 feet, each community adapting to the climate and soil of its micro-environment and skillfully utilizing its own resources. Because of the restricted growth on each level, resources must be exchanged by the communities to assure a balanced and adequate diet. Kaatan farmers and Apachetan herders, for example, provide each other with a mixed diet of carbohydrates and proteins (see Thomas 1972). Similarly, each community minimizes the risk of starvation because of loss from its crops by maintaining ritual links with a variety of levels, each of which has different risk and yield factors.

The variable growing seasons of each level of Kaata community and that level's resource suitability requires agricultural and pastoral specialization. The elders educate their children in the complicated folklore of the earth and its growing seasons; they show them which potato seed is suited for which particular place and how to read the signs of the weather. The gathering of the ritual items respects this specialization by having the participants travel to the area where the resource is found, but it also emphasizes the necessary resource exchange between parts of the mountain.

The gathering of these ritual items from the three levels symbolically referred to the patrilineage of Marcelino and the lineage of Carmen. Corresponding to the vertical ayllu, Marcelino and Martin climbed to the high puna area where the sun dies and the dead ancestors travel. The dead influence the living by causing sickness and death to those who do not continue their claim to the land. Following the symbolism of the horizontal ayllu, Carmen traveled across to Upinhuaya and Cañisaya for coca and incense, and then to her lower community, where she picked carnations and invited her brother's son to represent her ayllu at the lineage ritual.

Essentially, then, the gathering of ritual items was a classification and ordering of these items into a high, center, and low, according to the metaphor of the mountain. It was not as Douglas (1966:12) says, "positively reordering the environment, making it conform to an idea," but the converse—the idea came from the mountain. This idea of high, center, and low has sound ecological and geographical foundations, as well as an association with distinct communities and the man's and woman's lineage groups. The ritual orders the levels of high, center, and low, and symbolically puts them together, and this integrity influences the compatability of the man's patrilineage and the woman's lineage.

BEFORE AND AFTER MIDNIGHT

There is greater temperature variation between night and day than between winter and summer in the Andes, where within several hours the temperature drops sixty degrees Fahrenheit (Troll 1968:17). Such a day-night rhythm influences the biological, social, and cultural life of Andeans, as the winter and summer cycle influences Nordics. The lineage ritual symbolizes night and day by first feeding the dead ancestors with symbols of decay near the western sleeping house before midnight, and by then feeding the household, seasonal, and mountain shrines near the eastern supply house after midnight.

And so Sarito arrived at about 11:00 on a Wednesday evening. Marcelino quickly led him to the sleeping house, where Sarito began feeding the mummy sites. Kaatan houses form three sides of a rectangle with the open end towards the north, facing Mount Aqhamani. The sleeping house is to the west, symbolically relating sleep to death, night, and the higher level of the ayllu.

Sarito faced the place where the sun dies, and his two assistants spread three large wads of black llama wool. The assistants, Manuel Valencia and Pedro Quispe, represented female roles and the woman's lineage.[4] Kaata was also represented by coca, which Carmen had collected from the Great Shrine in Kaatapata, from Mojata apacheta, and from the shrines of the Secretary General, who is always represented at household rituals. Ritual emphasized that the integrity of each household's male and female ayllus is related to the solidarity of the community of Kaata and the communities of the mountain ayllu.

Sarito distributed twelve leaves into the llama wool, covered them with clumps of pig fat, and wrapped them all together by pulling the yarn tightly into a ball. Pedro carried the balls to the mummy sites, where Manuel had built a large fire in a broken pot. The fire blazed high from the dry straw as Manuel fed the balls into it saying, "Ancestors, this is a meal of coca and cheese for you to eat. Do not be angry when we feed the other places. Let them eat also. Do not hear men and dogs, for this is a meal for the ancestors."

The ancestor mummies had been fed black llama wool and pig fat. Black is a symbol of decay, death, and night; and pig fat comes from an animal who feeds on fecal matter, also deathly. These symbols of death are associated with the west side of the house where Kaatans urinate and defecate, where the ancestor mummy sites are located, where the dead person travels after burial, and where the sun dies. Moreover, the western higher level is associated with the patrilineage and the ancestors, who represent authority and claim to the land. For this ritual the ancestors were Marcelino's father and godfather. Neither Martin nor Marcelino fed the dead ancestors, perhaps for the reason that the ancestors were angry with both of them for neglecting to produce a male offspring to perpetuate their claim to the land.

After midnight, Marcelino led Sarito to the supply house to feed the household and ayllu shrines. The supply house, on the east side of the patio, is the storage room for bins of dried corn, potatoes, oca, and cloth. It is associated with abundance of offspring and food, the fruits of daily activity, and the lowlands. Sarito began preparing a meal for Marcelino and Carmen's household shrines. All Kaatan households have guardians, a patron and a matron, to care for the outside and the inside of their homes. The patron of the patio (*kanchayuh*) is a rectangular hole dug into the adobe bench lining the supply house. The patron protects the garden plots and patio, and he is responsible for all activities within these areas. The matron of the kitchen (*cabildo*) is the table in the supply house. The matron watches over the cloth, supplies, and food. She represents the female head of the household and the wife's lineage, and the patron symbolizes the husband and his patrilineage. Carmen, for example, usually feeds the matron. Before each meal, she places three coca leaves beneath the tablecloth, and all guests must likewise serve the matron before eating from Carmen's table. In similar fashion, Marcelino feeds the patron by giving him coca each time he goes to the fields.

The weather and mountain were invited to eat with Marcelino and Carmen. Sarito placed llama fat on four piles, carefully wrapping them, and instructed Pedro, "Each pile is for a different lord." He pointed to the piles and named them, "Lords of the season, lords of the mountain, patrons of the kitchen and patio." The lords of the season are owners of the agricultural year; the crop belongs to them. Watayuh, their name, means "the one who owns the year." Every year Sarito divines the mountains that will best foster the crops. Aqhamani, Sunchuli, and Sillaqa, the highest peaks of the area, were chosen for 1972. The permanent ayllu shrines (see page 59) are the lords of the mountain, referred to as condors (*mallkus*). Sarito told Pedro to feed these four and only these four because they constituted one whole, *tawantin*. Pedro burned the offerings in the hole alongside the supply house. Then all exchanged coca, alcohol, and ate soup: Marcelino with his plots of land, descendants, and ancestors; Carmen with her food, cloth, and children. Martin, associated with Marcelino, and Celia, associated with Carmen, all ate together with the lords of the season and the ayllu.

The symbolic incorporation of Martin into Marcelino's patrilineage was enacted by their respective positionings for the rest of the ritual. Celia and Martin stood in the center. Sarito placed a large silver cross around Martin's neck. Marcelino was given the staff and stood on Martin's right side. I stood to Marcelino's right. Carmen stood on Celia's left side, next to my wife Judy, then the oldest to youngest daughters. That is, the positioning was similar to that of a wedding ceremony. Marcelino said that he and Carmen were the vertical sponsors, who in the marriage ritual represent the groom's patrilineage, and that Judy and I were the level sponsors, who represent the bride's lineage.

Positioning is symbolic and its meaning can be understood by referring the positioning of the lineage ritual to that of the wedding, where the positioning and gestures were concerned with incorporating a woman into the man's patrilineage. The lineage ritual was concerned with Martin's involvement in Marcelino's household and land. Although Marcelino's desire for a male descendant was the major concern of the ritual, the social relationships between both families were also important. The ritual was both redressive of social conflicts and also a symbolic manipulation of cultural themes for the benefits of some actors. If Martin had held the staff and stood on the outside of Marcelino or if he had refused to participate, then this would have communicated an entirely different message to everyone.

THE SERVING OF THE LORDS

The major feeding of the ritual began when Sarito gave Marcelino the staff to hold and Martin the cross to wear. Pedro arrived with the incense pot and, placing it underneath our hands and in front of our mouths, he exhaled and said, "Huh!" The ritual items wrapped in the multicolored ritual cloth were touched to the head of each person. We prayed with all our hearts that the lords of the season and the ayllu would receive the gifts. Sarito took Marcelino's staff and gave him a large candle in return. The staff was set alongside of the llama fetus at the eastern end of the cloth. Sarito said that the staff was the godfather of the fetus, meaning that the ones who claimed the land were sponsoring a llama for the mountain. Eggs and bread were placed on the four corners, and a coin was put in the center. Sarito carefully wiped his seashells, which Carmen thrilled at seeing. He set these seashells on the ritual cloth, beginning with the bottom row, moving from west to east and upward. He began following symbolically the path of the sun as it dies in the west, is buried in the earth, and travels beneath the mountain to the east

POSITIONING OF ACTORS AT LINEAGE RITUAL

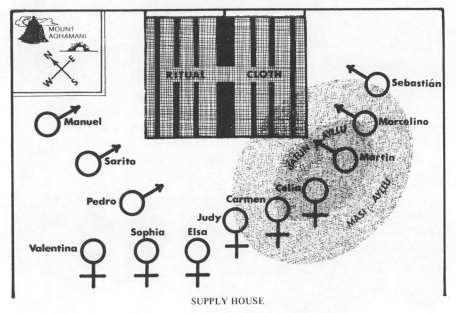

SUPPLY HOUSE

where it is born again. Designating the first seashell to two western masculine lords of the mountain, Wayna Qowila and Machu Qowila, Sarito said that the young Qowila would serve the old Qowila. He emphasized a principle of Kaatan society that the young served their elders—or perhaps that a grandson would serve Marcelino. Sarito set a plate to the central lord of the ayllu Phesqa Pata and to the lords of the lower ayllus Kalla Kalla and Qota Qota. The female guardians, Ik'ituana, Paya Tuana, and Machu Tuana were beseeched. According to the legend, it was on the shores of Lake Tuana that the first crops arose after the deluge. This flood destroyed the world, except for Kaatans who climbed to their rooftop site at Kaatapata. When Carmen was born, Mikyla dedicated her to Tuana, whom she would beseech for fertility.

At the upper edge of the ritual cloth, corresponding to the summit of the mountain, Sarito served plates to the staff and the llama fetus. The staff is a symbol of lightning as well as of authority and patrilineal claim to land. The ritual items were wrapped in the cotton, and tied around the staff and fetus's back. Sarito said that the staff and fetus would carry these plates to the dead ancestors. Light-

Praying to Mount Kaata

ning and ancestor sickness protect the ancestor's patrilineage.

As Sarito turned from north to west, south, and east, Aqhamani, Sunchuli, and Sillaqa, the three lords of the season, were each given a plate. These lords are associated with the three crops of potatoes, oca, and barley, grown each year in the central area; with the three ecological levels of land; and with their corresponding communities.

Sarito began filling the seashells with food around 2 a.m. Twelve select leaves of coca were placed on the cotton within each shell. Since coca is a universal symbol for Andeans, it is used for every class of ritual. Kaatans greet each other with an exchange of coca. Coca is also a form of payment for work, and cloths containing coca are always given to confirm a contract. Sarito sorted pink and white carnation petals and dropped them onto the coca as if they were the budding flowers of the green coca plant. Besides being symbols of the lower communities, pink and white carnations are the colors of the early morning sky. Flowers are signs of friendship and love for Kaatans, who place lilies in the hats of those they love. Whenever we visited their homes, we were asked to wait while they went to their garden plots to pick us a bouquet of flowers. On top of the carnation petals, Sarito placed chunks of llama fat telling the lord it was cheese.

Incense, dried ferns, lead figurines, pea-sized white and pink candies, confetti, and sugar were added to each seashell. Sarito scraped the coins and the eggshell over the plates, and whispered to the lords to serve themselves and to buy something with the money. The preparation of seashells took two hours, and Sarito worked methodically, occasionally joking with someone about the large noses on the figurines. Martin was very quiet, somehow aware that he was the subject of the ritual. Sarito poured wine and *pisco* (distilled grape liquor) on each plate and then announced that the meal was served and the lords were ready to eat. Marcelino was pleased, for the lords of the season and mountain had to be fed before the new sun was born, at the cock's crow.

Several orderings were discernible in the serving of the foods. The solid ritual foods were put on the seashells by beginning with the lower left corner and crossing to the upper right. Sarito repeated this upward movement until he reached the llama fetus. Wine, pisco, and alcohol, symbols of fertility, stood on the lower part of the cloth. Sarito sprinkled each plate with these liquids in the reverse direction and ended at his place near the lower left corner. Solids moved upward, and liquids moved down, just as on the mountain where solid food moves up and water runs down. The sun travels upward from east to west over the mountain during the day and descends from there under the mountain during the night. Solids and liquids are related to the cyclical factors of day and night, earth and sky, sun and rain, as well as the husband's patrilineage and wife's lineage.

Sarito followed an order of serving the foods, beginning with lower foods such as the seashells, coca, incense, and carnations, going to the center foods of eggs, money, llama fat, candies, and finishing with the figurines, associated with the higher level. The distinct foods were served from low, to center, to high; at the same time the plates were being served from high, center, to low, expressing a simultaneous back and forth movement.

The ritual gestures symbolized the movements from low, to center, to high, as one swing, and the reverse movement as the other swing. The gestures also symbolized the movements toward night and day. This ritual system of classification created the reciprocal cycle as sacred and as the order of the universe and environment. The kinship groups of Marcelino and Martin participated in these movements, which were sacred and eternally repetitive to them.

Ritual was a way for Marcelino to invite all the lords to eat at his household shrines. Marcelino hoped that by inviting Martin to feed his shrines there wold be an ordering of social relations. If the lords and ancestors, which are associated with parts of the mountain, were fed at the proper time, then this communion of people and places would ensure the organic integrity of the corporeal body (health to Erminia) and the solidarity of the social body (Marcelino's patrilineage).

About 4 a.m. we carried candles in procession across the patio, traveling in a semicircle from east to west and back again, where we faced the birth of the sun and Aqhamani. The rain began pelting us, and Judy's teeth were chattering from the cold. The temperature for this night near the end of the rainy season was somewhere in the forties.

Sarito moved rapidly; he was sick with bronchitis and anxious to get inside. He placed two filled seashells in Martin's left hand and underneath the same arm he nestled the loaded fetus and the pisco bottle. He gave Marcelino the staff, placing it under his left arm, and put two seashells in his left hand. Celia and Carmen were each given two seashells, and all the others one. Sarito told us to kneel and pray to the lords. The women sat on the ground. Sarito next took the fetus, two shells, and the bottle of pisco from Martin. He held these over Martin's head and prayed that the lords of the season and the ayllu receive these foods with Martin's best intention. He held them before Martin's mouth, who breathed heavily upon them, saying, "Huh." They explained, "Our heart, our work we are giving with huh." Sarito moved these items over the incense pot, which Pedro held. Sarito went toward the east and north and knelt, holding the fetus, pisco, and filled seashells toward the place where the sun was to be born. He implored that Chaqamita—the lord of the newborn sun; Aqhamani, Sunchuli, Sillaqa—the lords of the season; Zaqtalaya, Qowila, Pachaqota—the lords of the highlands; Qota Qota, Kalla Kalla—the lords of the lower region; and Phesqa Pata, Jatun Junch'a—the lords of the central area, serve themselves from these plates. He first faced the east, then the north, the west, again the east, and finally the center. Sarito beseeched the lords for good luck, food, crops, the birth of a grandson, and safe journeys. After we had processed counterclockwise around the courtyard five times in a spiral which decreased in size, we recessed to the supply house with the burning candles.

THE RITUAL EATING BY THE LORDS

Only the ritualists could watch the lords eat, so we were ushered into the cloth room of the supply house. Marcelino explained to us what was happening. Pedro carried each seashell to Sarito who was outside standing near the fire pot and the adobe hole for the patron of the patio.[5] Sarito emptied the contents of the seashells into the flames of the firepot. He beseeched, "Please receive this food, servant, and carry it to the lords of the season." Sarito turned toward the lords of the ayllu, moving in a spiral direction similar to when he offered the plates. The llama fetus was loaded with the cotton wads, which contained ritual items; and after the contents of the seashells had been burned in the fire pot, the fetus was buried in the earth shrines of the patron of the patio.

The last part of the ritual was the divination of guinea pigs to determine the sincerity of the participants and the acceptance of the food by the lords. During the earlier liturgy on the patio, Sarito had held guinea pigs next to the forehead and heart of Martin, Marcelino, Celia, and Carmen. After the lords were fed, Sarito took Martin's guinea pig and ripped open its skin with his thumb, laying bare its intestines. He emptied its blood into a seashell and read its heart. Sarito told Martin that its beating heart meant strong life in his lineage, but because a corner of the pancreas was folded over, he said that Martin had pain in his heart. The pig's liver was fine, and so Martin and Celia would prosper. Marcelino's guinea pig was not as revealing as Martin's. The pig's heart had stopped beating, which was an indication of weakness in the blood, symbolically associated with Marcelino's patrilineage. As Sarito read Celia's guinea pig, everyone crowded close to see and hear, but there were no straight lines on the liver to indicate a male child.

Sarito fed the guinea pig's viscera into the firepot as a dessert for the lords. The first cock crowed. Everyone was pleased that all the ritual activity had been completed before the birth of the sun. Carmen and Celia served plates of hot soup, followed by cooked corn and potatoes. Marcelino gave Sarito a sack of dried foods and thanked him.

The lineage ritual showed how Marcelino symbolically centered Martin within his patrilineage, thereby effecting a completion for Marcelino's lineage based on the expectation of a male grandson. Martin's son would continue the interests of Marcelino's ancestors in regard to land. At the time of the lineage ritual, Marcelino had only daughters and granddaughters, who would move away from their parents' land according to virilocal settlement patterns. This incompletion of Marcelino's patrilineage was associated with Erminia's ancestor sickness and caused by Martin's negligence in producing a male offspring which disturbed the ancestor mummy sites. Erminia's ancestor sickness was temporarily cured when they fed the ancestor mummies and Celia became pregnant.

NOTES

1. Turner (1957:330) regards ritual as a mechanism of redress, postulating "that ritual mechanisms tend to come into play in situations of crisis where conflicts have arisen in and between villages as the result of structural contradictions."

2. Rappaport (1967:17-30) studies how rituals affect New Guinea people's relationship with their land.

3. The divination initiated by Carmen altered the power in Kaata by rallying the mystical forces of the dead ancestors against Martin. (See Gluckman 1965:239, 264).

4. Manuel is married to Sarito's daughter and is settled with her in Sarito's vertical ayllu; thus he represents the horizontal ayllu.

5. The firepot is thirty inches in circumference and made from clay. Manufactured in Amarete, it is a ritual item employed only for feeding the different lords.

*

9

The River
and the Misfortune Ritual

After the lineage ritual, everyone smiled again, even Erminia. Her boils had disappeared. She toddled to our kitchen and ate raisins with us. She even shared them with our puppy, Boo, who caught the raisins as she threw them to him. Celia was in her ninth month of pregnancy, and Marcelino confidently expected a grandson. He had even decided to call him Manuel. The healing of the boils was a sure sign to Marcelino that his ancestors were working to prolong their patrilineage.

The birth was a secret, entirely the affair of Carmen and Celia. In the middle of July, Marcelino was surprised when Carmen walked through the gate and handed him a newborn infant wrapped in swaddling clothes. Carmen retreated to the kitchen as Marcelino unraveled the baby.

"A granddaughter," he said.

Judy and I were delighted to see the little creature, so red and wrinkled after birth. Marcelino cried. Still, he asked Judy and me to be godparents, and he smiled when we accepted.

During the following months, Marcelino often traveled to Curva, the village across the valley. He left in the evening and returned early in the morning several days later to do the necessary farm work during the day. Then he set out again on another nighttime journey to Curva. He said he had bought several cows, which were grazing in the pastures beyond Curva. He began drinking much more, and during the fiesta of Mama Santa Rosa he staggered out in front of a thousand spectators at the Kaatan bullfight, slipped, and fell into a mud puddle, soaking his snail-motif poncho and medicine bag. Those who loved him saw no humor in his predicament, but everyone else laughed. A man whom Marcelino had raised as an orphan helped him from the ring, and Carmen guided him home.

Erminia became sick again in October. This time she was afflicted with chronic diarrhea and vomiting. Her parents asked me to cure her; I gave her enterbioform and later lincocin, but she could not retain the pills because of the vomiting. She finally stopped vomiting and began to sleep. Celia carried the child to lower Chaqahuaya, where she and Martin lived.

I did not see Erminia and Celia for three days, and I complained to Marcelino that, if they wanted me to cure Erminia, she must continue to take the medicine. Marcelino doubted the power of the drugs and said that he intended to take Erminia to Bonifacio Quispe, a diviner.

Bonifacio read the coca and discovered that Martin Mejia's house had been affected by lightning, which had struck nearby while they were away. The coca also explained Erminia's sickness by revealing that she had lost a bar of soap in the Lajoni River, which passed close to their home. Celia had shouted at Erminia for this, and the river had grabbed Erminia's spirit (animo). The diviner said the river must be fed in order to return Erminia's spirit.

Bonifacio arrived at Martin's house Tuesday night to offer a ransom mass (misa de fianza) for Erminia's spirit. Martin gave Bonifacio a coca cloth with coca, llama fat, and carnations, with which he prepared a meal for the patron of Martin's patio and matron of Celia's kitchen, and for the river and the lightning. He divined a guinea pig which had been placed on Erminia's breast.

Bonifacio went to the Lajoni River, burned the offerings near the river and threw the ashes into it saying, "Come Erminia; don't remain behind." He then coaxed Erminia's spirit with a piece of candy in her stocking cap, saying, "Erminia! Come and get some candy!" He gathered Erminia's spirit and placed a rock inside her hat, which he held close to his heart. Running to Erminia's house, he fed her the candy, set the rock next to her heart, and placed the hat on her head. He assured Martin and Celia that Erminia would soon be cured. She began to recover the very next day.

A week before the ritual, Celia had quarreled with her mother-in-law over the shares of a llama both families had purchased. The old lady had screamed at Celia, calling her a thief. In desperation, Celia had slapped her mother-in-law. Celia's behavior was interrelated with her daughter's sickness; this relationship was symbolically communicated as shouting at Erminia near the river. The lightning, which had struck Martin's house, was the anger of Marcelino's ancestor at Martin, who had failed to produce a son for Marcelino's patrilineage. The stocking cap which covered the top of Erminia's head, was associated with the original time and place, and the rock, which had been washed down the river, referred to the erosion of land. The rock inside the cap linked the original time and place with the particular time and place, that is, the restitutive quality of the mountain cured Erminia's sickness. The river had taken Erminia's spirit. Bonifacio returned to the river, fed it, recovered the spirit, and cured Erminia. The river washed away the spirit and returned it. Misfortunes temporarily dissolved the corporeal and lineage bodies, but within the larger context of the mountain the disintegration of these lesser bodies was restored by the integrity and solidarity of the mountain body.

A month after Erminia held the rock near her heart, she contracted typhoid fever and died. Celia and Carmen dressed her in a snail-motif mantle with a red skirt. Martin put three coca leaves between her lips and placed a candle in her tiny hand and with Marcelino lowered Erminia into the earth. Everyone bid her a fast journey to the highlands and threw a handful of dirt over her body.

But Erminia's death did not heal hostilities between Marcelino's and Martin's lineages. Celia again struck her mother-in-law hard enough to blacken her eye. On behalf of the mother-in-law, I reprimanded Celia, who then avoided me for three weeks. Almost daily, Marcelino drank and fought with his neighbors. One afternoon after patching up his head wounds and his victim's wounds, I was asked by Marcelino to send another injured drunk to La Paz for medical attention. I told him angrily that he should stop his drinking and fighting for his own good and that of his family.

The final misfortune struck Martin after the Feast with the

Dead. A woman smashed his collarbone with a rock and broke it. Martin had fought with her husband in a drunken brawl and was swinging at him with a wooden flute when she hit Martin. A crippled collarbone would permanently prevent Martin from plowing, if it were not cured.

Marcelino and Carmen had other explanations for the injury; they complained that Martin had not set up a table for Erminia during the Feast with the Dead and that he had avoided her gravesite. During this feast, Celia had sat alone in front of Erminia's grave and had given bread, bananas, and oranges to those who prayed for her daughter. Carmen was certain the ancestor mummies were punishing Martin for his blatant disrespect toward the dead, and implied that they were angry that he had not produced a male descendant to continue Marcelino's patrilineage.

The incident of the broken collarbone was the climax of the feuding between the Mejias and Yanahuayas, who realized that another male would be lost if they did not help each other. In reconciliation, Marcelino called Juan Wilka to cure Martin, and Juan applied a compress of dried frog skins to the front and back of the broken bone. Several elders also visited Martin, and they recalled that Daniel Barrera had died the year before after his broken bone had protruded and become infected from the herb medicine. They talked about another person who had a broken collarbone and was never able to use the hand plow. After the herbs had failed, Marcelino asked me to cure Martin. Martin, who was bedridden with pain, cried as he showed me his doubled collarbone which was setting in its broken position. Celia begged me to do something, so I sent Marcelino and Martin into La Paz to have the bone set. The curers admitted that this was the only way to cure it, after their compresses had failed. Marcelino and Martin returned happy, not so much that Martin would be cured, but because they had the legal papers to sue the lady who hit Martin. A common enemy had united both families. I was pleased to have helped cure Martin, but was disappointed when one morning he crossed the patio carrying a hundred-pound sack and no cast. He had chipped it off because it had bothered him. Carmen and Marcelino were disgusted with Martin for removing the cast and called him an ass.

The typhoid fever which caused Erminia's death also infected my wife and me, and Marcelino's sister, who died in October.

Everyone decided that we should have a misfortune ritual. We felt a need to go to the river to wash away the misfortunes and to have the river restore whatever was lacking.

THE TWO SENSES OF THE RIVER

According to the mountain metaphor, Kaatans believe that personal calamities are connected to rivers washing away the mountain's body. The Kunochayuh River originating at the summit, crossing the levels, and descending to the lowlands, causes erosion as it descends rapidly from Apacheta, cutting into the land, causing landslides, and washing people to their deaths in the lowlands. In a metaphorical sense, sickness deteriorates the organic body as other misfortunes dissolve the agricultural and social body.

The river, however, has a restitutive nature in that it can restore what has been removed. Even though the river descends through the levels, it forms one continual link with the uma pacha. Moreover, the river is continuously restored, originating at and returning to the uma pacha. According to legend, the organ removed by sickness or the land taken by theft is not irretrievably lost. It is returned by the river.

Rivers form the boundaries of the ayllu, and if in ritual they refer to its dissolution, they can, at the same time, symbolize its completion. The deep gorges of the Chari and Kunochayuh rivers divide Kaata from ayllus Chari and Upinhuaya. The wide and turbulent lower Huruku and Ayllu rivers form the boundaries of ayllu Kaata with Chullina and Charazani. Kaatans say they are one ayllu because their mountain is bordered by rivers, which form many of the anatomical parts of the mountain body.

Rivers also traverse the heavens and the netherworld. The Milky Way is called *mayu* (river) because it connects the stars across the sky. Concomitantly, underneath the mountain are rivers along which the dead travel on their return to the highland's lake.

Legends say that high places are safe from destruction, such as the following account by Juan Wilka, a Kaatan curer:

When the chunchos took the headband from Matías Akarapi's wife's head, he became very angry, throwing his medicine bag into the valley and forming Green Lake.[1] He thought his sons would retrieve it, but they did not; so he threw all of their medicine bags into this lake. For this reason, those of Kaata do not have medicine bags. The only one who retrieved his medicine bag was a Curveño.[2]

Matías Akarapi spoke with the mountains as God. He was like a condor. When there were three kings, Melchior, Balthazar, and Caspar, Matías said, "I know." They asked him, "How do you know?" "I know from my coca," he said, "that Jesus is going to be born. He will be God."

In times past (*ñawpah pacha*), there was a judgment before Jesus Christ. A judgment came with water, 200,000 years before, and it rained for six months. Everything was buried, and when the water disappeared, the secretaries (*alcaldes*) said, "There will be another judgment with water. Build all the new cities on the high places." For this reason, Kaata is on a high rock, which is very fine, but Upinhuaya is in the corner, which is not fine. Our God is blessed, and any herb from Kaata is very powerful.

The second judgment was when our God had made the sun, *awqui sonk'a* (Grandfather Beard).[3]

In other words, cities built on high places are safe from floods, which are judgmental and destructive for those who remain on the leveled areas below the uma pacha. The flood washes away all the levels, communities, and peoples below the mountain top. Judgment carried out by the flood is returning to the uma pacha, a place and time of origination and completion. The river is associated with the flood in that it crosses the ecological levels and washes away the land, and is associated with the mountain top from which it continually flows, and to which it returns.

Because the river both removes and renews, it is the dominant symbol of the misfortune ritual. The misfortune ritual is a montage of the river's two senses: (1) the consecutive, passing-by-places sense of the river washes away misfortune and (2) the cyclical, returning-to-highlands sense restores the loss. The river returns what has been lacking, again completing the body.

The river's senses make it a metaphorical landmark for Kaatan history associated with irrigation ditches, mummies, and boundary

CYCLICAL AND CONSECUTIVE SENSES OF THE RIVER

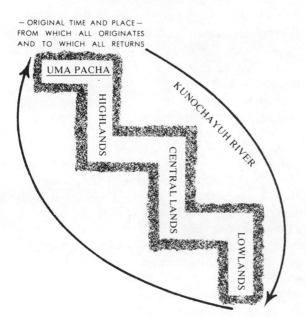

— ORIGINAL TIME AND PLACE —
FROM WHICH ALL ORIGINATES
AND TO WHICH ALL RETURNS

UMA PACHA

HIGHLANDS

KUNOCHAYUH RIVER

CENTRAL LANDS

LOWLANDS

Cyclical sense of time and place, from which all is originating and to which all is returning. Timely sense of completion and circulation: cyclical experience based on agricultural, seasonal, and diurnal cycles.

Consecutive sense of linear, past, and present events. Transitory experiences of sickness, loss of land, property, and relatives.

battles. The Kunochayuh River was the site of an irrigation system most probably constructed during the time of the Inca. This four-mile canal from the Kunochayuh River to the center of Kaata carried water along a pathway of geometrical patterns, two feet deep and three feet across. The builders created this engineering feat by using their technical ability to overcome two difficulties by channeling the river along the S contour of a very steep valley and shooting the water across two thirty-foot crevices into continuing canals. For the misfortune ritual, the participants make a circular return journey to Kaata from the river along the upper path of the irrigation canal, which their forbearers made so that the river would run horizontally to the center.

The river serves as a metaphorical reference for another layer of history marked by the arrival of the Spaniards and removal of the mummies. The lineage ritual pointed out that the ancestor mummies were associated with abandoned gravesites west of Kaata but they came to be associated with the river; at misfortune rituals plates are fed into the river for the ancestor mummies. Veneration of the ancestor mummies was transferred from their gravesites to the river as a result of early missionaries' efforts to eradicate ancestor worship by burning the mummies and throwing their ashes into the river. One historical source for this is the instructions given to the extirpator of idolatry during the early seventeenth century:

> Great care must be exercised in this to keep them from hiding anything, for they will do so if they can. Public punishment should be given to anyone who hides anything. . . .
>
> After the individuals have given up their objects, the sorcerers are to hand over the *huacas* (shrines) and *malquis* (mummies) that they are in charge of and which they have brought from their hiding places . . . [and] are to be piled up outside the town together with the mummies of malquis removed from the church and burned in a large bonfire in a remote place. I know a town, and not a very large one, where on such an occasion more than three hundred objects were burned at one time.
>
> . . . Therefore, the visitor and the fathers present sign these lists, as it is more important than is generally understood for the Indians to perceive and be persuaded that there is no intention during a visit of taking away from them anything that is rightfully theirs, but only objects which are without profit to anyone, hurtful to all, and an offense to the Lord our God because they are used in the service and ministry of the huacas.
>
> . . . Everything which would not burn in the fire must be thrown away where it can never be found. If possible, the Indians should be prevented from seeing this done and from knowing where the material has been thrown. As the Lord Archbishop has ordered, everything that has been placed under the crosses near the church should, when a good occasion offers, be taken out, dissipated, scattered, and thrown into the river, where there will remain neither memory nor trace of it. For a few months ago sacrifices of guinea pigs and other things habitually offered to the huacas were found around the cross beneath which the residue from the burned huacas had been buried. . . . but if the joy of the Indians is great, greater still is the joy of the persons who have taught and confessed them, seeing how different the town is from the way they found it — on its way to eternal life *ut cognoscant te Deum verum, et quem misisti Iesum Christum.* (Arriaga 1621: 130-134)

Arriaga implies that by throwing the mummy ashes into the river, they will be forgotten and all traces of them washed away. He was obviously unaware of the river as a means of returning relics to an original time and place. With an irony perhaps too subtle for the ordered Spaniard, the extirpators returned the ancestor mummies to the original time and place, where they could never be destroyed by the catastrophes of events and places. Another factor was the missionaries' inability to communicate their concepts of eternal life to the Indians. As a result, the Indians were inclined to view the Spanish beliefs according to their own ideas of origin and return.

The Kunochayuh River remains to this day a ritual site for feeding the ancestors and earth shrines. And Marcelino and Carmen still feed their dead ancestors by placing the ritual food near the gravesites west of their house and in the Kunochayuh River. During the misfortune ritual Kaatans usually set a plate to the ancestor mummies and the earth shrines which is thrown into the Kunochayuh River. According to its removing and renewing nature, the river washes away the causants of the misfortune according to linear time (the Spaniards) and returns what is incomplete (their ancestors) to the ayllu body by cyclical time.

The Kunochayuh River also represents a more recent historical event, the invasion of Kaata by Upinhuaya in 1904. This invasion site remains a landmark of Kaatan resistance and resilience regarding their mountain.

In other words, the Kunochayuh River passes through levels of land originating at and returning to the original time and place. The river is associated with the legendary time of the flood, the irrigation sites of the Incas, the ashes of the mummies, and the boundaries of the body which had been invaded.

WOMAN RITUALIST FROM THE CORNER

Kaatans usually choose women from Upinhuaya to perform misfortune rituals. Upinhuaya's position in relation to Kaata is one underlying basis for this preference. The oral tradition of the flood speaks about Upinhuaya being away in the corner. The ritualists from the corner are more apt to manipulate and expel the dissipative experiences than those from the center, who circulate the blood and fat. The Upinhuayan ritualists manipulate the thorns, rat, and river so that calamities cease to circulate. Upinhuayans' proximity to the Kunochayuh River is another reason they are able to manipulate this fluid symbol.

A woman always performs misfortune rituals due to her structural position in a society principled upon bilineal inheritance and virilocality. The pattern of removal and renewal, seen in a woman moving away from her land when she marries and her daughter returning again to regain access to her mother's inheritance, is repeated in the ritual when a woman sends objects which dissolve the land, body, and lineage, but also restore what has been removed. She feeds the river which crosses levels but yet returns; whereas the man ritualist feeds the mountain, which is permanent and symbolizes the patrilineage.

Selecting the best diviner of Upinhuaya, Carmen invited Rosinta Garcia to perform the misfortune ritual. Her sorcery is reputed to have killed seven people. One way she sends curses is by hiding a misfortune (*chije*) inside the skulls of a cat and a dog, clenching the teeth of the dog on those of the cat as if they were fighting each other. If the misfortune is discovered, the person can either throw it in the river, or retaliate by soliciting another sorceress, who engages in a mystical war with Rosinta. If either sorceress is caught in the act, she is taken to the sheriff who fines her a month's salary and makes her promise on the cross never to bewitch again. The sheriff of Charazani, however, fears Rosinta, so she is never arrested.

It was dark when Rosinta arrived through the back gate of Marcelino's house. Her wrinkled and leathery face reflected the powers of a wizardly ritualist. She quickly unpacked her ritual paraphernalia inside the supply house, and Carmen was thrilled to see the dead rat which she said was strangled by Rosinta. Nervously, Marcelino prodded Rosinta to move more quickly, but from the start she set her own pace. Methodically and confidently, she began removing the misfortunes. Cupping a bowl in front of her mouth, Rosinta blew puffs of incense around our heads and feet, then she balanced a cup of alcohol on our heads, associated it with the original time and place, and threw it to our earth shrine. She explained that the drops of alcohol were to ask permission of the patrons of the patio and kitchen and the levels of the mountain to perform this ritual for the river.

Rosinta sat in the eastern corner facing west, and all the Yana-huaya women sat around her with their instruments of weaving in a bundle in front of her. Near them were bundles of potatoes, oca, and barley which symbolized a personalized female entity called *tawichu*. The female symbolism of the misfortune ritual can be understood in relation to the male symbolism of the lineage ritual, which stressed the patrilineal claim to land.

Essentially, the movement of the lineage ritual had been toward the center of Marcelino's household, whereas the misfortune ritual, which dealt with the dissolutions of the body and land, moved away from the household. On a symbolic parallel, women, who menstru-ate, also move away from their father's land: they are physiologi-cally and socially more capable than men of manipulating symbols which deal with the losses of the body and land.

Gloria, Marcelino and Carmen's daughter, was absent from the ritual. Although she was in La Paz, she was symbolically present, however, by virtue of her hat, which lay between Celia and Sophia. This spot corresponded to her place as the third oldest daughter. Rosinta placed a cup of alcohol on Gloria's hat, and throughout the ritual Rosinta performed gestures with this hat as if it were Gloria. The hat is also a symbol of return for Andeans. Marcelino, for example, has his dead son Sabino's hat hanging on the wall to remind them of his return. As a gesture of binding friendship, Andeans weave the person's name and year on a stocking cap, which they then give to the friend.

After Rosinta purified the participants by incense and alcohol, she asked permission of the wind (*anqari*) to perform the ritual by throwing alcohol into the air so that the wind could carry it "to where the wind blows." That same wind also brought these misfor-tunes to the Yanahuayas. In retaliation, Rosinta poured another cup of alcohol for the community wind, and she passed this cup over our heads and went into the patio to throw it into the wind. This toast was to ensure that the wind of those who cursed the community would be destroyed.

The wind has two aspects because it serves as a metaphorical vehicle for cursing people, and also brings the rain clouds to blow away misfortunes. The wind's binal climatic properties parallel the river's two relationships to the mountain as both erosive and cyclical elements.

By contrast, the earth shrine does not possess the binal variability of the river and the wind, but each one is interpreted by its complementary shrine. For example, Chaqamita (shrine to the rising sun) is paired with Pachaqota (shrine to the setting sun). The earth shrines were the central symbols of the agricultural and lineage rituals, which symbolized a stable mountain body, but wind and river were the symbols within the misfortune ritual, because of their natural variability. They are fed a rat, moss, and cacti: rats eat the valuable supplies, moss cracks the rocks of their homes and fences, and the cacti which spring up in the fields are not only harmful to animals but difficult to remove.

The dead ancestors of Marcelino's patrilineage, the patron of the patio, the matron of Carmen's kitchen, and Mount Kaata ate with the wind and river. For these guests, Rosinta served six cotton wads of coca, llama fat, carnations, and incense into the shrine alongside the supply house. The wads disappeared into the fire within the shrine. Rosinta set aside another six wads to be burned and fed into the Kunochayuh River. The ancestors, patron, matron, wind, and mountain finished their meal on the banks of the Kunochayuh River. The river was named Mario, which Rosinta said was close to the Quechua word mayu, meaning river. We admired Rosinta's ingenuity, and became silent when she asked each of us to name two of our enemies, so she could send them a misfortune. I could not hear who the enemies were, but when Rosinta asked me, they all listened intently as I named Lionel Alvarez of Charazani. Alvarez had repeatedly reserved the cabin of his truck for our twenty-hour trip to La Paz. Then, when my wife and I crossed the mountain to Charazani, he informed us that someone else would ride in front. He had sold the seats for more money. When I named Alvarez as my enemy, Carmen and Marcelino smiled; they also disliked this mestizo. Alvarez was generally disliked because he crowded the Indians into the back of his truck and charged them high rates.

Midnight divided the misfortune ritual into different eating sites and ritual foods. Before midnight Rosinta fed llama fat and cotton to the ancestors, patron, matron, mountain, wind, and river in Marcelino's patio. After midnight, they ate principally pig fat and black llama wool as well as llama fat and cotton at the Kunochayuh River. The pig traditionally comes from below the mountain's levels, and its fat symbolizes negative power from the area. The llama is native to the highlands, but its dark wool symbolizes death. Both symbols together, however, suggest that the negative forces of death and decay from below the mountain are restored by the positive regenerative forces of the highlands. Although land and people erode and die on their journey down the levels to the lowlands, when they die, they return to the highlands, where they will generate again.

After midnight on Tuesday, Rosinta began preparing the meal for the river by divining with a gray guinea pig which had been placed on everyone's forehead. She opened its viscera with her fingernails and poured its blood into a cup with wine, eggs, and corn. After she removed the rib cage, she examined the protrusion in the front, which formed a small half-moon. She said it looked fine. On the guinea pig's pancreas she spotted two incisions, which she said were two mouths (*simikuna*). Enemies were bewitching us, she explained, and Marcelino identified one mouth as that of Dominga Ari. Dominga had become impoverished following the death of her husband, Mariano Yanahuaya. Twenty years earlier, Mariano, Marcelino's classificatory brother had usurped Marcelino's land, and Marcelino said that Dominga's blindness and poverty were the punishments from Marcelino's ancestors. In fact, Dominga had accused Marcelino of soliciting a sorceress to send these misfortunes. When two hostile Andean families suffer calamities, an exchange of sorcery is suspected.

Josefa Waque, the second mouth, was suspected of cursing me. This tough, seventy-year-old lady had been trampled by horses, severely damaging her coronal bone. She was dying when they brought her to be cured. After I shaved her head, I cleansed and bound the bone together with a bandage. She recovered in a month and came to me requesting her hair. When I explained that I had burned it, she angrily departed and suspected me of using her hair in witchcraft against her. At the same time, Dominga and Josefa became close friends, further arousing Carmen's suspicions about them.

When Rosinta showed the Yanahuayas the two incisions on the pancreas, they knew just what Dominga and Josefa had been up to. When would Sebastián learn? they said. They were happy, however, that I now considered Dominga and Josefa as my enemies, which I had not done in the past. I should not have given Dominga and Josefa food. The incongruity of giving food to a person cursing me was a social contradiction to Kaatans who see exchange as always being reciprocated with a likeness. One should exchange produce with produce, and misfortunes with misfortunes.

The snatching of hair, so essential to most Andean sorcery, is an attack on the person's uma pacha, as when the chunchos in the legend of the flood stole the Kaatan woman's headband. Snatching hair is removing from the person what is most original and cyclical to him, and symbolically it implies a dissolving of the body without returning it to the source. The river is the place which can break the misfortune cycle, nevertheless, and so return what is lost.

Rosinta's divination lasted more than two hours, and it was around 2:30 a.m. when she began the servings for the river. She laid the rat at the head of the ritual cloth and sorted out twenty wads of dark llama wool. Meanwhile Carmen had secretly snatched coca from some shrines and secretaries of the community, and Rosinta placed twelve of these leaves on each wad. Slivers of pig fat were put on the coca.

"Here's some cheese for the mice and rats," Rosinta said. Carmen jokingly commented that rats and mice were jungle varmints, who ate pig fat for cheese. Rosinta also served daisies, seeds, herb clumps, and moss. Once Rosinta had served the food, she wrapped the dark wool tightly around it. One wad was tied to the rat's back and two wads were given to each participant, setting one beneath the hat of the man or inside the headband of the woman, and the other between the left big toe and sandal. Two wads were stuffed into the crops (tawichu), the weavings, the kitchen, sleeping room, and dispensary. The sheep, horse, and burro corrals were each given two wads. While the wads drew the evil forces from their associated objects, we rested and ate in preparation for the lower journey to the Kunochayuh. Rosinta gathered the wads from the different places, each time breaking a llama thread from the spindle around the threshold of the door or the legs of the animals. Marcelino hurried everyone along, fearing that we would be seen by Josefa or heard by Dominga, if they were awake when we passed their homes. Rosinta finally collected all the wads, and we were ready to go, but she could not find her coca cloth. Carmen raced around looking for it, and then gave her another one.

We filed out the front gate into the mud and rain. Everyone had a large pack carrying dirty clothes, which would also be washed in the river just as our bodies would be. We stumbled along in the dark, Marcelino at the front and Rosinta at the end. The trail cut across the side of the mountain, and where Tala and Machu Pata peaks met, an erosion cut deeply into the side of the valley. The rocks and slippery clay made the passage across the landslide very dangerous. Several times Marcelino told me to help the elderly Rosinta, who hobbled along loaded with a large sack of dried food in payment for her night's work. However, she needed little help and kept pace with everyone in spite of her seventy years.

Somewhere I lost one misfortune wad stuck between my foot and sandal. The consequences of my carelessness frightened me, so I removed the wad from my hat and divided it into two. It was a very dark night, and no one noticed.

Two hours later, we arrived at the bridge crossing the Kunochayuh River and climbed another steep path three hundred yards up the mountain. Marcelino pointed out a cave alongside the river, and called it "lord of the devil" (*supayniyuh*). Marcelino explained its name:

> Once a Kaatan was crossing the river from Upinhuaya. He saw a
> man wearing a white suit and a black mask standing inside of this
> cave. Frightened, he dropped everything and ran to Kaatapata,
> telling everybody he had seen the devil.

We crouched inside the grotto, the women deep within it and Marcelino and I on the outside. Rosinta threw an offering of coca to the lord of the river, and prayed that our sorrows and misfortunes would go away. Carmen served us hot potatoes and oca. We talked about the river.

The Kunochayuh flowed rapidly in front of the grotto, descending twenty feet in about twenty-five yards. The river was about fifteen feet across, winding in and out of the gorges cut into the mountainside and flowing around and over large rocks pushed down by its swift current. Owing to the descent, it flowed down in steps of waterfalls close to one another, somewhat similar to the terraces of the land. Marcelino told us how he had played on the rocks of the river when he was a boy. He pointed out places where he used to sit which were now washed away, and ponds, now filled with boulders, where he once swam. Marcelino talked about the bridge:

> This lower bridge across the Kunochayuh was built ten years ago after the Agrarian Reform. Before this time Kaatans and Upinhuayans crossed far above the grotto, where the river was narrower and shallower. During the rainy season many people could not cross, and if they did they were carried to places below by this river.
>
> Upinhuayans, in times past, had another road to Charazani cutting across the lower fields of our ayllu. They would carry their dead to bury them in the cemetery of Charazani. These Aymaras had the strange practice of burying their dead away from Upinhuaya. A landslide washed their lower road away and now with the bridge they pass rapidly through Kaata. They do not carry their dead through Kaata, but now bury them in Upinhuaya.[4]

Marcelino gathered dry straw and wood to build a small fire inside the grotto. Rosinta placed one cotton wad in each of our hands. We presented the offerings to the lords of the mountain and the river, and prayed that our enemies would let us alone. Rosinta burned all the wads and threw the ashes into the river.

Then Carmen gáve Rosinta a large black-and-white guinea pig, which she dissected to examine the viscera. The still-beating heart predicted good health. Everyone crowded around as she showed us the two pancreases, dark red with white tips. She said this sign indicated lack of life in the Yanahuaya household and that the household had not been feeding the ayllu shrines. If they wanted life to grow they should begin to offer more rituals, and so Marcelino and Carmen immediately promised to have more lineage rituals for the lords of the ayllu.

We knelt facing the river's descent. Rosinta threw the yolk and white from a chicken egg into the waters, and then she removed the black wads from our hats, sandals, as well as from the women's headbands. As she took the bands, she broke the wool thread around our right and left hands, and right and left feet. She put the black wads into an old coca cloth with the guinea pigs, rat, coca quids, cigarette butts, and ashes. Everyone looked away, as Rosinta flung the cloth into the river, saying, *"Puriychej chijekuna!"* ("Begone misfortunes!").

And so Rosinta had removed the misfortunes and was anxious to return to Upinhuaya. She bid everyone good-bye as she crossed the river; for an instant she entered its icy waters, holding her skirt in her right hand and her sandals in her left. The water rushed around this diviner as she made one final step into the whirling pool and then out again. She rapidly ascended the zig-zag path rising steeply to the main road to Upinhuaya and disappeared into a cloud, just as she had come out of the darkness into the ritual house earlier that evening.

She left, having removed misfortunes from the Yanahuaya family. She had revealed that misfortune was an exchange between enemies which disintegrated the corporeal, social, and geographical body, just as exchange between these layers built up the body. Once again the Marcelino Yanahuaya family was made aware of the inter-relation of dead ancestors, ancestral land, backbiting, loss of land, and bodily sickness. The woman diviner had come "from the corner" to throw these misfortunes into the river, and so wash them away.

Our physical bodies needed cleansing also, so for this ablution Marcelino and Carmen began brewing a concoction of cacti, thorny weeds, and water. Carmen and her three daughters took the spiny water to the shores of the river. After they gargled with it, they stripped naked and thoroughly washed each other with it, careful to see that it entered every crevice. Marcelino and I were out of sight in the cave, as Kaatan women are very shy, even during rituals. After they had finished, Marcelino and I did as they had done. The earthen pot and wash basin were then floated down the river.

Carmen and Marcelino removed every trace of the ablutions; even the ashes were thrown into the waters, and the place appeared as if no one had ever been there. We returned to Kaata by the higher path. I had been warned by Marcelino and Elsa, "Once we have left the river, you may only look in front of you, not to the right, nor to the left, nor behind you." Carmen and Elsa were always more careful concerning the rubrics of the rituals, and Marcelino soon forgot the taboo as we climbed up the steep incline and he began to talk more about the river.

During his lapse, Marcelino told me about the irrigation canal. I was amazed to discover this engineering feat, which for a year I had been unaware of, set into the hills. I was interested in when it was built and when it was used. My curiosity irritated him and he remained silent as we walked along the stone mosaics. I kept saying,

"Allinyapuni!" ("Magnificent!"). Carmen and Marcelino looked pleased to hear this, and Marcelino began to talk:

> We cannot recall any time when our ancestors had used the canal. Our ancestors had carried the rocks from the lower valley to these highlands. They had carried them on their backs, not with llamas or alpacas. The rocks were fit into the sides and bottom of the canal. One by one they came up the lower river basin where they gathered the rocks and carried them up the mountain.

As he spoke he said repeatedly, *"Nin nispa"* ("Told, but continually telling"). He spoke as if "they" were still carrying the rocks up the mountain. We all paused to look down the mountainside through the cloud, as if expecting an ancestor loaded with a large rock to cross the horizon. The very shape of the mountains, which makes the mountains silent, also makes them echo.

This particular oral tradition recalls what part Kaatans played in constructing the canal and how people, not llamas, carried the rocks from the lowlands to the highlands to make the river flow to the center of ayllu Kaata. It emphasizes carrying upward the rocks which the river had carried downward. Through human activity the body, levels of land, and society can be restored to the original time and place. In similar fashion, the account of the flood depicts Andean man as carrying the llama to the mountain top where they both are saved from the washing-away effects of the flood.

Our return path was along this irrigation canal, and after an hour's journey we could see Kaata. Marcelino and Elsa told me not to look down at the path over which we had traveled to the river earlier that morning. I obeyed. Eventually, we arrived in back of Marcelino's house and climbed over the fence just as a traveler came around the side of the house. Marcelino said we had been very lucky not to have met anyone either going or returning. Our travels had made a large circle. By the lower route to the river, we had removed our misfortunes, and by the upper road across the highlands we had restored our losses.

We passed our hands and feet through the smoke of a fire inside the patio, which Carmen said was done to dispel any of the grief remaining from the misfortunes. Celia brought us large plates of pig soup, which we ate heartily after eleven hours of ritual activity.

I found the black wad which I had carelessly left behind. When I showed it to Marcelino, he was alarmed. We quickly burned it in the fire without telling anyone about it.

Shortly before noon, Josefa Waque came into the patio to beg for food. Carmen angrily chased her away, disturbed that one of the bewitchers had arrived so soon after we had removed the misfortunes. Carmen and Marcelino began to suspect the efficacy of the misfortune ritual, until they saw visible effects of Rosinta's powers that same afternoon. Dominga Ari and her son, Julian, began crying and yelling at each other toward suppertime, and at one point Dominga struck the boy. Marcelino smiled and said that the misfortunes had returned to her. Carmen later explained the cause of the yelling. Dominga had collected strands of her son's hair with the intent of bewitching him. Julian learned of this and took his mother to the sheriff, who severely reprimanded her. Marcelino complimented Rosinta's power by saying, *"Yachan"* ("She knows").

In essence, then, the river is instrumental in washing away misfortunes and in returning the parts to make the body complete. As a metaphor, the river is associated with different geographical places, periods of time, and social groups, as well as sickness, feuds, and loss of land. Another set of meanings is, however, attached to the river in the form of a continuous stream originating from and flowing to the original time and place (*uma pacha*). The river makes the body complete not only by washing it but by defining its boundaries and by forever returning what has been removed.

Kaatan geography, society, time, and history have two dimensions, which coincide with the river. The particular levels of land, ecological zones, distinct communities, ordered time, and layered history is one dimension. The other is understood in terms of a complete geographical body, social and cultural ayllu unity, and an original time and place. This original time and place is self-contained, cyclical, and constitutive of everything else. These two dimensions are of one body.

NOTES

1.   Green Lake is a large lake in the head of ayllu Kaata.

2.   Wilka, a native of Curva, emphasizes the importance of herbal curers from Curva in comparison to diviners of Kaata. He implies that only the people of Curva are entitled to carry the medicine bag. Nevertheless, Kaatans carry medicine bags with ritual paraphernalia.

3.   The sun is spoken of as a grandfather with a beard, which Marcelino explained, "The rays of the sun are like your beard, hiding the sun from our eyes. We cannot see him."

4.   The Agrarian Reform was primarily interested in linking Upinhuaya and Kaata with the capital of the province, Charazani, and with La Paz. The reform defined the communities' boundaries, which often split them from their ayllu solidarity, and connected them by roads with Bolivian centers of exchange. The gorged Kunochayuh River separated ayllu Upinhuaya from ayllu Kaata in the past when exchange patterns were more vertical than horizontal.

10

The Feast with the Dead

For Andeans, the finality of death is lessened by the mountain metaphor. Andeans become a part of the land which they work: as their bodies perish, their land increases. When they die, they enter into the mountain and journey upwards. The visible levels of the living are only one-half of the mountain; the other half consists of the subterranean waterways of the dead.

Andeans' world view is an extension of the mountain's three levels; they divide their universe into the heavens (*junaq pacha*), this world (*kay pacha*), and the netherworld (*ura pacha*).[1] Each place has an ancient, past, and present time, to which specific beings correspond.

The heavens are where the elders of lightning, sun, and stars have dwelled since ancient times; where God, Jesus, and Santiago have roamed since past times, and where dead baptized babies are descending to the uma pacha in present times. The heavens suggest origination and restitution by their permanent and cyclical features, whereas the experiences of this world are temporal and consecutive. The three times of this world are symbolized by chullpas, the cross, and the graveyard, which refer respectively to the ancestor mummies, Jesus, and the recent dead (those who have died within three years).

The earth shrines refer to space, time, and being. In the netherworld the ancestor mummies, past, and recent dead are journeying within the subterranean waterways to the highlands; it is the recycling area between death and life. Being, space, and time, our metaphysical concepts for the universe, are intertwined in each of the three gradient levels; thus the mountain serves as an expression of Andean cosmology.

On the second day of the Fiesta of the Holy Cross, Guillermo Bautista, while intoxicated, fell backwards from a wall where he sat enjoying the music. The house sat on a cliff, and the courtyard wall, which was only three feet high inside the patio, dropped twenty feet to a gravel road. Guillermo's head and shoulders crashed against a sharp rock. The dance stopped.

Four men carried Guillermo home. Guillermo's wife, Refilda, sobered instantly when she realized her husband's spinal column had been seriously injured. Guillermo was paralyzed from his neck to his toes. And for days they tried to cure him. An herbalist wrapped Guillermo's back with a compress of crushed frog legs and coca to no avail. Out of desperation, Refilda summoned Marcelino, who was Guillermo's godfather. By now Guillermo was motionless, barely able to move his lips. Marcelino wept when he saw his friend who had always been the life of the party. Guillermo loved to dance and play the flute.

As everyone realized, Guillermo was dying. But there was the possibility of taking him to a hospital in Ancoraimes.[2] Four men could carry Guillermo by stretcher to Charazani and from there he would be transported in the back of a truck to Ancoraimes, ten hours away. However, if Guillermo died on the journey or in Ancoraimes, then his body would be buried where he died, according to Andean custom. And if Guillermo were buried away from Mount Kaata, then he could not reach its uma pacha; neither could Guillermo banquet with his living descendants during the Feast with the Dead. It had to be decided, then, by coca, whether Guillermo was going to die. Marcelino summoned the diviner, Teodoro Yanahuaya.

Teodoro placed coca over Guillermo's heart for several minutes. He selected several leaves and marked them by tearing pieces from the side of the leaf.

"*Manan allinchu!*" ("Not good!"), he said finally, and Guillermo's wife broke into loud crying. The diviner had predicted Guillermo's death, said that his blood was running out, and that he would die away from the mountain if he went to Ancoraimes. To die in Ancoraimes would negate Guillermo's claim to the land he once worked because he would be buried there and not on the mountain.

The secretary of education wrote Guillermo's last will and testament in a notebook. Guillermo's wife, Refilda, sat close to him as he listed the land which he had inherited from his father and his mother. He named the distinct places of the lower fields, and then his terraces in each rotative field: Waterhole for the Skunk (*Añas Unoyuh*), Two Faces (*Iskay Uya*), Rounded Terrace (*Muyupata*), and Lord of the Black Bull (*Yana Toroyuh*).

As Guillermo named the places which he had plowed, planted, and harvested since he was four years old, everyone relaxed and mentally made the journey with him through the lower and rotative fields. They were happy, not so much to receive land, as to know that Guillermo was associated with so many places. By cultivating these places, Guillermo had become a part of the mountain, which would remain forever.

Life comes from and returns to the earth. Andean children grow with the earth of which they become a part at death. Together with their parents, they feed the earth, put it to sleep, give it drink, plow, germinate, nurture, and harvest its gifts. When Kaatan children are able to do these things alone, then they are adults. Each time this cycle of the earth involves them they become more of an adult, an elder, and finally a completed person.

Guillermo's inheritance was given equally to his children. It will be kept in trust for them by their mother and the eldest son. When they come of marrying age, it will be their land, and they will take care of their mother. The living Guillermo guaranteed his patrilineage in writing before the Secretary General and the sheriff, and everyone knew that the dead Guillermo would haunt these same people if his claim failed to be maintained.

JOURNEYING TO THE UMA PACHA

The misfortune ritual associated the river with originating and returning to the uma pacha, the head of the ayllu body. The burial ritual prepares the dead for a journey along the underground rivers to the uma pacha. The journey of the dead is described in Andean legend:

> When they captured a prisoner, they cut his face. "This is our strength," they said and made him dance. . . . the prisoner said, "Brother, you are going to kill me. I was a man of influence, but you are going to make me a *wayu* (person to be sacrificially hanged). When I am ready to go out to the field, you should feed me well and give me a lot to drink."
>
> After they heard this, some people fed and gave drink to the wayu. "Today you will dance with us in the open," they said. Then they carried the wayu around in a stretcher for two days. On the next day they hanged him with the corn, potatoes, and all they had given him. Regarding the things they hanged, people used to believe and say: "Bringing along these things he will return to uma pacha, the place of origin." (Huarochiri ms., 3169:F.94)

During the burial rite clothes, food, coca, chicha, and alcohol are given to the dead for the journey to the place of origin. The dead person is turned toward the summit of the mountain and given a candle for this nighttime trip.

Guillermo died eleven days after his fall. The first person to guide me to Kaata, he had been my friend. He possessed an impish quality which made him pleasantly entertaining at times and a pestering nuisance at other times. My last memory of Guillermo was the day I was recording his flute band for the fiesta. He spotted me and throughout the recording I can hear him shouting, *"Págame, págame"* ("Pay me, pay me"). He wanted me to contribute a bottle of alcohol to his band.

When Marcelino told me that he had died, I could still hear Guillermo asking me to pay him. I thought of the Kaatan places, mallkus, shrines, lords of the season, patrons of the patio and kitchen, which he had paid with coca, blood, and fat. Now we would pay him each time we fed the earth.

In preparation for burial, Guillermo first was washed in hot water. A tight cord was then tied around his throat and cotton stuffed in his nose and mouth to stop the odors. Marcelino and a relative dressed the body in new clothes and placed it on a table with two candles. Friends and relatives paid their respects by praying Hail Mary's and Our Father's and by putting coca into his bag for the journey.

The burial service began at noon the day after Guillermo had died. Refilda filled his medicine bag with cooked potatoes, oca, charqui, hot sauce, and llama fat, enough for a long day's journey. She wrapped his blankets and poncho around him for it would be cold inside of the earth as he traveled the underground waterways toward the highlands.

Four secretaries carried Guillermo's body, stretched out on two large poles and two smaller cross bars, from his home in Chaqahuaya to the small cemetery in Qollahuaya. The cemetery is about twenty yards long and fifteen yards wide, with an eight-foot adobe wall encircling it. All the dead are buried about five feet below the ground, close to the other members of their patrilineage. The wife is always buried near her husband, or if she dies before him, she is buried in his patrilineal plot of the cemetery. Since the dead are believed to be journeying, after several years another dead relative may be buried on top of, or in the same place as the other deceased.

Two secretaries carried the empty coffin which had been recently constructed of two large eucalyptus boards and alcohol crates. Fearing the power of a dead person, the police officials and truck drivers prohibit the transport of coffins from La Paz to parts of the Altiplano. Andeans believe that a dead person moving above the earth could snatch their blood and fat and take away their life and energy. Moreover, the transferring of the dead takes the life of the crops. From the time of death to the burial is the neither here-nor-there period, dangerous to Kaatans. Once the corpse is permanently clothed, nailed in the coffin, and placed in the earth, people can rejoice in having brought about the end of this period which lies between journeying with people above the earth while alive and journeying with people inside the earth while dead.

Thirty-six men sat on benches along the wall of the cemetery. The Secretary General measured the coffin with a cord and instructed the diggers as to the size of the grave. One man rapidly broke the earth with the hand plow and another shoveled. The grave-digging was a relay race; they plowed and shoveled in pairs to the point of exhaustion and then were replaced by another pair. The sheriff invited new diggers when he saw that the old ones were tiring. The grave reached the buried coffins, whose tin edges from the alcohol cans had rusted through. They uncovered the top of a skull and a large femur bone, which was rapidly placed aside. Suddenly they all exclaimed, *"Wajta!"* ("Another one!"). A fetid smell filled the grave, and everyone stepped back, holding their noses with their ponchos and placing coca leaves inside their nostrils. They had opened a decomposed skull. They quickly covered it and passed around coca and alcohol. The coca quids were placed alongside the grave, as were the empty alcohol bottles. Some of the men were crying and others were laughing.

Guillermo's eldest son had arrived from La Paz shortly after his father had died. He served everyone alcohol and coca, and so assumed his responsibilities as head of his father's patrilineage.

Only four women attended the burial: Guillermo's sisters and one classificatory mother, since his natural mother was dead. As is customary for all burials, only the mother and sisters are permitted. Guillermo's wife and members of her lineage were not allowed to assist at the gravesite, but remained at home to cook. Only members of Guillermo's patrilineage could set him into the earth and secure his claim to the land by burying him within it. The living members of the patrilineage were the hosts of dead Guillermo, and they would feed him for the next three years, during the Feast with the Dead. After three years of ritual feeding, he would complete the cycle, by climbing up the three levels to the uma pacha.

The grave was dug in half an hour, and the Secretary General approved it. Guillermo's body, wrapped in a lead-colored poncho, symbolic of night, was placed inside the coffin. They placed a candle in his hand and lit it. I took from my hat a white carnation, whose ruffled petals resembled a lazy cloud and whose two sisters, pink and red, inaugurate and terminate the day, and asked that it be given to Guillermo. They put it in his hand, saying, "This is a gift from Sebastián to take with you on your journey and to give to Him."

Four men holding rope straps lowered Guillermo to begin his journey. They covered the coffin hastily, while the women wailed. The dirt was tamped down with a rock, and they made a large cross from the four poles and placed it at the head of the grave. A wreath of red gladiolas formed a circle around the cross. All of the participants washed their hands in a pot of water over the grave, and later flowers were placed inside the pot. The burial service ended with a silent prayer and, as rapidly as Guillermo was buried, everyone descended to the deceased's house.

As we entered the courtyard, Refilda passed incense beneath our hands, and prayed, "May your sorrow rise with the smoke." The women arrived with pots of soup and cloths of solid foods, which they gave to their husbands. The husbands set the boiled food on the four sides of the courtyard where the men sat, and in the center of the circle of women. Everyone sampled the wide variety of potatoes, oca, and corn. The husbands then served us soup with rice, noodles, charqui, and barley. The Secretary General received the servings, lining them up in the courtyard. After he had drunk five bowls of soup, he served the rest to the other guests. We enjoyed each other's company and food.

When the meal was finished, the Secretary General called for a few minutes of silent prayer for Guillermo's journey. Then everyone shouted, "Have a good trip, Guillermo!" and we threw alcohol and coca toward the summit of Mount Kaata. We continued drinking until evening, when the Secretary General ended the festivities with his announcement that the sun had died in the highlands and Guillermo's journey had ended.

The ritualist at the burial service was the Secretary General of the community. The highest official told Guillermo's patrilineage and Refilda's lineage that, however much they suffered the consequences of Guillermo's death, they remained members of a community which shared grief and food. His ritual activity was to serve drink and food to the bereaved and to dispatch Guillermo on his journey to the uma pacha.

The burial site emphasized the journey of the dead to the uma pacha. The living travel down the three levels of the ayllu above the earth, and the dead climb back up the ayllu within the earth. The sun rises above the ayllu during the day, and it travels underneath the ayllu during the night. As a result, both the living and the dead are actively involved in the processes of the universe.

THE DEAD VISIT THE LIVING

Kaatans compare death to the eclipse of the sun: death is ecliptic, hiding the dead within the earth where they journey with the movements of the sun, the seasons, and the land. Within all these movements there is a time when the dead return to the community, November 2, the Feast with the Dead. This feast coincides with All Souls on the Catholic calendar, but it also marks the end of the dry season and the beginning of the rainy season. The rains cease in April and May, and the dry season continues until November. During this time of rest and relaxation, Kaatans harvest and celebrate. When the rains begin again in November, Kaatans plant their crops. They also elect their secretaries, who organize the people in communal projects, such as building up the terrace, repairing the roads, and white-washing the school.

The living invite the dead when the harvest and festive times have ended and planting and agricultural rituals begin. The Feast with the Dead is an annual rite of passage from the dry to wet season and from the activity of the dead to that of the living. The dry season connotates resting, and the wet season, growth. Between this pivotal point within the Andean year, the dead visit the living, and then they are sent on another year's journey with their share of the harvest.[3]

At noon on Wednesday, the Secretary General ignited a coffee can of dynamite. The explosion rocked the dead and announced their arrival to the living. Only those who had died within three years were invited to the feast, and in the hamlet of Qollahuaya three dead persons returned. Fortunato and Toribia Inofuentes had died two years earlier without descendants. Venancio Yanahuaya had bought their land from the secretaries for two hundred pesos and now had to claim them as his ancestors by ritually feeding them.[4] The third dead person to return to Qollahuaya was Juana Ticona. She also had died two years earlier, and came to visit her husband, Laborio Yanahuaya. The flickering of a candle told everyone that she had arrived. Rosela, Juana's sister, began to wail, lamenting over the fact that Juana had left her with so much work. She told Juana that it was difficult to cook and care for her husband, who was very stubborn. After Juana had died, Rosela had assumed her sister's responsibility to Laborio as his companion and cook.

Death seldom dissolves relationships between godchildren and god-parents or between the wife's and husband's kin, and often the next classificatory equal to the deceased assumes the role of the dead person.

Crippled from age and work, Laborio served us and Juana. He gave everyone a plate of pig's head soup, which Rosela had cooked. In the kitchen was an elaborate table with three tiers of food and drink. The lowest tier was covered with lowland products of coca, apples, bananas, and chicha. A platform stood on this surface and was filled with cooked potatoes, oca, ch'uño, beer, and plain breads, symbolizing the central lands. A square wooden box formed the third level, upon which sat a wicker basket with bread figurines. The third level symbolized the head of ayllu Kaata and place of origin for all the produce of the ayllu. The llamas, birds, fish, cows, and flowers within the basket were symbolic products of the three eco-logical zones emerging from the lakes and waterholes of the uma pacha.

Laborio served Juana a plate of soup. He complained to her about Rosela, saying how she ordered him around and that she would not go with him to the highlands, where he lived in a small hut near his sixty llamas and fifteen horses. A fly circled Juana's table, alighting on each of the levels, and everyone agreed that this was a sign of her presence.

At the end of the meal, Laborio's brothers assembled bamboos to be placed above the table. Three bamboos fanned out from the end of a wooden pole, to which they were tied. A cross was formed with another bar positioned horizontally. Flowers were arranged over the center and a string of oranges was hung beneath the cross-bar. The bamboos with the cross and the oranges symbolized the heavens of the saints and the sun.

Along the bottom of the tablecloth, Gregorio pinned three water color drawings which his nine-year-old son had done in school. No one could explain these drawings, but their place suggested some association with the netherworld, the devil, and the dead. Juana's table would be set over her grave on Thursday.

The table's three levels symbolized Mount Kaata, and its legs the netherworld. The Indians understand the mountain as a solid three-leveled center with an ephemeral heaven above a hollow netherworld foundation. The sun, living, and dead circulate above, below, and around the mountain.

TABLE FOR THE DEAD

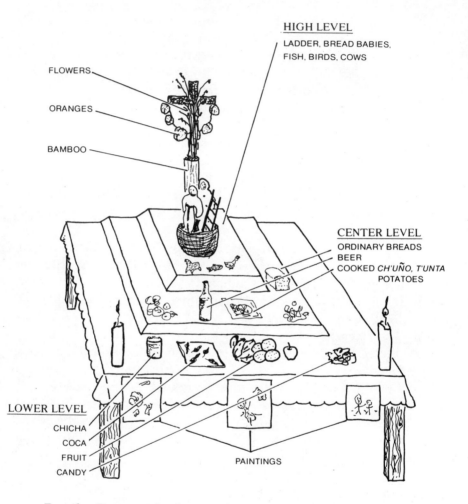

For the Feast with the Dead, Kaatans always place a glass of chicha on the dead's table, and when the Apachetans pray for the dead they sprinkle chicha on the earth asking the dead to drink. The Apachetan drinks several mouthfuls, toasting, and thus forming a bond with the dead person. Although cane alcohol is drunk at the feast, chicha remains the primary drink for both the living and the dead. Chicha was also the pre-Columbian drink of the dead, as the following tradition illustrates:

In the olden times they used to bring the dead all kinds of food, all of them well-cooked. When a man died, they said, "Our dead will return after five days. We shall wait for them." They used to stay awake each night until the fifth day of their death.

Already on the fifth day, a woman putting on her best clothes used to go to Yaru Tini saying, "I will wait for him," or "I will lead him." The woman went bringing food and corn beer. In Yaru Tini when the sun was already rising, the dead ones used to arrive. In the olden times two or three flies used to sit on the garment she brought, and there they remained for a long time. When the other fly we call *wanquy k'uru* left, she said to a small stone, "Come on, let us go to the village."

"This is he," she said to the stone, bringing it back with her. When she arrived, her home was swept clean and people began to serve food. Once they had offered the dead food, they gave the dead corn beer. After the dead one had eaten, they ate. (Huarochiri ms. 3169:F.98)

Apachetans descend from the highlands to receive bread in exchange for their prayers. Apachetans' relationship to the head of the mountain qualifies them to assist the dead, who travel to this place of generation. The ritualist's level is important in qualifying him for the distinct ritual. At New Earth, for example, Sarito had come from the center of the mountain, and for the misfortune ritual Rosinta came from the corner. This specialization of ritualists corresponds to the metaphorical understanding of the mountain ayllu. The Apachetans who offer ritual prayers are associated with the head of the body, to which the dead are ascending. The Apachetan's descent to Kaata is understood in terms of his return, when he will carry the dead's bread up to the uma pacha for him. The Apachetan eats bread and drinks chicha for the dead person, and when he ascends he will symbolically take the dead person with him.

After the Apachetan ritualists descended to Kaata, they traveled from house to house, playing the flute and praying for the dead person. It was dark when the first Apachetan entered Laborio's house to pray for Juana. The Apachetan took a glass of chicha, sprinkled several drops over the table's three levels and over the ground, and then swallowed a mouthful. A fly entered the room as he loudly prayed, *"Nanakan awquisa"* ("Our Father"). Everyone smiled as they saw Juana circling over the one who, with his prayer, would assist her ascent to the uma pacha. The Apachetan was given bread, fruit, and a glass of chicha for his prayers. Everyone exchanged coca bags and visited for a while.

Early Thursday morning, Laborio's brothers carried Juana's table to the cemetery, where they placed it on her grave. By midmorning the cemetery was filled with similar tables, constructed by the relatives of the dead. About forty Apachetan ritualists were making the rounds, praying for the dead. They carried large sacks filled with bread and fruit. Those who prayed fervently and offered candles to the dead were given beautiful bread figurines, oranges, and bananas.

All three hamlets bury their dead in the cemetery located in Qollahuaya. One cemetery symbolizes communality for the three hamlets. Kaatapata's and Chaqahuaya's chapels are shrines to the saints, who inhabit heaven, and Qollahuaya's cemetery is a shrine to the dead, who inhabit the netherworld. Each villa has an orientation to high, center, and low levels of ayllu Kaata, as well as an orientation to the above or below places.

All the commoners had congregated in the cemetery around the tables of the dead. They spoke in whispers out of respect for the dead; occasionally someone wailed or laughed. Subdued silence and reverence were the communal emotions, rather than grief and fear. They were at home with their dead, or perhaps it is that the dead are at home both literally and figuratively with the living.

When the sun was overhead, the dead departed to the uma pacha. Their relatives rapidly dismantled the tables and stuffed what was left into sacks. Everyone went from the cemetery to the homes of the sponsors, and by early afternoon the graveyard resumed its quietude.

The hosts sponsored departure banquets for the deceased, similar to that of the burial ritual. Once they had finished eating, people shared drinks, and the flute band, silent until then, played. The band was composed of six flute players, two drummers, and two playing the cowtail (wacachupa), which is a long wooden tube with a cow's tail and emits a low and resonating sound like a foghorn. The band zig-zagged through the streets while the dancing couples were swinging back and forth, until they completed a circle, traveling from Qollahuaya to Kaatapata and back again.

Later that afternoon Marcelino, a bit tipsy, arrived home and asked me to join him in prayers for our dead. He cried as he talked about Erminia, who so recently was the joy of their household. Two Apachetans came through the front gate, and they said some prayers for my dead mother, and for Marcelino's deceased relatives. Marcelino consoled me:

> Your mother is one with the earth. She is like Mother Earth, and she is here with us now. The dead visit us and they assist us in our work. They provide many blessings. As the sun and moon live, so the dead accompany us. When the sun burns out at the judgment, then the dead will never return.

Marcelino brought out two bread babies from his storeroom. He cuddled the breads as if they were newborn babies. When he gave me a male baby, I was about to eat it, being unaware of the second half of the Feast with the Dead. He stopped me and explained that the baby would have to be baptized before being eaten.

THE BAPTISM AND DEATH OF THE BREAD BABIES

The next morning, Friday, Carmen dressed the bread baby and wrapped a blanket around it. As I carried the bread baby in my arms with its head nestled inside the cloth, it looked almost alive. Five or six neighboring children were spying over the fence and laughing at the incongruities. Just as life and death balance each other, so also do sadness and joy. The second half of the Feast with the Dead would bring fun and laughter.[5]

Venancio Yanahuaya arrived with a flute band, and I asked him to be godfather for my bread baby. He was honored and grabbed me and the baby. We danced around the courtyard and through the streets of the hamlet to Luciano Juarez's house. Luciano was sponsor for the parody part of the Feast with the Dead. The youth had congregated in Luciano's patio. Young women, courted by their boyfriends, carried similar bread babies, and every child in the hamlet was perched on the courtyard wall. The community's catechist was the ritualist for the baptism and death of the bread babies. The Franciscan friars trained a man chosen by Kaatans to be catechism

Bread Babies

teacher for their community. The catechist then prepared these Andeans for baptism, communion, and marriage. Mario Quispe was the catechist for Kaata, and when the dancing had stopped, he announced that the unbaptized bread babies should be baptized. The giggling mothers and godmothers came forth with their bread bundles and shyly whispered to Mario when their baby was born. Maria, Venancio's wife, carried our bread baby up to Mario, who was pompously acting his role as notary and priest. Mario asked the date when the baby was born and then studied the almanac to find the corresponding saint for that day. He named our child Ernesto. The elders scrutinized Mario's ritual performance, careful to see that he complied with the rubrics of this liturgy. Mario toasted each newborn with alcohol and was intoxicated when he began baptizing.

The godmothers and godfathers circled around Mario, holding the babies in their right arms. After praying an Our Father and a Hail Mary, Mario sprinkled each baby's forehead with water, made the sign of the cross, and said the baby's name. He baptized all of them and finished the service with a blessing for everyone.

The godparents returned the babies to their mothers, who gave them alcohol, coca, and sugar. We hugged each other and began to dance, circling around and out of the patio, then up the eastern slope toward the chapel and plaza of Kaatapata. We swung back and forth in a slow-motion waltz. The lead couple ran far ahead of the band and doubled back, running behind and around the band. Entering the plaza, the band always moved in the direction of the sun, symbolically following its path from the lower eastern lands, across the central lands, and into the western highlands.

Saturday morning we crowded around Luciano's courtyard for the bread babies' death. This day was called Bread Baby's Shroud, referring to the white cloth, cut in the shape of a bird, which is placed on the dead's back before a Catholic burial. Mario set up an altar the same way as a priest does for Catholic mass; he covered a table with a white linen and placed two candles and a crucifix in the center. The godparents laid the bread babies on the table. Mario celebrated the Catholic mass, praying, "This is the body of Christ!" He spread his arms wide, said *"Oremos,"* and made the sign of the cross over the breads.

We picked up the consecrated breads after an elder explained that they had become the body of Christ and that we should dance with Jesus around the community. The dancing stopped, and we exchanged coca and alcohol. The babies were again set on the altar. Mario shouted in a trembling voice, "This is the death of these babies, eat their bodies!" He broke each bread in two and gave half to the parents and half to the godparents. The parents separated their piece into morsels, placing them in the mouths of the godparents, saying, "This is my dead baby; eat him." The godparents fed the parents with the other half. When they had served each other, they shared the other bread with the community. After a short time all had communicated, and another gesture of sharing alcohol and coca began and was consummated.

The parents and godparents drank and danced until Monday evening, when the Feast with the Dead ended. The six-day feast included three days each of serious and comic activities, lamentations and laughter—equally sacred gestures and emotions. The counterbalance of sentiments is as necessary for Kaatans as the cycles of the seasons.

The second part of the Feast with the Dead refers to the Catholic rituals of baptism, mass, and communion, which is a parody of birth, death, and eating of the Eucharist. It is possible that this folk tradition arose as an effort to counter-balance the enforced official Catholic rites, which were imposed on Kaatans by the missionaries in Charazani. Whatever the explanation may be, both halves are one ritual, as understood in the present time by Kaatans. Although they may be symbols from this or that religion, once they have become incorporated into Kaatan ritual, the very processes of the ritual give them new meaning. The Kaatan meaning of baptism, for example, is not to become sons of God, as Catholic dogma teaches, but to be the son of a godparent living on another level or in a different society, which perdures beyond death

Kaatans regard baptism, the mass, and communion as expressions of a reciprocal exchange between the living and the dead. The dead are fed during the first half, the living during the second. The living feeding the dead and the dead feeding the living are two halves of one reciprocal cycle. This reciprocal cycle is expressed in work exchange, in ritual obligations between natural and ritual kin, in exchange between levels, in recent and remote history, and in diurnal, seasonal, and agricultural time.

The feast set between seasons reunites the living and the dead and symbolizes that the upper and lower people are united on the same mountain. The symbolism suggests that the living are descending from the uma pacha and that the dead are ascending to it. This can be restated in ecological terms by saying that the highlands need the lowlands for exchanging produce; in societal terms by saying that baptism and marriage unite distinct levels; and in cosmological terms by pointing out that Kaatans ascend to the original time and place as well as descend from it.

The Feast with the Dead expresses to Andeans that the mountain body contains the living and the dead, gives form to their history, and underlies their social and economic structure. It is the conclusive ritual of the Andes.

NOTES

1. This division of the cosmological world into three parts was first suggested to me by Jorge Urioste.

2. Methodist missionaries staff a hospital in Ancoraimes, where they treat Methodists at no cost and where other poor cases pay half of the expenses, as Norberto Condori, a former Methodist, explained to the group. They would first have to remove the herbs, because the missionaries would not approve. These missionaries preached that herb curing was the work of the devil and that the sick man would be punished by the snake. Moreover, because the Indians had used herbs, their ancestors had been expelled from paradise, which was associated with the jungle.

3. The Feast with the Dead's timely position between these phases has made this fiesta a vulnerable time for imposing unpopular changes on the Bolivian Indians by the government. The popular Agrarian Reform party of the MNR was overthrown by the military during the Feast with the Dead in 1964. In 1973, President Banzer devaluated the Bolivian peso from 12 to the dollar to 20 to the dollar, causing inflationary prices for the Indians with no corresponding increase in their incomes. Another reason for selecting the Feast with the Dead as a time for revolution and devaluation is that the Indians would be too concerned with feeding their dead to become involved in counteracting the changes.

4. The secretaries ate and drank with Venancio and the dead, and they declared the property to be his. Only after the dead have been fed can property be exchanged or sold. During the feast, José Carmen Quispe, for example, gave title to a lower field to a lady whom he had injured, and Marcelino sold a house plot in Kaatapata for 500 pesos. The secretaries preside over all exchanges and sale of land. Their responsibility is to settle land disputes and to sponsor the Feast with the Dead.

5. For a study of the comic and the serious as expressions of ritual, see Bakhtin, 1968.

*

11

Conclusion

A distinctive mark of Andean culture is the application of metaphor to land and society. Andeans think about their territory and communities according to anatomical paradigms of animals and people. Early Peruvians planned the space in their ancient cities according to the metaphors of birds and animals (Schaedel 1978). They furrowed the outlines of large animals into the surface of the Nazca valley between 200 and 600 A.D. (Mason 1968:88). During the fourteenth and fifteenth centuries, the Incas designed Cuzco according to the metaphor of a puma (Rowe 1967:60). The spatial organization of Cuzco was also symbolic of their social structure (Zuidema 1964a, 1964b, 1968). The Huarochiri legends, preconquest oral traditions of the Central Andes, depicted the mountain as a human body with the summit of the mountain as the head, the central slopes as the chest and shoulders, and the places where two rivers diverge below the central slopes as the crotch and legs. Throughout the conquest, metaphors persisted, and today the people of Jesus de Machacha, a community near Tiahuanaco, Bolivia, still refer to their land as divided and integrated according to the parts of a cougar (Albo 1972:788-790).

Metaphors were, and still are, unifying principles between ecological levels and groups within the Andes. The mountain/body

metaphor of the Qollahuayas continues to unite distant and distinct
Andeans into an ayllu. The people of Apacheta, Kaata, and Niñokorin live far apart, speak different languages, and extract resources
characteristic of their levels—high, central, and low. These people
say they are united because their communities correspond to parts of
the mountain/body metaphor. Apacheta is the head, where the
bunchgrass and wool symbolize the hair, and the lakes are the eyes.
Kaata, surrounded by large rotative fields, is the trunk, where potatoes and oca, internal crops, are associated with the viscera and heart
of this metaphorical body. From Kaata, diviners circulate blood and
fat to the other parts of the human mountain. The lowlands of Niñokorin are the legs and toenails, where corn, vegetables, and orchards
abound on narrow strips alongside the rivers. The mountain/body
metaphor appears in Qollahuaya historical records, oral traditions,
place names, social structure, earth shrines, and rituals. Thirteen
earth shrines cover Mount Kaata and reflect the corporateness of the
communities. When diviners feed these shrines blood and fat, they
symbolically vitalize the mountain. After the mountain is fed it feeds
its people. The mountain/body metaphor is then complete.

The mountain/body metaphor has enabled these communities
to maintain cultural unity despite divisive external political forces.
Since the conquest, foreigners have divided ayllu Kaata for their
interests. First, the governor of Charazani turned the lands of Niñokorin into a hacienda during the seventeenth century, next the
Republicans made ayllu Kaata a part of canton Charazani in the
nineteenth century, and finally in this century the Agrarian Reform
Commission insisted that the communities be autonomous. Since
1954, Agrarian Reformists have forced the people of Apacheta,
Kaata, and Niñokorin to define their boundaries, elect secretaries,
and establish economic links with Charazani and La Paz. As a result,
the communities are feuding over boundaries, exchanging fewer resources, and decreasing their ties through marriage. Fortunately,
economic and political forces have not destroyed ayllu Kaata because Qollahuaya diviners have perpetuated a cultural solidarity of
ayllu Kaata by means of the mountain/body metaphor.

In other parts of the Andes, as well as those described above,
verticality and resource exchange have become diminishing factors
for cultural and social unification of Andean communities. By verticality Murra (1972:429-468) means the strategy of controlling as

many distinct niches as possible; in the Andes, altitude is the great ecological variable. Through resource exchange, upper and lower levels are held together by their participation in an ecosystem wherein there is a sharing of specialized resources from different micro-climates, necessary for each level's and each society's energy demands (Thomas 1972). Vertical exchange is being replaced by horizontal links (trucks and airplanes) to economic centers where goods are purchased at competitive prices and sold by middlemen at profitable gains (Buechler 1968, Doughty 1970).

An almost exclusive concern with economic and political factors in Andean studies has guided scholars away from the study of under-lying symbolic patterns, which are not dependent on external influences for their continued existence. Economic and political power, on the other hand, changes and requires external domination to hold the communities together. Power operates by dominance and clear recognition of differences, whereas rituals serve as ties between the communities. For this reason, verticality, which emphasizes ex-ternal control, is not an adequate explanation of ayllu solidarity in Kaata nor does it explain basic Andean patterns. In contrast, the mountain metaphor continually pervades the Kaatan ayllu and com-poses its people into social and cultural units analogous to the human mountain.

Neither can the ayllu be adequately explained by traditional theories of social structure. It is not merely the "network of relations connecting the inhabitants amongst themselves and with other people of other regions" as Radcliffe-Brown (1952:188-204) defined social structure. Following the tradition of Radcliffe-Brown, Andeanists have attempted to describe the ayllu according to social principles and kinship relations. This restricts the membership of the ayllu to only those related by blood and marriage, and it cannot explain the formation of ayllu membership by people living in the same territory, such as the colonizers of Inca times and the Peruvian immigrants of this century. The colonizers were united to one another in ayllus by sharing the same territory and earth shrines. The Peruvians symbolically became part of ayllu Kaata in 1956 when lightning struck a tree in their settlement and this site, Phesqa Pata, became an ayllu earth shrine. The Andean ayllu is formed not only by social relationships but also by symbolic systems, such as the mountain/body metaphor.

Nor would it be sufficient to interpret the ayllu only in terms of contemporary structural anthropologists, such as Lévi-Strauss (1953:525) and Duviols (1974). These anthropologists are primarily concerned with universal structures of the mind: they catalog binal distinctions within social and cultural categories, but fail to explain how these pairs are composed into holistic frameworks unique to the culture. Although Andeans perhaps share similar structures of the mind with us, they do not conceptualize a dualism between mind and matter. According to their epistemology, inner self is identical with outer self. Andeans do not conceptualize the metaphor as an idea independent of their mountain and bodies.

The ayllu is formed by a continual process of matching terms and constituting separate parts into wholes; it is the mountain, the communities on three levels, and their bodies insofar as they reflect one another and come together to form the mountain/body metaphor.

This interpretation of the ayllu does not exclude social networks, verticality, resource exchange, and binal distinctions; rather it incorporates them within the Andean framework of the mountain/body metaphor. This methodology utilizes the underlying symbolic pattern of Andeans to explain how they put their parts together into meaningful patterns. This research centers on their interpretations and symbolic patterns. Validity can be determined by how well this model can explain the ethnographic data. Does this underlying symbolic pattern integrate the diversities within the culture? Finally, how does it interrelate to their ecology, economics, cosmology, history, politics, and social organization?

In addition to the Andes, this type of analysis may be employed to explain the cultural continuity of other complex agrarian civilizations such as China and India. It provides a theory for how ancient civilizations, such as Chavín and Tiahuanaco, united vast populated regions by symbols, shrines, and rituals.

PROPERTIES OF THE METAPHOR

Although we can learn about the Andean society by understanding the mountain/body metaphor, we can increase our knowledge of this metaphor by studying its analogical, systemic, separated, and telluric characteristics. These properties express basic ideas about Andean cosmology, ecology, politics, and social structure.

The metaphor is essentially a comparison of analogous qualities between Andeans and their environment. They understand their own bodies in terms of the mountain, and they consider the mountain in terms of their own anatomy. Sickness, for example, is a disintegration of the human body similar to a landslide on the mountain, and health is restored by feeding the complete mountain. The three communities are analogous to the major parts of the body and to the three ecological levels. Kaatan society looks to the mountain for its social structure. Marriage is always between spouses from high, center, and low levels. The woman crosses the levels to live with her husband on his land, but her daughters return to the mother's level to regain access to her inheritance. The man remains on the land of his ancestors who protect it, and belongs to his ancestors' jatun ayllu. The jatun ayllu is the metaphorical relationship of those living on the land with the dead ancestors, who previously worked the land, and it is more important for a man to live on the land and care for the dead than to be descended from the ancestors.

Qollahuaya time and history is marked by changes on the mountain. An irrigation canal reminds them of the Incas, who made the river run uphill, and a broken-down hacienda recalls the Spaniards, who occupied Niñokorin. The rotative fields have a resting and working cycle similar to day and night, or life and death of these Andeans.

Finally, Andean cosmology is embedded within the earth shrines on Mount Kaata. Qollahuayas originate from Pachaqota, the highland lake, and travel down the mountain during their lifetimes. When they die, they are buried beneath the earth, where they begin their travels to the top of the mountain. Their journey from life to death is the reverse of the travels of the sun, like two contrapetal strokes propelling one another. The analogous quality of the metaphor enables Andeans to identify closely with their environment because they look to their mountain for their understanding of self and society.

Although the terms of analogy come together, like mirrors reflecting one another, they do not become one another. The analogies are never one to one: the body metaphor never corresponds completely to the communities, earth shrines, ecology, and physiography. The analogies involve imagination, ability to understand meanings of Andean languages, embellishment by oral tradition, and, most of all, the external application of the metaphor in ritual. The mountain and its people change with the seasons, sickness, natural catastrophies, migration, and conquest. When the terms change, diviners gather the people together to match the body metaphor with their land and communities.

Sometimes, the body metaphor does not reflect the mountain metaphor. Such was the case during the ayllu rite of Potato Planting in November, 1972. The ayllu leaders from Apacheta refused to send a sacrificial llama because of boundary squabbles. The secretaries of Kaata wanted to cancel this ritual, until the people of Kaatapata agreed to provide the llama. Sarito said, "A llama must always be fed to the mountain body because there will always be a highlands. A body can't exist without a head." Sarito had reinterpreted the metaphor to make Kaatapata, the high hamlet of community Kaata the head for this ritual. Nonetheless, the ritual still expressed the incompleteness of ayllu Kaata without Apacheta.

External economic and political forces have often caused discrepancies between the body metaphor and the mountain metaphor. As a result, the struggle in the Andes is an attempt to remove the discrepancies between the analogous terms. This provides a cultural explanation for "violence" in the Andes, which Aymara ethnologists have overemphasized. Moreover, it places the cause of the "aggression" on foreigners, who have divided the land of Andeans without regard to basic Andean patterns.

The analogous terms not only reflect each other but they also function together within a system. The mountain with its levels and the Qollahuayas with their communities are in reciprocal exchange with one another. The three communities are united to one another in a symmetrical relationship in which there is an even exchange of resources and spouses in marriage. The central theme of most rituals is the feeding of the mountain, so that the mountain gives the people food. Diviners circulate the blood and fat to the earth shrines, and secretaries circulate the resources between communities. These leaders are catalysts for the agricultural, ritual, and social life of the ayllu. Qollahuaya leadership, then, is not the controlling of people, but rather passing along the ingredients which unite them. These ingredients include food, people, and symbols.

Metaphorically, ayllu Kaata is an organic entity brought into being by exchange, work, and ritual. This summation can be understood in Andean terms and rituals. Andeans express this wholeness by adding the suffix *nti* to their words: *Tawantinsuyo* (Inca Empire) means the four places insofar as they constitute a whole, and five is the symbol for this gestalt. *Llahtantin runakuna* (ayllu leaders) refers to the secretaries from Apacheta, Kaata, and Niñokorin coming together to form the leadership for ayllu Kaata. More significantly, the word for body, *uqhuntin*, means all the parts of the body in summation, but with additional qualities beyond this summation. In other words, the body metaphor implies that the ayllu is more than the summation of its parts and that it is a system analagous to Andeans' ideas about their own bodies. With a varying degree of success, ritualists bring the people together and try to create this gestalt. One successful example, New Earth, was an occasion when the parts came together, and the participants experienced the wholeness of their ayllu. These Andeans talked about this liturgical celebration for days after as being *"muy completo."*

Within this system, the mountain/body metaphor distinguishes specific meanings rather than condenses diverse meanings into a diffuse symbol. The mountain, for example, has many-layered references associated with a specialization and a particular people, who live there. The metaphor separates ecological niches, communities, and earth shrines. The lineage has its household shrines in the kitchen and patio; the community has its shrine corresponding to its level; and the ayllu has thirteen shrines across the mountain. Corresponding to these stratified shrines are distinct, yet similar, rituals. Moreover, there are certain times when these shrines are fed by specific rituals and ritualists, highly skilled in these matters.

The thirteen ayllu shrines are interpreted according to their association with ecological levels and parts of the human anatomy. The three community shrines, for example, are Chaqamita, Jatun Junch'a, and Pachaqota. Chaqamita, located to the east near the legs, is related to the sun's birth, fertility, and corn, making it a suitable shrine for Niñokorin, whose Corn Planting rite reverences this site. This lower lake is also a shrine for Curva and Chullina, neighboring ayllus. Earth shrines, when shared by several ayllus, religiously unite separate mountains, and so Qollahuayas claim that they are one people because they worship the same shrines.

Pachaqota, a large lake on the head, is the eye into which the sun sinks; it symbolizes death, fertilization, and llamas. Apachetan herders celebrate the rite of All Colors on the shores of Pachaqota. Jatun Junch'a, associated with the liver and heart, lies in the hamlet of Kaatapata. Diviners feed this shrine a llama fetus during the rite of Chosen Field. The high, central, and low lands have community shrines reflecting their ecological zones, but from the viewpoint of the ayllu, the community shrine is only one part of the body metaphor. The people from the three communities feed all thirteen shrines during the ayllu rites. Apachetans, for example, contribute a llama fetus to the lower shrine, just as Niñokorins supply chicha to feed the highland shrine. Although the shrines are located on levels of the mountain, they are integrated parts of the mountain/body metaphor.

At other times and shrines, priests perform rituals to the saints. Kaatans interpret Catholic shrines according to the mountain/body metaphor. The chapel in the center of Kaata is where the saints are kept; Qollahuayas carry these statues around the plaza on the saint's name day. Qollahuayas reverence these statues because they are made from plaster of Paris which is associated with the uma pacha. The cross is placed near Mojata apacheta on Good Friday. This apacheta is where Andeans discard their coca quids to dispel their tiredness. In an analogous fashion, perhaps they are also unloading the burden of the crucifixion.

Finally, the mountain/body metaphor is telluric, which means that its primary association is with the earth and its natural manifestations. Andeans, for example, incorporated the Catholic symbolic system, which is conceptual, theological, and belief oriented, by stratifying it into the places of the mountain, which continued to be associated with the earth. The deeper Andean meanings were still associated with the mountain. For some time, it expressed two distinct meanings for two civilizations. Once the civilization passed over the mountain, like the sun, its symbols remained, not with their conceptual component, but with their icons set into the earth. Qollahuayas express this in their pictograph of the sun, which has a little sun, Inca staff, and a cross woven inside of it. The same sun has passed over the same mountain, containing within it signs of sequential events. The mountain is more basic to Andean civilizations than historical epochs.

Andean religion has a tradition of telluric symbolism, such as the sacred geography and megalithic statues of Tiahuanaco and Cuzco. Their oral tradition speaks of the divinities as incarnating into rocks (Huarochiri ms.3169), and a large rock was the principal shrine for important pre-Columbian rituals on the Altiplano (Bandelier 1910:237). Pachamama, Mother Earth, is always toasted before any Andean drinks a beverage. The natural configurations of rocks typify animals and people. Passes, waterholes, rivers, mountains, lakes, rocks, and caves are ritual sites. The telluric quality of Andean shrines enables them to be metaphors of the ecological order.

In the Andes and elsewhere, ethnographers should look deeper than the empirical realities of behavior and kinship; they should include the symbolic patterns by which people understand themselves and their society. It is by becoming engaged with Andeans in their way of life that one can see beneath their surface violence to the symbolic system of the "real life." The Andean symbolic system is not the explanatory model of the anthropologist but the people's own metaphors of society. It is an analogous process by which a people understand themselves in terms of their land. Furthermore, violence is merely a symbol of tension within the metaphor, when the people and their land are not analogous. Ritual provides the occasion when people and land look at each other, and the Qollahuayas contribute to this tradition by their ritual expertise. They feed the mountains in five Andean countries, and Andeans still travel to *Kuntur Qutu*, Mountain of the Condor.

*

Epilogue

We left Mount Kaata the day before Christmas. Marcelino gave me an old medicine bag and a hat. He smiled when I told him that the hat would protect my uma pacha. Carmen gave Judy a headband and said that it would bring many babies. Sarito met us at the edge of the city. Pressing three eggs in my hand, he whispered, "Your shrine is Mount Kaata and it will forever be calling you back."

We climbed to an earth knob, set like a bump on the mountain's side. Sarito stopped me. He took little steps around the knob and pressed coca leaves inside its rocks. "This is your shrine, feed it for a safe journey."

The road followed a ridge away from Kaata and cut through Mojata Pass. Woolly clouds were rolling up the valley. Kaata appeared and disappeared through the clouds. Thinner ones, some hazier than others, lay like puffs of incense around its three levels. We walked into a cloud. My eyes smarted from the reflected brightness, and the dampness chilled me. Marcelino and Sarito had disappeared into the vapor, and we felt visually closeted inside a world which was spatially immense. The cloud continued its journey to the highlands.

*

Bibliography

Albo, Javier
  1972   "Dinámica en estructura inter-comunitaria de Jesus de Ma-
          chaca." *América Indígena*, vol. XXXII, 3:773-816.

Arriaga, Father Pablo de
  1621   *The Extirpation of Idolatry in Peru*. L. Clark Keating, ed. Lexing-
          ton, Kentucky: University of Kentucky Press, 1968.

Bakhtin, Mikhail
  1968   *Rabelais and His World*. Helene Iswolsky, trans. Boston: MIT
          Press.

Bandelier, Adolf F.
  1904   "Aboriginal trephining in Bolivia." *American Anthropologist*,
          VI:440-46.
  1910   *The Islands of Titicaca and Koati*. New York: The Hispanic
          Society of America.

Bastien, Joseph W.
  1973   *Qollahuaya Rituals: an Ethnographic Account of the Symbolic
          Relations of Man and Land in an Andean Village*. Ph.D. disser-
          tation, Cornell University.

Bennett, Wendell
1946 "The Andean highlands: an introduction." *Handbook of South American Indians*, II, 1-147. Washington: Smithsonian Institution.

Bolton, Ralph
1972 *Aggression in Qolla Society*. Ph.D. dissertation, Cornell University.

Bourricaud, Francois
1967 *Cambios en Puno*. La Ciudad de México: Instituto Indigenista Interamericano.

Buechler, Hans C.
1968 "The reorganization of counties in the Bolivian Highlands: an analysis of rural-urban networks and hierarchies." In *Urban Anthropology: Research Perspectives and Strategies*, edited by E. Eddy. Southern Anthropological Society Proceedings, No. 2, University of Georgia Press.

Buechler, Hans C. and Judith Maria
1971 *The Bolivian Aymara*. New York: Holt, Rinehart & Winston Co.

Carter, William
1964 *Aymara Communities and the Bolivian Agrarian Reform*. Gainesville: University of Florida Press.
1968 "Secular reinforcement in Aymara death ritual." *American Anthropologist*, LXX:238-63.

Cobo, Bernabé
1890-95 *Historia del Nuevo Mundo*. Sevillá: Marcos Jiménez de La Espada.

Comacho, José Maria
1947 "El Pueblo Aymara." *Boletín de la Sociedad Geográfica de La Paz*, 69. La Paz.

Costas Arguedas, José
1961 *Diccionario del folklore Boliviano*. Sucre: Universidad Mayor de San Francisco.

Cunow, Heinrich
  1891   Das Verwandschaftsistem und die Geschlechtsyerbaende der Inka.
          Das Ausland, LXIV.

Diez de San Miguel, Garcia
  1567   Visita hecha a la provincia de Chucuito. Versión paleográfica de
          Waldemar Espinoza Soriano. Lima: Casa de Cultura.

Douglas, Mary
  1966   Purity and Danger. Middlesex: Penguin Books.

Doughty, Paul L.
  1970   "Behind the back of the city: 'Provincial' life in Lima, Peru." In
          Peasants in Cities, edited by W. Mangin. Boston: Houghton
          Mifflin Company.

Durkheim, Emile
  1968   The Elementary Forms of the Religious Life. Translated by Joseph
          Ward Swain. New York: The Free Press.

Duviols, Pierre
  1974   "Duality in the Andes." Paper presented at Andean Symposium
          II. Nov. 20, 1974. A.A.A. meetings in Mexico City.

Forbes, David
  1870   On the Aymara Indians of Bolivia and Peru. Journal of the
          Ethnological Society of London, England, II:193-305.

Garcilaso de la Vega
  1609   Comentarios reales de los Incas, vol. I. Lisbon.
  1943   Comentarios reales de los Incas. Edited by Angel Rosenblat.
          Buenos Aires: Emecé Editores.
  1961   The Incas. Edited by Alain Gheerbrant. New York: Avon Books.

Gibson, Charles
  1966   Spain in America. New York: Harper & Row.

Girault, Louis
  1969   Textiles Boliviens: Région de Charazani. Paris: Musée de l'Homme.

Gluckman, Max
1954   *Rituals of Rebellion in South-East Africa*. Manchester: Manchester University Press.
1965   *Politics, Law and Ritual in Tribal Society*. Chicago: Aldine Publishing Company.

Heath, Dwight; Charles Erasmus; and Hans Buechler
1969   *Land Reform and Social Revolution in Bolivia*. New York: Praeger Publishers.

Hickman, John Marshall
1963   *The Aymara of Chinchera, Peru: Persistence and Change in a Bicultural Context*. Ph.D. dissertation, Cornell University.

Hjortsjö, Carl-Herman
1972   "Anthropological investigation of an artificially deformed and trepanned cranium from Niñokorin, La Paz, Bolivia." *Etnologiska Studier*, XXXII:145-58. Göteborg: The Ethnographic Museum.

Huarochiri Manuscript
16 c.   Manuscript 3169. Quechua text attributed to Francisco Ávila. Biblioteca Nacional de Madrid.

James, Preston E.
1959   *Latin America*. Indianapolis: Odyssey Press.

Kaatan Manuscripts
1592   Por mando: el capitán Arias Pando Maldonado, corregidor y justicia mayor. 12 de Junio. Partid de Larecaxa.
        (This document and others are held in Kaata).
1609   Documento por Francisco de Alfaro, oidor de su majestad en la audiencia real de La Plata en Ácora, 25 de Julio.
1611   Auto: en el pueblo Charazani, 19 de Junio. Juan Ramirez Vargas, juez de real audiencia La Plata.
1633   Decreto: el licenciad Diego Muñox Cuellar. 30 de Junio. La Plata.
1757   Testamento último por Juan Miguel Sirena. 15 de Junio, Matías La Cruz Alvarez. Charazani.
1760   Testamento último por Juan Miguel Sirena. 3 de Octubre. Estancia Niñokorin.
1796   Petición por Micaela Slavilla. 4 de Agosto, y 6 de Septiembre. Niñokorin.
1796   Decreto por juez real, Josef Sánchez Barreda. 6 de Octubre. Charazani.

1797   Juramento por Gaspar Quispe. 25 de Octubre. Kaata.
1904   Copias de documentos de 1880-1904 por custodio Angeles, notario de Provincia Muñecas. Chuma.
1919   Testimonios por Eduardo Pastén. Charazani.
1928   Testimonios de Kaata contra Chari. Kaata.

Karsten, Rafael
1935   *The Life and Culture of the Jibaro Indians of Eastern Ecuador and Peru.* Helsinki: Helsingfors.

Keen, Benjamin
1973   *Latin American Civilization: The Colonial Origins.* Boston: Houghton Mifflin Company.

La Barre, Weston
1948   *The Aymara Indians of the Lake Titicaca Plateau, Bolivia.* Memoirs of the American Anthropological Association, No. 68.
1946   "The Uru-Chipaya." *Handbook of South American Indians,* II:575-85.
1950   "Aymara Folktales." *International Journal of American Linguistics,* XVI:40-45.

Leons, Barbara
1967   "Land reform in the Bolivian Yungas." *América Indígena,* XXVII: 689-713.

Lévi-Strauss, Claude
1953   "Social structure." *Anthropology Today,* edited by A. L. Kroeber. Chicago: The University of Chicago Press, pp. 524-53.
1969   *The Elementary Structures of Kinship.* Translated by James Bell and John von Sturmer. Boston: Beacon Press.

Loukotka, Cestmir
1968   *Classification of South American Indian Languages.* Edited by Johannes Wilbert. Vol. VII. Los Angeles: Latin American Center U.C.L.A.

Lowie, Robert H.
1948   "The tropical forest: an introduction." *Handbook of South American Indians,* III:1-56. Washington: Smithsonian Institution.

Lynch, Thomas F.
1971   "Preceramic transhumance in the Callejón de Huaylas, Peru." *American Antiquity,* XXXVI:139-48.

Maps
    1936   Approximate Map of Sorata and area. Hoja no. 20. Mapoteca VICA. Ministerio de Colonización. La Paz: Comisión Cartográfica.
    1955   Aerial photographs by the Servicio Geodésico Interamericano. La Paz: Instituto Geográfico Militar.
    1963   Khata, Bolivia. Hoja 5748 I. Carta Nacional Bolivia. La Paz: Instituto Geográfico Militar.
    1963a   Villa General Gonzalez. Hoja 5748 II. Carta Nacional Bolivia. La Paz: Instituto Geográfico Militar.

Marzal, Manuel
    1971   *El mundo religioso de Urcos.* Cuzco: Instituto de Pastoral Andina.

Mason, J. Alden
    1963   "The Languages of South American Indians." *Handbook of South American Indians*, VI:157-317. Washington: Smithsonian Institution.
    1968   *The Ancient Civilizations of Peru.* New York: Penguin Books.

Mauss, Marcel
    1974   *The Gift.* New York: W.W. Norton and Co.

Means, Philip
    1931   *Ancient Civilizations of the Andes.* New York: Charles Scribner and Sons.

Métraux, Alfred
    1967   *Religions et Magies Indiennes Amérique du Sud.* Paris: Gallimard.

Mishkin, Bernard
    1946   "Contemporary Quechua." *Handbook of South American Indians*, II:411-70. Washington: Smithsonian Institution.

Monast, Jacques
    1966   *L'Univers Religieux des Aymaras de Bolivie.* Cuernavaca: CIDOC.

Morúa, Martín de
  1922-25 *Historia del origen y genealogia real de los reyes Incas del Perú.* Edited by H. H. Urteaga y C. A. Romero. Lima: Collección de Libros y Documentos Referentes a La Historia de Perú, IV:1-253; V:1-72.

Murra, John V.
1962   "Cloth and its function in the Inca State." *American Anthropologist*, LXIV:710-25.
1972   "El 'control vertical' de un máximo de pisos ecológicos en la economía de las sociedades Andinas" in *Visita de la Provincia de León de Huánuco en 1562*. Edited by John V. Murra. Huánuco, Peru: Universidad Nacional Hermilio Valdizan.

Nordenskiöld, Erland
1953   *Investigaciones arqueológicas en la región fronteriza de Perú y Bolivia*. Translated by Carlos Ponce and Stig Rydén. La Paz: Biblioteca Pazeña.

Oblitas Poblete, Enrique
1963   *Cultura Callawaya*. La Paz: Editorial "Talleres Gráficos Bolivianos."
1968   *La lengua secreta de los Incas*. La Paz: Editorial "Los Amigos del Libro."
1969   *Plantas medicinales en Bolivia*. La Paz: Editorial "Los Amigos del Libro."

Otero, Gustavo Adolfo
1951   *La piedra mágica. Vida y costumbres de los Indios Callahuayas de Bolivia*. México, D.F.: Instituto Indigenista Interamericano.

Paredes, M. Rigoberto
1936   *Mitos, supersticiones y supervivencias populares de Bolivia*. La Paz: Arno Hermanos.

Parish Records
1783-86   *Matrimonial Libro No. I*. Charazani: Parroquia San Juan de Charazani.
1787-94   *Matrimonial Libro No. II*. Charazani: Parroquia San Juan de Charazani.

Pérez Bocanegra, Juan
1631   *Ritual formulario; e institución de cura, para administrar a los naturales de este Reyno*. Lima.

Polo de Ondegardo
1571   *Informaciones acerca de la religión y gobierno de los Incas*. Edited by Carlos Romero. Lima: Collección de Libros y Documentos a la Historia de Perú. III(1916):45-188.

1940   *Informe del Licenciado Juan Polo de Ondegardo al Licenciado Briviesca de Muñatones sobre la perpetuidad de las encomiendas en el Perú.* Edited by Carlos Romero. Lima: Revista Histórica, XIII:125-96.

Poma de Ayala, Felipe Guaman
    1936   *Nueva crónica y buen gobierno.* Travaux et Mémoires, vol. XXIII. Paris: Institute d'Ethnolgie.

Ponce Sanguinés, Carlos
    1957   *Arqueología Boliviana.* La Paz: Biblioteca Paceña.
    1969   *Tunupa y Ekako.* Publicación 19, especially pages 145-60. La Paz: Academia Nacional de Ciencias.

Posnansky, Arthur
    1945   *Tihuanacu: The Cradle of American Man,* I & II. Translated by J. F. Shearer. New York: J. J. Augustin.
    1957   *Tihuanacu: The Cradle of American Man,* III & IV. Translated by J. F. Shearer. La Paz: Ministerio de Educación.

Radcliffe-Brown, A. R.
    1952   *Structure and Function in Primitive Society.* New York: The Free Press.

Rappaport, Roy
    1967   "Ritual regulation of environmental relations among a New Guinea people." *Ethnology,* VI:17-30.

Romero, Emilio
    1928   *Monografía del Departamento de Puno.* Lima.

Rowe, John Howland
    1946   "Inca culture at the time of the Spanish Conquest." *Handbook of South American Indians,* II:198-330. Washington: Smithsonian Institution.
    1967   "What kind of settlement was Inca Cuzco?" Presentation at the 11th Annual Meeting of the Kroeber Anthropological Society, Berkeley, April 22, 1967.

Rydén, Stig
    1957-59   "Andean excavations I-II." *Monograph Series No. 4 and No. 6.* Stockholm: Statens Etnografiska Museum.

Sauer, Carl
   1963   "Geography of South America." *Handbook of South American Indians*, VI:319-407. Washington: Smithsonian Institution.

Schaedel, Richard
   1978   Conversations with Schaedel at The University of Texas at Austin, February 1 and 2.

Squier, E. George
   1877   *Peru: Incidents of Travel and Exploration in the Land of the Incas.* New York: Harper and Brothers.

Stark, Louisa R.
   1972   "Machaj-juyai: secret language of the Callahuayas." *Papers in Andean Linguistics*, I:199-227.

Thomas, R. Brooke
   1972   *Human Adaptation to a High Andean Energy Flow System.* Ph.D. dissertation, Pennsylvania State University.

Toledo, Francisco de
   1882   *Informaciones.* Madrid.

Troll, Carl
   1968   *Geo-Ecology of the Mountainous Regions of the Tropical Americas.* UNESCO, 1966. Kommission Bei Ferd. Bonn: Dummlers Verlag.

Tschopik, Harry
   1946   "The Aymara." In *Handbook of South American Indians*, II:501-73. Washington: Smithsonian Institution.
   1951   *The Aymara of Chucuito, Peru.* Anthropological Papers of the American Museum of Natural History, New York, vol. XLIV, part 2. New York: The American Museum of Natural History.

Turner, Victor
   1957   *Schism and Continuity in African Society.* London: Manchester University Press.
   1967   *The Forest of Symbols.* Ithaca: Cornell University Press.
   1969   *The Ritual Process.* Chicago: Aldine Publishing Company.

Urioste, Jorge
  1971   Lecture delivered at Cornell University, Ithaca, in November.
  1973   *Chay Simiri Kaymi: Language of the Manuscript of Huarochiri.* Ph.D. dissertation, Cornell University.
  1975   Conversations with Urioste at the University of Nevada, Las Vegas. April 15.

Valverde, Vicente
  1539   *Documentación de Indias*, III:98. Cuzco, March 20.

Viscarra, F. J.
  1901   *Rolletes Aymáru-Aymara.* La Paz: Palza Hermanos.

Voegelin, C. F. and F. M.
  1965   "Languages of the world: native America fascicle two." *Anthropologic Linguistics*, VII(no. 7):75-80.

Wassén, S. Henry
  1972   "A medicine-man's implements and plants in a Tiahuanacoid tomb in Highland Bolivia." *Etnologiska Studier*, XXXII. Göteborg: The Ethnographic Museum.

Wolf, Eric
  1955   "Types of Latin American peasantry: a preliminary discussion." *American Anthropologist*, LVII:452-55.

Zuidema, Thomas
  1964a   *The Ceque System of Cuzco: The Social Organization of the Capital of the Incas.* Leiden: E. J. Brill Publishers.
  1964b   "El Calendario Inca." *Congresso Internacional de Americanistas*, XXXVI(no. 2):25-30.
  1968   "A Visit to God." *Bijdragen Tot de taal—land en volkenkunde*, 124:22-39.

Glossary

Agrarian Reform: marks the end of the hacienda and serfdom for Andeans and the beginnings of land distribution (see Chapter 3, n. 3).

Altiplano: a high plain or plateau (12,500 feet) between eastern and western ranges of Peru and Bolivia. It is where most Aymara-speaking Andeans live.

Apacheta: the highlands (14,000-17,000 feet) of Mount Kaata. One hundred twenty Aymara-speaking families are scattered throughout this extensive pastoral area. These Aymaras herd alpacas, llamas, sheep, and pigs. Apacheta is the head of the mountain body.

apacheta: the earth shrine on the pass of the mountain, that is, the highest point of the trail. Travelers rest at this site, discard their coca, and pray, "With this quid may my tiredness leave me, and strength return." Mojata pass is the apacheta of Mount Kaata.

Aqhamani: snowcrested mountain (17,454 feet), which towers in front of communities Kaata and Niñokorin. For the 1972 agricultural season, Aqhamani was the guardian of the harvest.

ara padrinos: (see horizontal sponsors).

ayllu: distinguishable groups whose solidarity is formed by religious and territorial ties (llahta ayllu), by permanent claim to land and lineage (jatun ayllu), by affinal ties (masi ayllu), and by work (mitmaj ayllu). Qollahuayas understand ayllu as the vertical triangular land masses

211

divided into high, center, and low ecological zones, where communities live. It also refers to the penis, lineage, and community.

ayllu Chari: an ayllu bordering on Kaata's southwest side, corresponding to the right arm of the mountain body.

ayllu men: a title given to representatives from the highlands and lowlands, who perform roles at the mountain rituals; also called llahta runa.

ayllu Upinhuaya: triangular land mass bordering on ayllu Kaata's northwest side, but separated by the Kunochayuh River; left arm of the mountain body.

cabildo: (see matron of the kitchen).

cacique: term referring to local leader during Inca and early colonial times.

chaqi: anatomical part of the body from the knee to the foot; the lower agricultural areas (10,500-11,500 feet) along the Ayllu and Huruku rivers, whose narrow strips produce corn, wheat, barley, peas, and beans.

charqui: dried llama or alpaca meat.

chicha: beer made from fermented maize.

chijes: any misfortune, such as sickness, death, or loss of property, which is symbolized by a ball of wool wrapped around pig fat.

chullpa machula: pre-Columbian mummy shrines of rock cubicles found on Mount Kaata and other parts of the central Andes, which are associated with dead ancestors.

chunchos: the people living in the jungle, whom Andeans consider culturally inferior because they do not wear clothes and eat salt.

ch'uño: dehydrated potatoes.

ch'uspa: intricately woven coca bag, the size of a wallet.

coca: (see Chapter 1, n. 4)

Cocamama: (see Chapter 1, n. 5)

completion: the bringing together of the parts of the ayllu and only these parts insomuch as they constitute one whole.

condenado: an ostracized person who marries a classificatory cousin or someone from the same level.

curanderos: a distinct branch of Qollahuaya religious specialists dedicated to curing by herbs.

diurnal temperature climate: greater temperature variation between day and night than between summer and winter.

elder guide: (see machula watayuh purijchej).

horizontal ayllu: relatives and level of land of the wife; also called masi ayllu.

horizontal sponsors: the best man and bridesmaid of the bride, who represent the lowlands and cloth; also called ara padrinos.

huacas: pre-Columbian term for Andean earth shrines.

illa: the reflected image on the lakes of the uma pacha related to the origin of animals and people; the white strings tied between the threads of the weaving, instrumental in forming the distinct pictographs.

jatun ayllu: (see vertical ayllu)

jatun padrinos: (see vertical sponsors)

jichu: a long-stemmed, tough grass, which grows in clumps in the puna region and upon which the herds graze; also used for thatching roofs.

kanchayuh: (see patron of the patio)

kinre: the sides of the body; inclined slopes along the trunk of the mountain body, where the terraced rotative fields lie.

lords of the mountain: the permanent ayllu shrines on Mount Kaata; also called mallkus.

lords of the season: the mountain guardians of the agricultural year and the crops; for example, Aqhamani, Sunchuli, and Sillaqa were these lords for 1972; also called watayuh.

lower fields: land from 10,500-11,500 feet, along the Ayllu and Huruku rivers, which alternates one year with wheat and barley, and the following year with corn, beans, and peas; also called wajos chacras.

Machaj-Juyai: secret language employed only by Qollahuaya herbal curers for their curings. Oblitas (1968) claims that this is the secret language of the Incas. By contrast, Stark (1972) says it is the vestiges of the extinct Pukina.

machula onqosqa: a sickness, such as boils on the face, associated with ancestors angry over the living's relationship with their land.

machula watayuh purijchej: ancestor lord of the season—elder guide, title for the chief ritualist of Mount Kaata, bestowed upon him by the secretaries and commoners. Sarito Quispe held this title for 1972.

maki: anatomical part of the body from the hand to the elbow; the parts of the mountain where the rivers diverge from the central lands.

mallkus: (see lords of the mountain); condor.

masi ayllu: (see horizontal ayllu)

matron of the kitchen: a shrine, which is the eating table inside the supply house, associated with the female head of the household and her activities; also called cabildo.

mestizos: a class which has partially abandoned Andean traditions of dress and language and which has adapted to Western customs.

ñawi: eye; the lakes found on the mountain's head.

Niñokorin: lower part of Mount Kaata, where wheat, corn, peas, and beans are grown; community of eighty families, located a thousand feet up from the lowest point of the triangular land mass; left leg of the mountain body.

Nuño Orqo: Tit Hill, located on the trunk of the mountain body.

originarios y tributarios: colonial categories applied to Kaatans, which defined them as tribute-paying Indians, who had lived on their land since time immemorial.

Pachamama: Mother Earth; earth in general.

paña sillu: right toenail; the community of Lunlaya, found on the lowest part of the mountain, where it touches the Ayllu River.

Pariya Qaqa: Igneous Rock, an important Andean divinity of the Huarochiri oral tradition.

pasado runa: an elder; a man who has filled all the secretarial and fiesta posts.

patron of the patio: a shrine dug into the adobe bench lining the supply house, associated with the patrilineal claim to land and garden plots; also called kanchayuh.

peso: Bolivian monetary unit, the equivalent of eight cents or two hours' wages for a Kaatan in 1972.

pinquillo: bamboo flute, twenty inches long, with six holes on top and one on bottom.

pongo: menial work tribute required of the Indians by the owners of the hacienda and the officials of the pueblos.

puna: the highest inhabitable ecological zone of the Andes (14,000-17,000 feet), utilized by herders for grazing cameloids and sheep.

qari yachaj: male diviner.

qhariciri: a legendary personage who by cutting off the fat of the Indians snatches their power.

qochu: the sacrificial llama fed to the earth during the agricultural rituals.

Qollahuaya: place of the medicine, or place of the Qollahuayas, located in Province Bautista Saavedra in midwestern Bolivia.

Qollahuayas: an Andean people famous for ritual and herbal curing throughout the Andes.

qolla kapachu: medicine bag.

Quiabaya: community of fifteen families on lower fields; right leg of the mountain body.

reduction and mission: Spanish institutions applied to Kaatans, placing them and their land under the supervision of the Franciscan Friars, who catechized and controlled them.

rotative fields: the central lands (11,500-14,000 feet) which produce potatoes, oca, and barley for three years and then rest for four; also called qhapanas.

sonqo: heart; place from which blood is pumped; Kaata.

sullu: dried llama fetus.

Tawantinsuyo: Andeans' name for the Inca empire, which means "four parts and only these four parts insomuch as they constitute a whole."

tinka: ritual action of bringing together separated or contrasting parts, such as the patrilineage and wife's lineage, the highlands and lowlands, and the levels of the ayllu; often expressed as completion.

tinku: mock battle between two groups.

t'unt'a: dehydrated potatoes, made by first soaking them in a stream, later freezing, and then drying them, similar to making ch'uño.

uqhamapan: and so be it forever, Amen.

uqhuntin: Kaatans' definition of their body, which means these parts and only these parts insomuch as they form one inner self.

uma: head of the human body: uma pacha is the highlands and head of the mountain, where the hair of the llamas and the grass of the hills grow; place of origin and return for people, animals, time, and history.

warmi yachaj: female diviner.

Index

Abjjata, 79
Acculturation, xviii
Adultery: divination of, 10-11
Age groups, 86
Agrarian civilization, theory for, 192
Agrarian Reform, 32-34, 35 n. 4; and ayllu Kaata, 41; dividing ayllu, 190; laws, 35 n. 3; and secretary roles, 62-63
Agriculture, 7, 138; lords of season, 141; and ritual cycle, 178
Akapana, 60
Albo, Javier, xxiii, 49, 189
All Colors, rite of, 53, 57, 196
Altiplano: inhabitants of, 3; languages of, 3
Altitude (as ecological variable), 3, 6, 8, 39-41, 138, 191
Amarete, ayllu of, 5
Amulets, 138
Ancestor graves. See Chullpa
Ancestors, 14; cause of sickness, 119, 130, 133, 154; and cloth, 111; description of, 130-31; feeding of, 139-40, 162; guardians of lineage, 133; mummies, 158

Ancestor sickness, 119, 130, 133, 154
Animo, 152
Apacheta, community of, xix, 32, 34, 47, 194; herding in, 40; in metaphor, 47, 194; rite of All Colors in, 53
Apacheta, shrine of, 4, 69, 196
Apiris. See Emissaries
Apolo: coca growing in, 8
Araucanian, xxi
Arm in metaphor, 48
Arriaga, Father Pablo de, 60, 158
Astrology, 61
Audiencia de La Plata, 26
Ayllu: composed in ritual, 70, 122, 146, 179, 192, 195; definitions of, xxiii-xxiv, 121, 127 n. 7, 189-92; expressed in weaving, 109; incompleteness of, 194; leaders of, 70, 73, 75, 77, 81, 194, 195; in metaphor, xxiii-xxv, 81, 146, 190-92; shrines of, 57-60, 195; social structure, xix, 42-43, 115-20, 191-93; specialization, 6-10, 37-41. See also Horizontal ayllu; Llahta ayllu; Mitmaj ayllu; and Vertical ayllu
Ayllus, Qollahuaya, 5, 29-30; exchange

216

†